Henry Martin

The History of Brighton and Environs

From the Earliest Known Period to the Present Time - together with a short

historical description of towns and villages of interest within twelve miles of

Brighton

Henry Martin

The History of Brighton and Environs
*From the Earliest Known Period to the Present Time - together with a short historical
description of towns and villages of interest within twelve miles of Brighton*

ISBN/EAN: 9783337151713

Printed in Europe, USA, Canada, Australia, Japan

Cover: Foto ©Andreas Hilbeck / pixelio.de

More available books at **www.hansebooks.com**

THE

HISTORY OF BRIGHTON

AND ENVIRONS,

FROM THE EARLIEST KNOWN PERIOD TO THE PRESENT TIME:

TOGETHER WITH

A SHORT HISTORICAL DESCRIPTION OF TOWNS
AND VILLAGES OF INTEREST WITHIN
TWELVE MILES OF BRIGHTON.

By ALDERMAN HENRY MARTIN,

LATE MAYOR OF THE BOROUGH OF BRIGHTON.

BRIGHTON:

PUBLISHED BY JOHN BEAL, BOOKSELLER & STATIONER, EAST STREET.

1871.

ENTERED AT STATIONERS' HALL.

WILLIAM CURTIS, PRINTER, GAZETTE OFFICE, BRIGHTON.

PREFACE.

In submitting this *History of Brighton* to the Public, the Author deems it necessary to offer a few remarks with reference to the introduction of the Work and circumstances connected with its origin.

In the early part of the past winter the BRIGHTON MUSEUM COMMITTEE, desirous of extending the attractions and usefulness of our excellent local Museum, resolved to inaugurate a series of instructive and entertaining lectures, to be delivered at the Royal Pavilion in the evenings on which it is thrown open gratuitously to the ratepayers of the town. The result of this laudable effort exceeded expectation, · and the lectures were pre-eminently successful. The writer of this book assisted in the above project, and was invited to lecture upon and illustrate a large and very valuable collection of prints, views, &c., relating to the early days of this fashionable town, and which were kindly presented to the Museum by Robt. Furner, Esq., an esteemed inhabitant, who with other members of his family have been for many years associated with Brighton, and prominent in advancing its interests.

On the 6th of February, 1871, the compiler, in compliance with the request before alluded to, gave his first lecture on "Old Brighton" in the Banqueting Room of the Royal Pavilion, and on the 6th of March following, his concluding one upon the same subject, for which—at the next meeting of the members of the Committee—he received a cordial vote of thanks for the same, together with a desire that, at their expense, they might be published. The Author embraced this opportunity for writing a history of his native town,— —a task of no mean importance, involving an outlay of much time and labour, but undertaken *con amore*,— and if he has succeeded in contributing additional interest thereto, he is fully rewarded.

This volume, coupled with the Author's sincere regards, is most respectfully dedicated to His Worship the Mayor (Richard Mallam Webb, Esq.), the Brighton Museum Committee, and their valuable Honorary Secretary (George De Paris, Esq.). He further thankfully acknowledges the kindness of Messrs. Bellingham, Gay, W. J. Smith, and Stent, for their loan of rare books and prints: these have been of great assistance to him in the preparation of the work now submitted for public favour, which he trusts will prove satisfactory to subscribers and the public generally.

Brighton, April, 1871.

INDEX.

—o—

ILLUSTRATIONS.

—o—

THE HISTORY OF BRIGHTON.

ETYMOLOGY OF THE TOWN.

The town has been severally called Brightemston, Bristelmeston, Brighthamstan, and in Domesday Book it is called Brighthelmstun. The Saxon word *tun* signifies *town* or dwelling, and an adjoining village is called Preston or Priestown. The name doubtless was derived from St. Brighthelm, a Saxon Bishop, who gave the name to the town, and who resided here during the Heptarchy, for we find that Ella with his three sons (Cimen, Wiencing, and Cissa) effected their landing at West Wittering, south west of Chichester, A.D. 447, and defeated the Britons, who endeavoured to oppose him, and took possession of all the maritime parts of the county. Ella thus laid the foundation of the kingdom of the South Saxons, from which the county derives its name. Brighthelm accompanied this army. One of his successors resided at Aldrington, and held a considerable portion of land until the year A.D. 693: in this year the Bishop was killed in battle. This is stated by Stillingfleet and other writers, but no mention is made of where the battle was fought.

After the death of Brighthelm the town appears to have belonged to the ancestors of Earl Godwin, who were called *Thanes,*—noblemen of considerable possessions in Sussex. The first of whom we have any account was Ulnoth, Lord of the Manor of Brighthelmstun. He
A

was appointed commander of the ships sent by the County of Sussex, in 1008, to oppose the invasion of the Danes. In 1019 we find that Ulnoth's son, Earl Godwin, accompanied King Canute to Denmark, then invaded by the Vandals. Here Godwin distinguished himself, and in reward the King created him *Earl of Kent, Sussex, and Surrey.

About 1046 Earl Godwin became unpopular with Edward the Confessor, and Brighthelmstun and his other possessions were seized, but Godwin regained them by force and, being reinstated in favor, enjoyed his possessions until the 17th of April, 1053, when he was suddenly taken ill at Winchester, where the Court of Edward was then held, and died four days afterwards. Harold, the eldest son of Earl Godwin, succeeded to the chief manor of Brighthelmstun. This nobleman was distinguished for his qualities as a statesman and warrior, and his public and private virtues so endeared him to the nation that they looked upon him as the fittest person to succeed the reigning monarch. Upon the death of Edward, 1065, he was chosen King, but owing to a secret arrangement made between the King and William Duke of Normandy, the latter made a claim, and asserted his right by force of arms. After Harold had defeated his brother Tostin and the King of Norway, at Stanford Bridge, near York, William landed at Pevensey. Harold immediately proceeded southwards, and with the addition of some levies hastily collected at Brighthelmstun and his other manors in Sussex, encamped within nine miles of the invaders. On the 14th October, 1066, he gave battle with the Normans, and, after performing all that valour and judgment could do against a brave enemy, closed his life on the field of battle near Hastings.

---

* It is asserted on good authority that the dangerous shoals on the Kentish coast, called the Goodwin Sands, were formerly part of the possessions of this nobleman, before they were severed from the main land by the inroads of the sea—hence the name.

Harold's possessions,—Brighthelmstun and his other manors, having fallen into the hands of William the Conqueror, the town with the rape of Lewes, to which was attached the Castle and its demesne,was conferred on his son-in-law and one of his generals,William, Lord of Warrenne in Normandy, afterwards created Earl of Surrey in England.

The South Saxon monarchy lasted about 320 years, during which the most memorable occurrence was the conversion of Adelwach to Christianity by Wilfrid, first Bishop of Sussex, in the year 650, as borne out by a reference to that remarkable and valuable work of antiquity, Domesday Book, which was begun in 1086, and compiled in six years : written *in one handwriting* on 380 double pages of vellum, and without doubt the most important and interesting document possessed by any nation in Europe. It is also remarkable that of the 63 Hundreds in the division of the County of Sussex one half of them retain the same names now as were inserted in this book. For a proof we shall enumerate the following in this neighbourhood, viz. :—

Brighthelmstun	Brighthelmstone.
Hov	Hove Villa and Ecclesia.
Newtimbreham	} Newtimber.
Nivembre	
Prestetun..............	Preston.
Panninges	Poynings.
Wordinges	Worthing.
Stanninges	Steyning.

The Saxons divided the county into rapes, the latter peculiar to Sussex, a division strictly adhered to at the conquest; they are six in number, with their castles and respective baronies, namely, Chichester, Arundel, Bramber, Lewes, Pevensey, and Hastings. Brighthelmstun is in the Hundred of Whalesbone and annexed to the Rape of Lewes: in Domesday Book this Hundred was called Wellesmere, but in process of time,—most probably at the institution of Constables, under Edward I., the boroughs of Preston and Patcham (in the Half Hundred of Dean) were united to Brighthelmstun and composed a new Hundred, called Wellsbourne. The name is, without doubt, taken from the so-called well at Patcham: years since on the rising of the springs in the immediate neighbourhood, the well overflowed, and the water ran down the high road into the town,[o] inundating in its progress the basements of the houses in its route, and crossing the Steine, into the sea (by means of the sewer hereafter spoken of as made by order of the Prince of Wales and Duke of Marlborough) Prior to the construction of the sewer there was a large pond opposite the Castle Tavern (corner of Castle Square) which overflowed down the valley, hence the name Pool Valley or Lane. The parish of Brighton is divided into Five Manors, but they are so intermixed that the boundaries can scarcely be traced. Brighthelmstun was of considerable importance, likewise, during the period of the occupation of this kingdom by the Roman legions, after the landing of Julius Cæsar, as we find many traces of the same from the Castra or Camps in the neighbourhood, one of which was the Steine.

The Romans encamped on this spot,— so-called, — from being connected with *stein* or *stone* road-ways or pavements to the Metropolis. In all probability one passed through the town of *Steyning*, traces of the same having been discovered at different times in the neighbourhood. There are other Roman encampments lying in a line from south to north, from the Brighton one, the first being at Hollingbury Castle, and the second at *Ditchling* beacon, on the summit of the South Downs, and a *larger one* about a mile and-a-half eastward and about a mile from the sea, all being enabled to signal to each other in cases of emergency.

A military Roman way was discovered a few years ago on St. John's Common, also in the enclosed lands

---

* January 11, 1811.—In consequence of the flooded state of the *London Road*, the coaches into Brighton from London were compelled to come into the town by way of *Preston Drove* and over the *Church Hill*.

adjoining, in the parishes of *Keymer and Clayton;* and on the west side of Glynde Bridge near the railway station a paved Roman causeway was discovered, lying 3ft. below the turf upon a bed of *silt* or blue clay 20*ft. thick*, and close to it was found a large brass coin of the reign of Emperor *Antoninus Pius.*

The possessors of the lordship of Brighton are as ancient as any that we meet with, for in *Edward the Confessor's time, Godwin*, Earl of Kent, was Lord of this Manor, with many others *in this County*. He left it to his *son Harold, who was afterwards King;* he being conquered by *William the Norman*, the manor became the Conqueror's, who then gave it to one of his generals, William de War-renne (of Bellencombre, in Normandy) in reward for his services, also the earldom of Surrey, the whole rape of Lewes, and large possessions in Norfolk, Suffolk and Yorkshire. De Warrenne afterwards married his daughter Gundrada. She was the fifth daughter of William by his wife Matilda, of Flanders. In return for these favours, De Warrenne exerted himself to the utmost on behalf of his father-in-law, and was made one of the chief Justiciaries of England. About the year 1070, the Earl and Countess determined on a pilgrimage to Rome, having previously resolved to erect a monastery for the saving of their souls and those of their ancestors and successors. In the course of their journey they visited the great abbey of Clugni, in Burgundy, and observing there a discipline superior to that which was practised elsewhere, decided on making their projected monastery a branch or cell of that institution. Accordingly on their return to England, and probably to their residence in Lewes Castle, they summoned certain monks of Clugni to lay the foundation stone of the establishment, and they under the guidance of one of their number, Lanzo* by name, were soon energetically

---

* Lanzo was the first Prior of Lewes, and continued as such for more than 30 years. "He was a man," says Malmsbury, "surpassed by none for the gifts of the Holy Spirit."

engaged in the pious work. In a few years there sprang up, just outside the southern walls of Lewes, one of the most influential monastic houses that England ever possessed. Its endowments were enormous, and its Prior held a seat in the great Senate of the realm.

Gundrada died in childbirth, at Castle Acre, in Norfolk (where with her husband she had founded a second large Clugnaic Priory) 27th of May, 1085. Her body was brought for interment to Lewes, and buried beneath a slab of black marble in the chapter house of the Monastery. The Earl himself was buried in the same place three years later, under a tomb of white marble. The posthumous history of Gundrada is very remarkable. We have seen that she was buried in the chapter house of Lewes Priory. Some years later, when her flesh and that of the Earl had mouldered to dust, the bones of each were collected and placed, in two leaden coffins or cists, under the respective slabs of black and white marble just mentioned : these remained as objects of pious regard until it pleased Henry VIII. to dissolve the monastic establishments throughout the realm. In 1587, the Vicar-General Thomas Cromwell, levelled one of the finest monasteries in England to the ground. Small heed was given then to founders and foundresses, whose tombs were mostly thrown aside as useless things. Some kind soul who did not like that of a Princess being desecrated, bore it away from the scene of desolation, and Mr Mark Anthony Lower, in his work *The Worthies of Sussex*, thinks it might have been Edward Shirley, Esq., who resided at Isfield Place, and held the office of cofferer to the King; and singularly enough the slab was employed (its beautifully carved surface hidden from view) to prop up the tomb of that gentlemen himself. There it remained until Dr. Clarke, Rector of Buxted, discovered it in the year 1775, and reported it to Dr. (afterwards Sir William)

Burrell,* and the latter, with the consent of the representatives of the Shirley family, removed the slab to Southover
Church, and placed near it an inscription, stating the
circumstances under which it was found. Scarcely any
antiquarian discovery in England during the last century
excited so much interest as did this last relic
of Gundrada. But a still more remarkable incident
connected with Gundrada's bones occurred in the year
1845 : in the formation recently of the South Coast Railway, which crosses the site of the Lewes Priory, the
excavators engaged in the work found, at no great
distance from the surface, the identical leaden coffins
alluded to, inscribed respectively with the names Gvndrada
and Willemus. These with their contents were, by the
antiquarian zeal of the neighbourhood, preserved,
and a subscription raised for the erection of a sacellum,
attached to Southover Church. At length the bones of the
Conqueror's daughter, so long divorced from the memorial
which had covered them, found themselves again beneath
it. The history, then, of Gundrada's mortal remains is as
follows : originally buried 1085, re-interred about 1145,
separated from their tombstone 1537, tombstone brought
back to Southover 1775, re-deposit of the bones under the
original memorial 1846.

We find it stated (9th year of Edward II.'s reign)
that John, Earl of Surrey, for want of heirs of his own
body settled the Lordship of Brighton on that king,
only reserving his *life interest* in it and his other estates.
From the Crown it passed to the Earls of Arundel,
one of whom, Richard, being attainted in the reign
of King Richard II., his estates were seized and
this Lordship with several others were given at that
time to Thomas Mowbray, then created Duke of Norfolk,

* The Grandfather of the present Sir Percy Burrell and Walter
Wyndham Burrell, Esq., the present Sheriff of the County, and who left all
his manuscripts to the British Museum.

In King Henry VII.'s reign it was in possession of Maurice Lord Berkely, but after him no mention is to be found of it. By the statute of Winchester, 13th Edward I., this town had a constable appointed for itself exclusively, shewing its importance at that period.

STORMS & INCURSIONS OF THE SEA.

Brighton in former times, suffered considerably from its greatest enemy *the sea*, although its greatest friend in modern days, confirmed by the fact that from the year 1260 to 1340 upwards of 40 acres of land were submerged, the sea making frequent inroads on the *lower town* which existed *under* the *Cliff*. Between that period and 1665, 22 *copyhold tenements* belonging to the Manor of Brighthelmstone—Lewes alone,—were washed away, amongst them 12 shops with 4 *stake places* attached to them for fishing purposes, and 3 cottages and 3 parcels of land adjoining. There still remained under the Cliff 113 tenements with capstans and *stake places*, which were destroyed by the memorable storms of 1703 and 1705. The one of 1703 began about midnight on the 27th of November, and continued with *unabated fury* for 8 *hours*. Many houses were demolished, others unroofed, the church leads were torn off, and two mills belonging to the town thrown down and much injured, the town presenting the appearance of a place severely bombarded by an enemy. The storm of 1705 commenced at *one o'clock* in the morning, attained its greatest fury at *three*, and raged *until eight*. It completed the destruction of all the buildings of the lower town which had escaped the fury of former inundations. Every habitation under the Cliff was utterly demolished, and its very site concealed from the owners' knowledge beneath a mound of beach. The roof of the Parish Church again suffered much, the leads of the same being completely stripped away. A record of this event is preserved in the tower of the church beneath the bell storey, on the wall of which is nailed a tablet of sheet lead measuring 4ft. 6in. by 2ft. 6in., taken from the roof of this sacred edifice on the restoration of the church in 1853. It is inscribed in raised cast characters *Richard Masters, Richard Tuppen, John Masters, Church-wardens,* 1705. Irrespective of the 40 acres swallowed up by the sea from the years 1260 to 1340, the adjoining parishes of *Hove, Aldrington and Portslade* suffered considerably more, the first to the extent of 150 *acres, Aldrington* 40, and *Portslade* 60.

In *Magna Britannia* published in 1720, it is stated that "Hove had been a considerable place but is now almost swallowed up by the sea." As regards Aldrington it is stated by Camden, Stillingfleet, and other antiquarians to be " the Portus-Adurni of the Romans, or *Port* of the *River*," and was no doubt a place of considerable importance. It has still the ruins of a church,* but for many years had not a single inhabitant excepting the toll-keeper at the gate, on the high road from Brighton to Shoreham. With reference to Portslade, this village derives its name from *Slade* or way to the *Port*. As regards the inroads of the sea, Dr. Mantell remarks that "at Brighton they have been very extensive, and the whole of the ancient town was situated on the spot now covered by the sands, and the *present Cliffs* were behind the town like those of Dover." Mr Lyell in his *Principles of Geology*, says, " the sea has merely resumed its position at the base of the Cliffs, the site of the old town having been a *beach* which had for ages been abandoned by the ocean."

The town consisted, in the reign of Queen Elizabeth, of seven *streets* and as many *laines*. The most spacious of them, " *South Street*," devoured by the ocean, it is supposed formed the sea front of the town *under the Cliff*. At the

* The Living of Aldrington is worth £100 per year, and every successor to the curacy, on his induction, preaches once on a temporary pulpit; the Church being a heap of ruins.

beginning of the year 1700 there stood a house, 350 yards from " Wood's original Baths," (now the site of "the Ladies' Swimming Bath " belonging to " Brill's Baths Company," and near the Pump House Groyne), belonging to Mr Male, a respectable rope maker. At high tides the sea came up to the walls of the York Hotel, also up the west side of the circular bath, at the end of East Street, and flowed down Pool Valley into the sea again. The last memorable occasion was that of the *great storm* of the 23rd of November, 1824. Formerly it was the custom to unload *coal brigs* in front of the town, but this plan was abandoned in consequence of the numerous wrecks that took place, and the great risk attending the same. On one night during the last 40 years no less than half-a-dozen wrecks took place *between* Ship Street and West Street—the port of Brighthelmstone. The limit of the said port was from opposite the *Old Ship Hotel* to the bottom of *West Street,*—denoted by *two stones* each bearing the inscription : " The Port of Brighthelmstone :" the eastern stone was removed at the commencement of the sea wall, the other remains close to the fountain at the latter spot. The Insurance Offices refused to ensure longer any ships except upon such terms as made it almost *prohibitory.* It was of frequent occurrence formerly that one or two ships suffered in the same way, during the winter months, it being on a *lee shore,* and a gale springing up from the south or south west caused the damage. The principal *coal merchants* had at that time capstans and *buoys,* and to this custom is due the origin of so many gaps or roadways to the beach, to enable the coals to be brought to their several depositories. The coal duty was first levied in 1773 by Act of Parliament, and was 6d. *per chaldron,* afterwards increased to 1s., subsequently to 3s. and then altered to 2s. 6d. *per ton,*—being one-sixth less than the same, as at the present time,—to enable the authorities to erect groynes, jetties, and other defences, to stay the encroachments of the sea. Every *chaldron* of

coals cost in the year 1819, £3 16s. 3d., made up
from the following incidental expenses upon freighting a
vessel :—

	£	s.	d.
Freight per chaldron	1	18	0
Nesham Main, at	0	17	0
King's Duty, at	0	10	0
Town Duty, at	0	3	0
Spoutage at Newcastle, ditto	0	0	6
Cartage from beach, ditto	0	4	0
Metage and trimming, ditto	0	1	0
Ramsgate and Dover lights, ditto ...	0	2	6
Beer to men, at...	0	0	3
	£3	16	3

Beyond Mr Male's house before-mentioned was his extensive
rope walks, extending *east* and *west*, *parallel* with the *sea*, and
we may imagine from the number of fishing craft belonging
to the town, coupled with the fact that hemp grew close
at hand, that he must have done an extensive trade. On
reference to the *Court Rolls* it will be found that most of
the *ground* now occupied by *Black Lion Street* and *Ship Street*
was called the *hemp shares*, being at that time *plots* or *gardens*
for the exclusive use of the fishermen. Besides these plots
the ground on which stands Brunswick Square and Terrace,
&c., was devoted to the growing of *flax*, for the use likewise
of the fishermen. It might be incidentally named that
Male's predecessor was a man of the name of Anthony
Smith, who made all the cordage, &c., for the fishery, and
in 1670, for *being a nonconformist*, suffered great persecution.

In the year 1580 the number of fishing boats was rated
at 80, able mariners 400, and 10,000 nets. At the present
time many of our mackerel boats have nets to the extent of
two miles in length : they can be *shot* in an hour, but it
takes from three to seven hours to get them in,—according
to the weather. The boats now in use are of a heavier

calibre than formerly, inasmuch as the season for commencing the voyage is entirely changed. At the present time they, soon after Christmas, proceed to *Plymouth* and Mount's Bay, Cornwall, where the fish are taken in considerable numbers; formerly our fleet of mackerel boats proceeded to sea on the 1*st of May*, with the *garland* at the *mast head*. It was invariably the custom that a few *of the finest* fish of the first catch were sent as a present to the Prince of Wales, then resident at the Royal Pavilion, or at Windsor Castle. Two *red mullets* were once sold for a guinea, these to be applied to the same purpose. Fishing is not so profitable an undertaking as formerly : the highest price that has been known to be obtained per 100 for mackerel is from £12 to £20 ; the lowest 10s. to 12s. It is recorded in *" Yarrell's History of British Fishes "* that in May, 1807, the first catch of Brighton mackerel sold at Billingsgate for 40 guineas per 100, and reckoning them at *short tale*, viz., *six score*, this would amount to the enormous sum of 7s. each, the highest price ever known in that celebrated Metropolitan market. The old fishermen complain that the number of fish has diminished and attribute this fact to the use of small mesh nets and the *fishery* being continued at unseasonable periods. A boat has been known to take two lasts of fish (20,000), in two nights. Dark nights are necessary for mackerel fishing. On moonlight nights the fish keep at the bottom of the water.

The boats are likewise used for the herring voyage, which commences about October. Herrings as well as mackerel were taken formerly in larger quantities. The boats proceed generally to the North and South Foreland, and have been known to have taken two or three lasts each in a single night. The herring fishery commences much earlier on the Yorkshire coast : but let us hope there are better days in store for this class of the inhabitants, and that we may again see, as formerly, large heaps of fish on the beach, for nothing can be more advantageous than a *glut* (as it is termed) affording the humbler classes a cheap meal, and others an abundance. Formerly a custom prevailed among the old Brightonians to salt down for the winter's consumption of the family a number of herrings : a favorite dish was made therefrom, called *Solomon Gundy* (a corruption of the word *Salmagundi*), consisting of chopped-up *pickled herrings, apples, and onions, mixed with oil and vinegar.*

Another old custom was observed connected with the commencement of the mackerel voyage by the fishery population, called "bending in." On completion of the necessary preparation for the same, and the nets being put *on board*, it is celebrated in the following manner : the crews of the boats with their wives and families partake of bread, cheese, and beer *ad libitum*, on the beach, on the eve of their going to sea, and many are the wishes expressed for a prosperous voyage, &c. Formerly this custom was carried to a much greater extent than at the present time, inasmuch as the crews regaled themselves with hot suppers, but this latter portion of the custom is now of rare occurrence : the expense of this is chargeable to the boats. A mackerel boat and nets are worth from £500 to £700.

At the back of Mr Male's house was a walled in yard and excavated *well*, and during the prevalence of one of the storms related the whole of these premises were inundated and lost under the beach. Mr Male then purchased some land and a dwelling on the site of the mansion afterwards erected by Mrs Fitzherbert, on the Steine, in 1804, at the *corner of Steine Lane.* As late as the year 1781 the mouth of the well was visible at low tides ; but since that period the still further encroachments of the sea has rendered this last relic of the *old town no longer visible,* as it is now buried in deep water at low tide. In 1823, on Messrs. Cheesman and Co., builders, excavating the foundation of the house at the *south east* corner of Brunswick Square, the sea dashed over the road into the same ; but from that period to the present time it has gradually receded, mainly to be

16

attributed to our groynes, which appear to be effectual
bulwarks against its encroachments. The principal of
them appears to be the concrete one on the Junction Road,
which cost upwards of £5,000. Various have been the
improvements during the last half century, the first being
a road made on arches to connect *Middle Street and West
Street* in *front of the sea* (the communication prior to this
being the narrow street at the back, called South Street),
opened by George IV., Jan. 29, 1822 (anniversary of second
accession), and the whole road from the bottom of
East Street to the extremity of the parish was named the
" King's Road." Other improvements followed, the great
sea wall being commenced in 1834, from the bottom of
Ship Street opposite the Old Ship Hotel, obliterating all
traces of the ruins of the old block house* that stood on this
spot, built in the first year of the reign of Elizabeth. At
a Court Baron on the 27th of September, 1558, the Lords
of the Manor granted the inhabitants a parcel of land for
the purpose of building and fortifying the same as a protection against the incursions of the French. A few years
prior, viz., July 18th, 1545, the town had been attacked by
them under Admiral Donebatte with 200 ships, and 26
galleys, which arrived off Brighton " but the beacons were
fired, and the inhabitants thereabouts came down so thick
that the Frenchmen were driven to their ships with the
loss of divers of their numbers, so they did but little hurt."
They then proceeded to the Isle of Wight, and two thousand of their men landed, and one of their captains was
slain with many others. They then returned to their vessels
and attempted to land at Seaford, but "were again repelled by
Sir Nicholas Pelham and others, with such power that was

* The Block House, built by Queen Elizabeth, extended 400 feet from
the East to the West Gate, and was 14 feet high. The East Gate remained
till the year 1777, and was then taken down to afford room for constructing
a battery that stood on a portion of the site of Old Battery House, at the
bottom of East Street, the powder magazine of which was recently
found—on excavating for the erection of Markwell's Royal Hotel, a few
years prior the site of Mahomed's Shampooing Baths,—belonging to the
western part of the said battery.

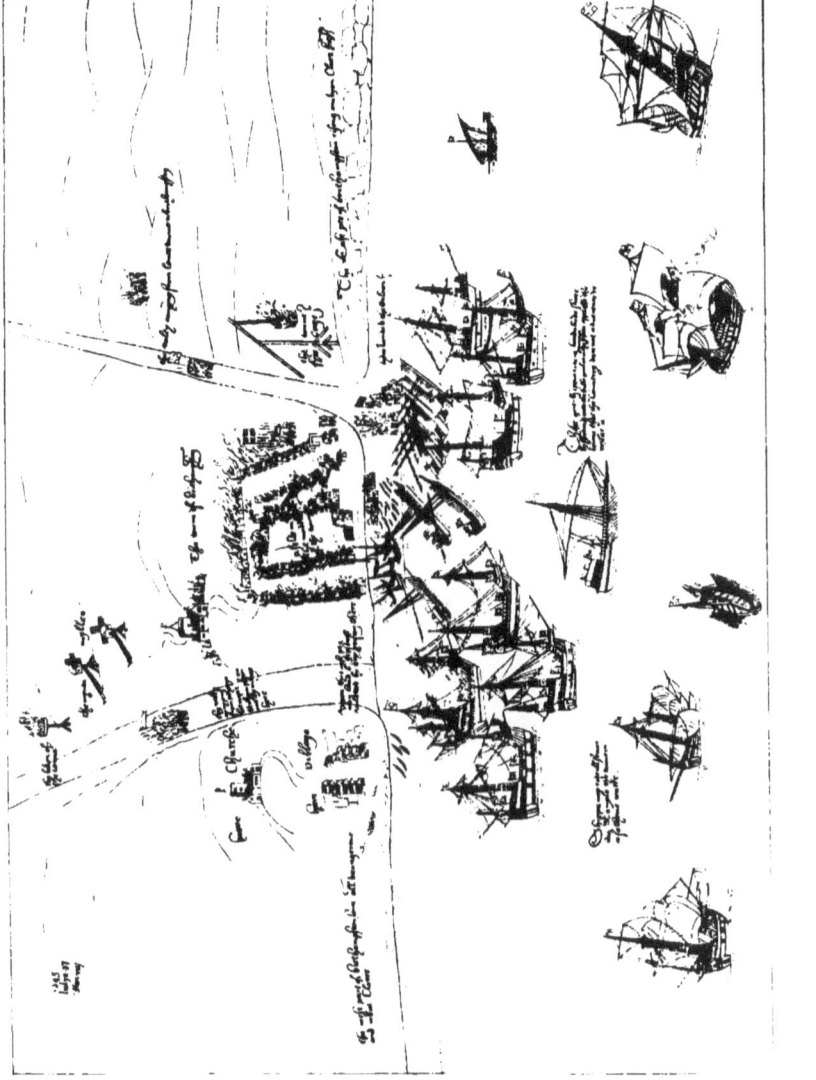

raised *in the sodden* that they *turned stern* and so got them *home again* with the loss of several thousand prisoners, without achieving any act worthy to be mentioned." This Sir Nicholas Pelham (an ancestor of our much respected and worthy neighbour, the Earl of Chichester, Lord Lieutenant of the County) was buried in the church of St. Michael's, Lewes, and this exploit is thus recorded on his tomb,

> "His valours proofe, his manly virtues prayse
> Cannot be marshalled in this narrow roome ;
> His brave exploit in great King Henry's dayes
> Among the worthye hath a worthier Toombe,
> What time the French sought to have sack't Seafoord
> This Pelham did *repel*-em back *aboord*."

There is an engraving of this attack in the British Museum.

Like all other buildings in that locality the old block house fell a prey to the insatiable ocean's attacks in January, 1749. The sea wall being completed it enabled the authorities to make a new carriage road round the circular Bath, at Junction Road, and considerably widen the existing roads along the sea frontage, and to form the beautiful slopes, &c., in front of Kemp Town. The Chain Pier* was commenced September 18th, 1822, under the immediate superintendence of Captain Samuel Brown, (afterwards knighted), and opened for the admission of the public the year afterwards, viz : on the 25th November, costing £30,000, and proving a great attraction to the town. Another pier, equally attractive, has been erected opposite Regency Square, by a company of gentlemen desirous of contributing to the comfort of our numerous visitors. It was commenced on Easter Monday, 1863, and opened by the Mayor of Brighton (Alderman Henry Martin), on October 6th, 1866, with a procession, &c., and a dinner at the Royal Pavilion, in commemoration of the event.

ANCIENT CUSTOMS OF THE TOWN.

It appears from the ancient records of the town that perpetual jealousies and strife existed between the fisher-

* It is not generally known that the Chain Pier is exactly in the CENTRE of the *Sea Front*, in the *Parish of Brighton*, consequently the *lower side of New Steine is in the* WEST PART *of the town.*

men and landsmen, touching the application of a quarter
share from boats, and in consequence of a memorial to
the Lords of the Council, from the former, respecting the same, a commission was sent here in
1580 to settle every difference, assess the town rates, and
arrange the public concerns of the parish. The number of
landsmen who at that time paid parochial rates and taxes
as 102; the number of fishermen amounted to 400.
The decision of the Commissioners, viz., the Earl of
Arundel, Lord Buckhurst (Lord of the Manor), Sir
Thomas Shirley (of Preston), and Henry Shelley, Esq.,
gave satisfaction till 1618, when a fresh arrangement was
entered into. The orders and regulations of these two
commissions were directed to be " written in two several
books of parchment," one of which was to be delivered to
the Earl of Arundel and Lord Buckhurst, the other was to
" be *kepte* in a *cheaste* locked with three locks in some convenient place in Brighthelmston." Provision was also
made for the safe custody of the key of the chest, and for
the annual reading of the regulations by the Vicar of the
Parish,—" *openlye* in the presence of all the fishermen and
others of the parishioners, contributories, in some convenient time and place." The " Book of all the '*Auncient*
Customs*'* is dated the 23rd of July, in the 32d year of
Queen Elizabeth, 1580, and is kept in the office of the
Vestry Clerk;" and in the same book will be found the
following, based on the application of the fishermen
to the Lords of the Council, for redress, as they
imagined they were paying (through the means of the
quarter share payable by every boat returning from
any voyage) a larger proportion than the landsmen.
It states as follows:—" The auncient custom for payment
and employing the quarter share: Item—the master of
every boat at Brighthelmston, at St. Stephen's Day next,
after his return from any fishing voyage, *wheresoever* or
whomsoever it was *begun, had* or *continued, hath used* to divide

and pay out of the whole profits of the said boat, without diminution or deduction to any stranger going in the said boat to be made, the said quarter share unto the Church-wardens of Brighthelmston for the time being, and half-a-share for the Vicar there for the time being, and the other he hath for his own use." Item—" the said wardens used to employ the said quarter share especially upon the building of forts and walls towards the sea for the defence of the said town, and for provision of shot and powder and other furniture for that purpose, and at all times to have in readiness in some convenient place in the town, to be kept in store safely, 4 barrels of powder and 40 round shot and 10 chain shot for every piece, and to be applied likewise for the entertainment of soldiers in time of wars, and other public service of the Prince and maintenance of the ' Parish Church.' "

Orders for the Churchwardens—" Imprimis. There shall be yearly at the time accustomed *two* substantial *fishermen* and *one* such landsman, chosen by consent of the *Constable, Vicar, or Curate,* and the chief of the town, for Churchwardens." Item : the said Churchwardens, or any of them, shall not employ nor disburse any of the money to be kept by the sea-faring and land-wardens to any other use than for the reparation of the church, and for neces-sary public charges for the town, without the consent of the Constable, the Vicar, or Curate, and six substantial men of the parish, first had in writing, of which six four shall be fishermen and *two landsmen,* upon pain of paying all sums of money laid out contrary to this order, at and upon the charges of the said wardens. And if they shall neglect to collect such quarter share of the fishermen for the town's uses, after his or their knowledge that it is due, within six days, then he or they for *every time* so neglecting *shall* pay unto the poor man's box, of Brighthelmston, three shillings and fourpence, or else answer it before the Com missioners."

B

Item.—" There shall be selected by the said Commissioners, out of the *auncientest*, *gravest*, and *wisest* inhabitants, eight fishermen and four landsmen for assistants to the constable in every public cause, whereof every one shall be ready, and give his attendance upon the constable as oft as need shall require, and whosoever shall presume to call together any assembly to the intent to practice or put in use any manner or device, or art, touching the government of the said town, without the privity, consent, and command of the said constable and assistants, shall forfeit for every time so doing forty shillings. And to the intent that the said *twelve* grave and *wise men* may have continuance, therefore, upon the death or removal of any of them, to choose and supply such other of the said town as by them, or the more *part of them*, shall be thought meet, provided that such choice shall be always ratified and allowed by the Stewards of the Lords of the said town, or by such one of them as shall happen to keep court in the said town, next after such choice made or otherwise, *the same choice to be void*, if such choice shall by the said Stewards, or by such one of them as shall fortune to be present as aforesaid, be disallowed until a sufficient man in the judgment of the same Stewards be chosen."

Item.—" That so much of the said quarter share as shall amount to the *double value* of the contribution (of the landsmen) shall be kept employed and accounted for indifferently by all the Churchwardens in such sort as is aforesaid, and the residue of the said quarter share shall be remaining in custody of the Seawardens, who shall not employ or disburse any part or parcel thereof but for the common profit of the town, and that only with the consent of the Constable *being a fisherman*, the Vicar, and six other *fishermen being of the twelve* in writing first had and obtained, and thereof shall make a true and particular account in writing, in the presence of the said Constable,

Churchwardens, and Fishermen at tho time accustomed."

Item :—" Forasmuch as the town is overcharged with
multitudes of poor people, which daily are thought to
increase by means of receiving *under tenants*, lodging of
strangers, and tho disorder of tippling-houses, and that
the Constable cannot without further assistance take upon
him the whole oversight and charge of all parts of the
town ; in this behalf it is thought meet that every one of
the twelve shall have assigned upon him some street or
circuit near his dwelling-house, where he shall, as deputy
to the Constable, have special charge for the keeping
of good order, and especially to see that the order for
the avoidance of under tenants be duly observed, and
that none lodge or keep tippling-houses ; and ' Whereas,
there hath been a controversy of long time between
the said fishermen, being the greater part of the parish
and the husbandmen and artificers there, as well as for
that for the reparation of the church as all other
public charges, which hath been great as building of forts
and walls, provision of shot and powder, and other necessaries, for the defence of the town against foreign enemies,
have been sustained and borne by the said quarter share
of the said fishermen only, except a small annuity or rent
yearly of two windmills (one of which is now utterly
decayed), as well for the utter *extinguishment* of all such
controversy and division, as also for the better increase of
amity and neighbourly friendship among the said parties,
the said Lord Buckhurst and Richard Shelley, Esquire, have
likewise named to be set down here in writing at tho place,
and in the day and year aforesaid, the names of all such
husbandmen and artificers which are of ability in the
said town, and the several sums of money which every
one of them by their several consents have granted yearly
to be paid for and in name of a contribution towards the
charges aforesaid, and to be paid " on St. Stephen's

Day," and in carrying out the foregoing arrangement, 73 of the class named attached their *marks* or *signature* to the document or signs, and the number that could not write their names amounted to 66. Consequently it will be found that at that period education had not made much progress amongst some of the principal inhabitants. The *marks, signs,* or *characters* of a large proportion named are of a novel kind, and it is conjectured by some antiquarians that they are the symbols of the trade or occupation of those who assented to the arrangement. This opinion is formed from the circumstance of Stoneham, the then Constable of the town, being a *ship carpenter*, and attaching a *hatchet* to his name, and for the same reason the supposition is that Oston, from his sign, was a butcher (it being *a heart*). Good, a wheelwright (from a wheel), J. Ducarde (the younger), a husbandman, from his mark, a harrow, &c.

BRIGHTON WORKHOUSES.

No record can be found in the annals of the parish relating to the relief of the poor prior to 1690, at which time existed a tenement for that purpose, situated in East Street. In the year 1727 the first mention is made of a workhouse being built,—in the *town book*, in Feb. 26, 1727, "That a mortgage be effected on the workhouse to indemnify Thomas Simmons in paying the moneys he made of the materials of the Block House to the Constable and Churchwardens, by them to be disbursed in payment of materials, and the workmen employed about building the Workhouse," and on May 10th following another entry to the following effect :—" Order in vestry for Churchwardens and Overseers with all speed to borrow £50 to pay for materials and workmanship about the Workhouse in the building of it, to be repaid out of the poor rate or taxes to be raised in the parish on or before May 10, 1728. At a public vestry meeting held at the Old Ship, October 18, 1727, it was agreed that the Churchwardens and Overseers should take up with all convenient speed and borrow £100, upon interest at 5 per centum per annum, towards building the New Workhouse. It is evident this Workhouse was of a very limited extent, for in 1733, a portion of the Alms-houses in connection with the chauntry of "St. Bartho-lomew," and which was sold for £17, was added to the building. (The spot is now occupied by the *east* portion of the "Brighton Market.") In consequence of the great increase of the "poors-rates,"—which amounted in 1736 to 8d. in the £ *rack rent*,—it was then considered an almost intolerable burthen to the parish. This increase in the rates had arisen from the *inroads* of the sea and the injury experienced by the town from the civil and foreign wars of that and the preceding century. The pressure of taxation was so great upon the inhabitants,—although the following order of the Commissioners had rigidly been carried out by the authorities, *to wit*, " That if any owner or lessor of any house within Brighthelmston shall admit any tenant or tenants, *under tenant* or *under tenants* into his said house, except the said tenant or tenants shall by the opinion of the Constable and Churchwardens in writing—first, to be set down,—be thought of sufficient ability to *maintain* himself and his family *without burthening the town*, then the said owner or lessor shall forfeit, for every month that any such tenant not being estimated as aforesaid shall inhabit or dwell in his said house, to the poor man's box, 3s. 4d.,"—that an application was made by the authorities of the town to the Justices, at the Quarter Sessions at Lewes, for assistance, who had the power under the Act of Parliament, the 18th of Elizabeth, to make an order on the parishes in the neighbourhood that had few poor of their own, which was accordingly done, and these parishes had to assist by way of contribution, as under, yearly:—

Patcham	...	...	...	...	...	£17	16	7
Hangleton	...	...	...	...	...	4	16	9
East Aldrington	...	...	...	...	6	1	1½
Blatchington	...	...	...	...	...	4	2	6
Ovingdean	...	...	...	...	...	6	0	10½
						£38	17	10

Formerly the recipients of parish relief were compelled to *wear a badge* to proclaim their poverty. The following is the Vestry minute from the parish books, viz. :—"At a meeting of the 'Churchwardens and Overseers,' held August 27th, 1696, an accompt was given that Susan Stone, the *widdow* of *Thomas, refused to ware* the town badge; the letters on the same being 'B.P.,' upon which she was *putt* out of the weekly pay." The Workhouse in the Bartholomews existed until 1822. In that year the one built on the Church Hill was completed. The cost was £10,000, in addition to £1600 for the land (between 13 and 14 acres) purchased in 1818 and paid for by a rate made expressly for that purpose. A portion of it was used as the northern cemetery of the Parish Church. The building was calculated to hold 460 inmates, including children. It received its first occupants on the 12th of September, and in that year the number was 95, although the average number before removal was 150, showing the antipathy of the paupers to be 'transported' out of the parish, as they were pleased to term it,—that other means of subsistence were found by them, in preference to being kept at the expense of the parish is evident. Herewith is subjoined the following statement, a most interesting document of the rapid increase of poors-rates :

Abstract of the receipts and expenditure of the
Directors and Guardians of the Poor from the 25th of
March, 1817 to March, 1818 :—

RECEIPTS.

Collected from Poor Rates paid into the
Treasurer's hands from Easter, 1817, to
Easter, 1818, viz. £10,983 10 9
Reimbursement from parishes 89 14 11
Poor's earnings 85 12 5
Bastardy 201 13 0
                                    _____
                                    £11,360 11 1
                                    _____

EXPENDITURE.
Weekly list to paupers 4,413 12 8
Other charges summed up 7,801 18 2
                                    _____
                                    £12,215 10 10
                                    _____
Excess of Expenditure £954 19 9
                                    _____

In this year, 1818, it was resolved, for the better classifica-
tion, &c., of the inmates, to build a new workhouse, and
the ground was consequently purchased for that purpose
at the price already named. This workhouse, like its
predecessor (after having had many additions and enlarge-
ments) was found to be totally inadequate for its requirements, and consequently, in February, 1853, the then
Board of Guardians determined (after a long controversy)
to receive the report of a Committee appointed for that
purpose, to dispose of the Workhouse and grounds and
erect another Industrial School. This Committee was
appointed in May, 1852, and consisted of the following
gentlemen, viz.:—Henry Nye, Arthur H. Cox, Henry
Martin, Wm. Lambert, Jno. Yearsley, Wm. Beedham,
Wm. Embling, Edmundus Burn, and Henry Schilling;
and it will be seen what sad havoc death has made among
them, inasmuch as there is but a third remaining, viz.:

Messrs. Burn, Cox and Martin, at the present time, 1871. The Rev. Jno. Allen, the present Vicar of Patcham, at the time mentioned was an ardent supporter of the scheme, being Chaplain to the Workhouse.

Ground was purchased in 1854 on the Race Hill, to the extent of 7 acres, at £325 per acre, for the site of the Workhouse (subject to a tithe rental of about £8, for which half an acre and ten perches of land were given up at the north-east corner of the site as compensation for the payment thereof); and for the Industrial Schools on the Warren Farm beyond the Race Course, to the extent of 20 acres, at £100 per acre. The Schools were completed, and occupied on the 14th day of August, 1862. The Industrial Schools cost £8223, the farm buildings £1513. The greatest difficulty was experienced in supplying the same with water. A well was sunk to the unprecedented depth of 1285 feet before water could be obtained in sufficient quantities for the purposes required. The commencement of the building of the Workhouse remained in abeyance till May 11, 1865, when the first stone was laid and the building commenced. It was finished in 1867, and received its first occupants on the 12th September following. The cost of the new building was £35,438 10s 5d; internal fittings, £5679 14s 6d; total of the whole, £41,118 4s 11d,—leaving a surplus of £244 19s 7d in favor of the parish, consequent on the removal of the Old Workhouse. The land and materials of the Old Workhouse, on Church Hill, realised £42,363 4s 6d.

The population of Brighton for the last century was as follows, viz. :—

In 1761 it amounted to	... 2,000	In 1831 it amounted to	... 40,634
" 1786 "	... 3,600	" 1841 "	... 46,661
" 1794 "	... 5,669	" 1851 "	... 65,573
" 1801* "	... 7,339	" 1861 "	... 77,693
" 1811 "	... 12,012	" 1871 to about	... 90,000
" 1821 "	... 24,429		

* The year the first Census was taken.

The Census to be taken this year, on April 3, it is believed
will shew the number of inhabitants to be about 90,000,
and that more accommodation in the Workhouse will be
required, from the fact that the inmates the last week in
March numbered: Workhouse, 778 ; Schools, 271 ; total,
1049 ; the relief, in cash and kind, to the out-door
poor, to £283 11s 10d ; number of persons relieved, 4871.

BARTHOLOMEWS AND THE VICARAGE.

It is a singular fact that the authorities of the town
have never defined the extent of the Bartholomews,
which for local convenience should be done, and more
especially for the inhabitants residing in the immediate
neighbourhood.

The Bartholomews is frequently mentioned in the
chronicles of the town. It was a kind of chauntrey or
free chapel, dedicated to St. Bartholomew, and was
destroyed by the French, the neighbouring parish church
of Aldrington sharing the same fate, and Hove and New
Shoreham partially so. Afterwards a dwelling for two or
three monks, who officiated, was attached to the same.
The Lord of the Manor of Brighthelmston granted a piece
of land for the purposes thereof to the priory of St.
Pancras at Lewes (in the parish of Southover) under a
quit rent of 3d per annum. In the year 1513 the French
made another of their descents on the town, under
Primauget, and partially destroyed this building by the
fire which devastated the parish, caused by their landing.
The north portion of the same, which escaped the devouring
element, was fitted up as the residence of the Vicar of
Brighton (after the Reformation) and which for many
years was called the Prior's Lodge. The Rev. T. Hudson
built a new Vicarage house thereon, about 1790, in lieu of

the old building, which was pulled down. This in its turn was vacated by the late Vicar, the Rev. H. M. Wagner, in 1835, and pulled down in 1837 : a garden was attached to the same of about a quarter of an acre, and the premises were situated at the eastern end of Prince Albert Street.

In the beginning of the sixteenth century the Rev. Edward Lowe was Vicar of the Parish, his successor was the Rev. Jno. Bolt (spoken of hereafter), and who died Nov. 2nd, 1660. He was succeeded by the Rev. — Falkner, who was Incumbent till 1705, when the Rev. Wm. Colbron succeeded him and held it till his death, on the 20th of July, 1750 (being an ancestor of the late Town Surveyor of that name). The next Vicar of Brighthelmston was the Rev. Henry Michell (grandfather of the late Rev. Henry Michell Wagner), who was made Rector of Maresfield at the age of 25 years, and five years after the Bishop of Chichester collated him to the Vicarage of Brighton and the Rectory of West Blatchington. In 1747 he married the only daughter of the Rev. Francis Reade, of Bedford, by whom he had sixteen children. A marble tablet, near the belfry of the Parish Church, speaks of his profound learning and estimable character. He died on the thirty - first of October, 1789, and was succeeded by the Rev. Thomas Hudson, who had for several years been Curate, and who commenced the first Chapel of Ease to the Church in this town, situated in Prince's Place, and known as " The Chapel Royal," the Prince of Wales laying the first stone on the twenty - fifth day of November, 1793. Mr Hudson died in 1804, and was succeeded by the Rev. Robert James Carr, D.D., after-wards Dean of Hereford and Bishop of Chichester and Worcester. He was succeeded by the Rev. H. M. Wagner, in July, 1824, who died October 7th, 1870, at the age of 77 years, and was succeeded by the present Vicar, the Rev. Dr. Jno. Hannah, D.C.L.* We fervently hope ho will be spared for many years to carry out the onerous duties of his holy ministry, so well commenced in his new sphere of action,—this large and populous parish of Brighton, in which his resources, both mentally and otherwise, will be severely taxed, but we trust, under Divine Providence, he may overcome all obstacles, and finally, when removed from his earthly labours, reap his reward. It will not be inappropriate to call attention to the long periods the incumbency of this parish has been held by all of his predecessors, and which is somewhat remarkable, viz. :—

The Rev. Edward Lowe	...	... 60 years.
" Rev. Jno. Bolt ...	...	... 56 "
" Rev. Jno. Falkner	...	... 45 "
" Rev. Wm. Colbron	...	... 45 "
" Rev. Henry Michell	...	... 50 "
" Rev. T. Hudson ...	...	... 15 "
" Rev. R. J. Carr† ...	...	... 20 "
" Rev. H. M. Wagner	...	... 46 "

The following anecdote is recorded of the Rev. H. Michell and connected with the celebrated Dr. Samuel Johnson, who came to Brighton on a visit to the Thrale family, who resided here regularly in the winter season, at a house in West Street, now partially the site of the " Concert Hall." Johnson was courted, admired and

---

* Born in 1818. Elected Scholar of Corpus-Christi College, Oxford, in 1837. Took a first class in Classics, and was elected Fellow of Lincoln College in 1840. After holding a small living in Oxfordshire a short time, was elected to succeed Archdeacon Williams as Rector of the Edinburgh Academy, in 1847. Was elected by the Scottish Bishops to succeed the Bishop of St. Andrew's, as Warden of Trinity College, Glenalmond, in 1854, where he was also Professor of Theology, and held these appointments till 1870. Was elected by the heads of Colleges in Oxford to preach the "Bampton Lectures" in 1870, and is also Rural Dean of Brighton and Hove. Is a Fellow likewise of the Royal and Antiquarian Societies of Scotland, &c.—It is understood that Dr. Hannah has received the appointment subject to a re-arrangement of *districts* connected with the establishment.

† Elected Bishop of Chichester.

received almost as a member of the family, and as such often visited them : " The Thrales often went to the Baths and Dr. Johnson went there also. The weather was cold, and Michell and Johnson meeting in the bath-room they sat down near the fire to warm themselves and converse. For a time their conversation was amicably and peacefully exchanged; but at last some knotty and difficult question arose, and not being able to adjust the matter, Michell seized the poker and Johnson the tongs, with which they enforced their arguments by thumping the grate violently and vociferating. The ladies were alarmed, and who were most unscientifically dancing the country dance, was interrupted; nor was it resumed till *Wade*, the Master of the Ceremonies, and the politest in the world, had pacified the wranglers."

The first stone of the present Vicarage was laid on Midsummer-day, 1834, and in the following year the structure was completed and accepted by the Bishop of the Diocese, on the unanimous recommendation of six Commissioners, namely, three laymen and three clergy-men, to the effect that the exchange would be in every respect beneficial. The ground on which it is erected is exactly two measured acres. The living is a Vicarage, in the gift of the Bishop of the Diocese ; but in the event of the Vicar being selected by the Crown to fill a vacant Bishopric the Crown has power to fill up the vacancy caused by such preferment. Annexed to it is the Rectory of West Blatchington, the Church of which is in ruins, and the living but small.*

The *Magna Britannia*, states that " The Church here is a Vicarage, but meanly endowed. The Vicar claims the old Episcopal custom of a penny per head (commonly called smoke money or a garden penny)

---

* Divine Service is performed at the Farm House on every Sunday afternoon by one of the Curates attached to the Parish Church of St. Nicholas, Brighton.

as also he requires as his due a quarter of a share out of
all fishing vessels, which formerly was very advantageous
to the Incumbent, when *the town was in its prosperity* but now
'tis of no *considerable profit to him*. The Parsonage Tythes
are about £100 per annum, but they are in the hands of an
impropriator, who allows the Vicar no benefit from them,
by which means the minister's maintenance is very small
and therefore the gentlemen of the *neighbouring parts* have
made an augmentation to it, by subscription of £50 per
annum, yet on this condition, that he shall instruct 50
poor boys of the *town*, in *reading and writing*. The Church
stands about 40 *rods* from the *town*, at a little distance
from the sea. There was formerly another Church, near
the *middle* of the town, which it is said was *burnt down*
some years ago by the French," alluding no doubt, to that
of St. Bartholomew already treated of.

In 1794 the salary of the Vicar of Brighton was solely
derived from the subscriptions of the nobility and gentry
resorting to the place. Books for that purpose were
placed in the Libraries, and the Vicar, prior to the
Reformation, had to pay to the Vicar of Hove yearly the
sum of 7s. 6d.

The Parish Church is supposed to be the oldest building in Brighton, being mentioned in the survey of the parish
in Domesday Book, 1086, and stood within the manor
held by William de Watteville, under William de Warrenne,
son-in-law of the Conqueror. It was valued before the
Conquest at £10, after the ravages of the Revolution at £8,
and at the time of the great survey at £12 a year, and
was thus described by an author of about half a century
ago :—" It appears to have been erected and repaired at
several different periods, as if it had been exposed to the
ravages and depredations of the French for centuries, and
during their hostile visits the churches were generally
plundered and set on fire ; hence we find this building
exhibiting styles of architecture of *different ages*. The

architecture is of that order usually denominated Gothic, or the ancient English. The external is flint, and very evidently the work of different periods. It consists of a nave, two side aisles, a chancel, in which is a rood loft, and a chantrey, or chapel, and a tower opening into the west end of the nave. The tower, porch, and buttresses at the east end of the church appear to be of later workmanship than some other parts. The chantrey, or chapel, which has been added to the original church by some pious person, is of the time of Henry VII. or Henry VIII. The architecture of it is different from every other part of the church, and is of inferior taste and workmanship, and of a much later date. The interior, before it was disfigured and encumbered with galleries, was plain, but yet handsome, having four equilateral pointed arches on each side of the nave, and octagonal columns with plain moulded capitals and bases. At the east end of the nave is a large arch opening into the chancel, and at the west end is a similar one opening into the tower. The large eastern window in the chancel, under which formerly stood the high altar, appears to be of the time of Henry II., and is a very beautiful structure, the mullions rising to the spring of the arch and then forming a rose. In this part there are a few remains of painted glass. Under the rood loft is a very beautiful screen executed in a different style to every other part of the church, the arches being formed from four centres, usually denominated the ' Tudor Arch,' and, according to the fashion of that age, was decorated with painting and gilding." In the church-yard leading to the porch is the shaft of a very ancient *stone cross*, which there can be no doubt was dismantled at or soon after the Reformation, and as regards the curious font the Church contains, it belonged it is thought to the Saxons *some time* previous to the *Norman* conquest. It is of a circular form, and has excited much observation among antiquarians. The sculpture upon it is in four sections. The first represents the Lord's Supper, and consists of seven figures: our Saviour in the centre, with glory crowned, is in the act of giving the blessing, and on the table are various drinking vessels and the bread. The next compartment contains a kneeling figure; the third which is larger, has a boat on the sea with the sail unfurled, and two figures, one presenting a small barrel or vessel to a bishop, who has his mitre and crozier and is giving bread to a female. Both figures are in the water : these are supposed to represent the first preaching of Christianity among the South Saxons. The fourth division consists of three arches, in each of which is a figure, the centre appearing to be the principal, the whole sculptured in *basso relievo*. Over these compartments is a line of *zig-zag* and lozenge work and beneath them is a row of exceedingly handsome ornamental work of leaves and flowers. The church stands 160 feet above low water mark, and is dedicated to St. Nicholas, Bishop of Mira in Lycia, who lived about the fourth century and was the reputed saint of fishermen, on account of various miracles he had performed in their favour. It was a noted land-mark for seamen, prior to its being surrounded by houses, and the tower of the edifice nearly represents the four cardinal points of the compass. It was given originally in the reign of Stephen, by Ralph de-Cheney, to the priory of Lewes, but it appears from the terms of an award or arbitration between Richard de-Wich, Bishop of Chichester, and William de-Ruslous, Vicar of St. Pancras, near Lewes, made in 1252, still extant in the episcopal archives at Chichester, that the Priory obtained no full possession of this church before that period. By this award, as soon as the then Rector of Brighthelmstone should die, or resign the living, the Prior of St. Pancras was to appoint the Vicar who was to have all the offerings of the altar, and as far as they belonged to altarage, and the *small tithes* (the great tithes belonging to the Priory) with a

convenient residence in the Bartholomews, and to have
the *third* of the *tithe* of hay. This order of things
continued until the suppression of Lewes Priory in 1538,
upon which the appropriation and patronage of this parish
were granted by Henry the VIII. to his Vicar, General
Cromwell, who, in that very year, ordered a public
register of baptisms and burials to be kept at Brighthelmstone and in every *other parish* in the *kingdom.* On
the death and attainder of Cromwell the Church was
conferred by the King on his repudiated Queen, "Anne
of Cleves" (who resided in the adjoining parish of Preston),
and on her death, in 1557, it again fell to the Crown, and
under Queen Elizabeth, if not sooner, the patronage and
appropriation of this Church seems to have been severed.
The former was attached to the See of Chichester and has
continued so to the present time, and the latter has passed
through several hands.

It is presumed that the Church of St. Nicholas, and
grounds were not used as a place of sepulture by the
inhabitants till after the destruction of the church and
chantry, or free chapel in the Bartholomews, from the
fact that the oldest tomb that we have on record and that
can be found or traced in the same does not date farther
back than that of the Rev. Jno. Bolt, who was Vicar
here, and a preacher of the Gospel for the long space
of 56 years. He died on the 2nd of November, 1669,
and was BLESSED with 29 CHILDREN and two wives, as
stated on his tomb, which was situate at the North East
corner of the Church, close to the entrance from Church
Street. The tomb was brick-built, the covering stone being
of perriwinkle, or Sussex marble. It became much dilapi-
dated, and from its very peculiar appearance passers-by
mischievously amused themselves by knocking off pieces,
but its final demolition took place in 1853, on the restoration of the present Church. The grounds connected with
the Church destroyed in the Bartholomews and the free

chapel likewise, were unquestionably the burial-places of the inhabitants, from the fact that on several occasions, during excavations, to wit, for the erection of the Market, the Town Hall, and the LATE VICARAGE, a number of skeletons, skulls, bones and other vestiges of mortality were brought to light.

NICHOLAS TETTERSELL AND THE ESCAPE OF CHARLES II.

In the churchyard of the Parish Church we have a tomb (next the chancel door) to the memory of Captain Nicholas Tettersell, who, for the sum of £60, conveyed Charles II. from Brighton to Fecamp, a town, situate just opposite Brighton, and near Havre, in France, in his little vessel, the "Surprise." The unfortunate King had been defeated at Worcester, Sept. 3, 1651, by the Parliamentarians; had wandered about the country for six weeks, and during the latter portion of the period was concealed in a farm house at Ovingdean,—now in the occupation of W. J. Green, Esq.,—waiting the first opportunity to cross the Channel. This soon offered and was successfully carried out, and the event has been treated on by Mr Harrison Ainsworth, in an historical romance called *Ovingdean Grange*. After the Restoration in 1671, " The Surprise " was moored opposite Whitehall, and a great number of persons visited and inspected it. In consideration of the important, loyal, and valuable services rendered by Capt. Tettersell to his Monarch, the name of the craft was altered from " The Surprise " to " The Royal Escape." It was entered as a fifth rate in the Navy, and he was made Captain of the same; in the year after, the King granted a reversion of the emoluments of the captaincy to his son, and pay likewise to a servant for each, to be paid by the naval authorities at Deptford, where the

c

vessel remained until the year 1791, when, being thoroughly
decayed, it was broken up. The family of Tettersell
continued to enjoy a pension, granted at the same time,
of £100 per annum. Sir Jno. Bridger, the grandfather of the
late Sir Henry Shiffner, of Coombe, near Lewes, was the
last of the family who received the pension. A ring that
was given by Charles to Tettersell is still in possession of
the family, and was exhibited, with many other relics and
works of art, in the Dome of the Pavilion, on the occasion
of the Southern Counties' Association meeting in this
town in the summer of 1867. Tettersell died July 26,
1674, and on his tomb is the following inscription :—

" P. M. S.

CAPTAIN NICHOLAS TETTERSELL,

THROUGH WHOSE PRUDENCE, VALOUR, AND LOYALTY, CHARLES II. KING
OF ENGLAND, AFTER HE HAD ESCAPED THE SWORD OF HIS MERCILESS
REBELS, AND HIS FORCES RECEIVED A FATAL OVERTHROW AT
WORCESTER, SEPT. THE 3D, 1651, WAS FAITHFULLY
PRESERVED AND CONVEYED TO FRANCE,
DEPARTED THIS LIFE THE 26TH DAY OF JULY, 1674."

"Within this marble Monument doth lie
Approved faith, honour, and loyalty ;
In this cold clay he hath now ta'en up his station,
Who once preserved the church, the crowne, and nation!
When Charles the Greate was nothing but a breath,
This valiant soul stept 'tween him and death :
Usurper's threats, nor tyrant rebels' frowne,
Could not affright his duty to the crowne ;
Which glorious act of his, for church and state,
Eight Princes, in one day, did gratulate——
Professing all to him in debt to bee,
As all the world are to his memory ;
Since earth could not reward the worth him given,
He now receives it from the King of Heaven.
In the same chest one jewel more you have,
The partner of his virtues, bed, and grave."

"Susannah, his wife, who deceased the 4th day of
May, 1672, to whose pious memory and his
own Honour, Nicholas,
Their only son, a just inheritor of his father's virtues,
hath paid his last duty in this monument, 1676."

———

"Here also lies interred the body of Captain Nicholas
Tettersell, his son, who departed this life the 4th of the
calends of October, 1701, in the fifty-seventh year of his
age."

With reference to the escape of King Charles II.,
the following has recently appeared in a new edition of
Bunyan's Pilgrim's Progress. After describing the fallen fortunes of that Monarch, following his defeat at Worcester,
during a space of six weeks, we read : " At length he
arrived at Brighton, then a little fishing town, and succeeded in escaping in a little vessel to France. The same
left Shoreham, and at night stood over to France, and
returned to Poole, no one discovering that they had been
out of their course."

A letter recently found among the archives of Devonshire House shows the important aid Charles received
from the mate of the vessel, Richard Carver, who was a
Quaker. He recognised the King, who pretended to be a
bankrupt merchant, flying from the bailiffs. Carver
assured him that his life was safe in his hands, and kept
the crew in ignorance of the quality of their passenger.
When they arrived on the French coast, off Fecamp, he
rowed him to the shore, and in shoal water carried him
on his shoulders to the land. Many years had passed
away, when Carver, on his return from the West
Indies, found a vast number of Quakers imprisoned for
conscience sake. Whitehead and Moore, the leading
members of the Society of Friends, entreated his
sympathy, and with him gained access to the King, who

at once recognised him, and enquired why he had not
been to claim his reward before. He answered that he
had been rewarded with the satisfaction of having saved
His Majesty's life, "and now, Sir, I ask nothing for
myself, but for my poor friends, that you should set them
at liberty, as I did you." The King offered to release any
six, and we may imagine the sailor's blunt answer:
"What! Six poor Quakers for a King's ransom!!"
His Majesty was so pleased as to invite them to come
again, and ultimately ordered their release. Probably
this Richard Carver here referred to was a relative of
Derrick Carver, of Brighton, who suffered martyrdom
at Lewes, for conscience sake, in the reign of Queen Mary.

PROSPERITY OF BRIGHTON & DR. RUSSELL.

Amongst the many causes that have operated to
give to Brighton pre-eminence among fashionable watering
places may be mentioned its vicinity to the metropolis,
being within 1¼ hour's ride of the same, and the railway
system is admirably carried out, with safety and convenience to passengers. The facilities afforded to visit
the adjacent towns and villages on its system cannot be
too highly praised, and the number of attractions that are
constantly held out for the gratification of our numerous
visitors have doubtless helped to promote the welfare
and prosperity of the town.* The efforts of its Mayor
and Corporation to increase its attractions, to foster the
same, and to assist materially Brighton's development and
advancement, have made the town in reality " the Queen
of Watering Places " and "London Super-mare." They
have recently resolved to pay £7000 towards the
Aquarium, now in progress, and this will be the means
of still further improving the sea frontage by the new

---

* It is stated, upon good authority, that at one period during the
season of 1870, there were upwards of 50,000 visitors in Brighton.

road extending from the Albion to the Suspension Pier. To the southward of the same, near the centre of the position now covered by this new promenade, there existed a battery in the year 1734,—but the inroads of the sea have swept it away, a result similar to what has befallen other portions of our sea front. It is also in contemplation to continue the road to Kemp Town,—thus forming, as it were, "the Rotten Row" of Brighton,—an under-cliff, like unto that of the Isle of Wight, and an agreeable resort for invalids and promenaders during the winter months. This work, when carried out, will prove a most advantageous and attractive one for the town, the eastern part of it in particular.

Previous to 1750 the town was not visited, for the sake of pleasure and health, by many persons of distinction, but remained in comparative obscurity. In that year Dr. Richard Russell removed here from Malling, near Lewes, took up his abode, and succeeded, by his talents and writings, in calling the attention of the public to the advantages arising from the use of sea-water. His works not only extended his fame, but brought into repute the town that he had adopted for his residence, and Dame Fashion soon patronized his efforts, as the following extract from a Brighthelmstone Guide, published in July, 1777, will show :—

This town, or village of renown
Like London Bridge, half broken down,
Few years ago was worse than Wapping,
Not fit for a human soul to stop in;
But now, like to a worn-out shoe,
By patching well, the place will do.
You'd wonder much, I'm sure, to see
How its becramm'd with quality:
Here Lords and Ladies oft carouse,
Together in a tiny house;
Like Joan and Darby in their cot,
With stool and table, spit and pot;

And what his valet would despise,
His lordship praises to the skies;
But such the *ton* is, such the case,
You'll see the first of rank or place,
With star and riband, all profuse,
Duck at his doorway like a goose:
The humble beam was placed so low,
Perhaps to teach some clown to bow.
The air is pure as pure can be,
And such an aspect of the sea!
As you, perhaps, ne'er saw before,
From off the side of any shore:
On one hand Ceres spreads her plain,
And on the other, o'er the main,
Many a bark Majestic laves
Upon the salt and buoyant waves;
The hills all mantl'd o'er with green,
A friendly shelter to the Steyne,
Whene'er the rugged Boreas blows,
Bemingled with unwelcome snows:
Such is the place and situation,
Such is the reigning seat of fashion.

Sea-bathing became more general, especially for persons afflicted with scrofulous diseases and glandular complaints, and, consequently, from the influx of visitors, Brighton began to flourish. Dr. Russell may, with justice, be called the founder of its prosperity (although it was destined for the Prince of Wales, afterwards, still further to develop its resources). He was born in the parish of St. Michael's, Lewes, and was the son of Mr Nathaniel Russell, a respectable surgeon there; was educated at St. Anne's Grammar School in that town, and joined his father as assistant. Afterwards went to Leyden, the most celebrated University in Europe for medical knowledge, and on his return to England was elected Fellow of the Royal Society and Doctor of Physic. He died in

1759, at the age of 72, and was buried in the family vault in South Malling, Lewes. The place of his residence in this town was on the spot now the Albion Hotel, formerly called Russell House (afterwards the residence of the Duke of Cumberland). In honor of his memory, Russell Street was named after him. It was admitted by all that he had done this town an incalculable degree of good. In the card room of the Old Ship Hotel there is an excellent likeness of the doctor, painted at the expense of Mr John Hicks, the then landlord, out of compliment, as the establishment at that time was the resort of the Materia-Medica visiting this town. Dr. Russell's works on the use of sea-water obtained a world-wide renown. After his death he was succeeded by Dr. A. Relham, who wrote a treatise on the invaluable efficacy of sea-bathing, and the salubrity of the town and neighbourhood, and the Rev. Dr. Mannington, of Jevington, wrote the following epigram on the abilities of Dr. Russell:—

> " Admiring ages Russell's fame shall know
> Till oceans' healing waters cease to flow."

And the following by Mr Serjeant Kemp, his grandson :—

> Brighthelmston was confessed by all
> To abound with females fair,
> But more so since fam'd Russell has
> Preferred the waters there.
> Then fly that dangerous town ye swains
> For fear ye shall endure
> A panic from some bright sparkling eye
> Which Russell's skill can't cure.

FIRST VISIT OF THE PRINCE OF WALES.

In the year 1782, being 20 years of age, the Prince of Wales paid a visit to his uncle, the Duke of Cumberland, at his residence at the southern extremity of the Steine, near the spot on which the Albion Hotel now stands, and the year after he repeated his visit, having evidently taken a great liking to the place. On this last occasion he took up his abode at a house belonging to the late Thomas Kemp, Esq., which formed the nucleus of the Pavilion, both visits of his Royal Highness being celebrated by the inhabitants by illuminations and other manifestations of joy in honour of the auspicious event. After purchasing this residence the Pavilion was commenced in 1784, and completed in 1787. The east front of the building was 200ft. in extent and consisted of a circular building in the centre supported by stone Doric pillars and crowned by a dome, and on each side there was a range of bow-fronted apartments one story high above the basement, with balconies and verandahs, the entrance front being towards East Street. A large barn that stood on the spot adjacent to the present County Bank was removed to assist the approach, and when visitors were travelling from London on the Cuckfield Road, and entered Brighton direct to East Street, passing Marlboro Place (then called North Row), there were two remarkable objects which struck the eye—a lofty, hideous, wooden weigh-scale, on the right hand at the bottom of North Street; and the barn spoken of on the left hand, opposite to it, in the same street, abutting nearly to Castle Square. This unsightly object —the weigh-scale—served to assess the toll which all weighty matters, such as hay, corn, bricks, &c., paid on entering the town. At the present time, when heavy goods are weighed while they are in the waggon, the horses are driven over a platform and just exceed the machine, while the carriage rests entirely upon it, and self-acting mechanism underneath calculates the toll, as in existence at the Western Road and King's Road Toll Houses. But our primitive weigh-scale here spoken of raised the carts and waggons a few inches in the air to the great dismay of the driver and his horses. The ground whereon

this novel machine stood was purchased by Mr
Hall, surgeon, and some handsome property erected in
its place, now occupied by Mr Page, bookseller, &c. Near
this spot (in July, 1811,) the last person in this town was
pilloried, of the name of Fuller, who underwent the punishment for endeavouring to pass a forged note. The platform
was about 10ft from the ground, consisting of a frame and
upright pillar, around which it revolved, and was made
with holes and folding boards, through which the head
and hands of the culprit were put. From 12 to 1 o'clock
he continued to take the circuit of an area of about 18ft.,
under the superintendence of the High Constable and his
Headboroughs, who had escorted him thither from the
King and Queen Inn, to which house he had been brought
from Lewes by the authorities of the House of Correction.
A large concourse of people assembled to witness the
punishment.

In 1793, his Royal Highness and the Duke of Marlborough, whose house stood at the north end of the Pavilion,
made a spacious sewer for carrying off a stream which flowed
occasionally from the Level and the well at Patcham and
sometimes inundated the Steyne, and from thence
emptied itself into the sea. The back of Marlborough House
was to the west, where the public road passed from
East Street to the bottom of Church Street. In consideration of the great expense of this most important
improvement the Lords of the Manor, with the consent
of the homage, gave his Royal Highness and the Duke of
Marlborough consent to rail in or enclose a certain portion
of the Steyne adjoining their houses respectively, but NEVER
to build or encumber it with anything that might obstruct
the prospect or be in any shape or way a nuisance to the
Steyne. In 1800, His Royal Highness purchased more property from Mr Weltjie, and, the year following, THAT called
Elm Grove Gardens, and the shrubberies and pleasure
grounds of the Duke of Marlborough, which grounds London

Road intersected by running in the REAR of the Pavilion,
With a view to connect the whole, the inhabitants of the
town gave permission to the Prince to enclose the old road.
This was given in the year 1803, but it was not till 1805
that an order from the Sessions, at Lewes, was obtained,
authorizing the same, and one of the conditions arranged
with his Royal Highness was to the following effect,
" That should the Prince at any time cease to require the
use of the same, proposed to be given up by the inhabitants,
or should the Pavilion and grounds at any time pass from
his occupation or be sold, then and in either of the said
cases the said portion was to revert to the use of the inhabitants."* The Grove Gardens adjacent were formerly a public
promenade and the resort of tea parties, the entrance
to the same being in Prince's Place, out of North Street.

The Pavilion is supposed to have cost upwards of a
million pounds, and the late Baron de Bode's money, to
the extent of a quarter of a million, was absorbed in this
edifice. The Baron's claims were before Parliament several
Sessions some few years since. Lambelette and several
celebrated Italian painters resided for years in Brighton
engaged in the decoration of the Pavilion. It has been stated
from authority that the Dome of the Music Room and
embellishments alone cost £10,000, the acoustic properties
of which cannot be surpassed. George IV. himself was
an accomplished player on the violoncello and a thorough
musician, and his private band consisted of about 50
performers, selected from the most eminent in the profession, the following being the names of the same :—
Malsch, Kramer, Eisert (conductors and leaders), Mencke,
Calhoun, Bennewitz, Schonerstadt, Spillerberg, 2 Rehns
(brothers), Schmidt, 2 Kirchners (father and son), 2
Behrns (ditto), 2 Andres (brothers), Andre (son), 3

---

* This very important provision was the means of saving this valuable
property to the town.

Turners (father and 2 sons), 3 Sillers (ditto), 5 Hardys (brothers), 2 Bests (brothers), 2 Bests (sons), Niebour, Gutteridge, Wœtzig, Albrecht, Tucker, Hammer, Dusart, Gilbert, Distin, Tuckwell, Bode, Krone, Schröder, Haussman, Medhurst, Egerstorff, Mennich, Hanedorn, Tidzer, Grabenstein, Chamerozvow, Mason, &c. It will be seen from these names that many of our resident professors belonged to this eminent band, and others of their descendants are still in this town.○

The King's first intimacy with Captain Blomfield arose from the circumstance of his enquiring of Colonel Slade, of the Royal Artillery (then stationed in the town), if he knew of any person who could play on the violoncello. The Colonel replied that he only knew of Captain Blomfield, who, in consequence, was invited to the Pavilion. His Royal Highness was so pleased with the Captain as to make him Master of the Household, and subsequently knighted him. A few years ago he was created Lord Blomfield, and his decease only occurred a short time since.

George IV. was a great patron of the arts and sciences and his benevolence and philanthropy were unbounded. A large number of the poorer inhabitants of this town were recipients of his bounty, and others were in the receipt of weekly stipends, and although Mr Thackeray, in his lectures on " The Four Georges,"† would not accord one atom of praise to the last George, yet there were traits in his character

---

* Many of the deceased members of this celebrated Band lie interred in the south-west portion of the Old Church Burial Ground, nearly opposite Upper North Street.

† These lectures were delivered at Brighton, as well as other places, and Mr Thackeray made a personal application at the Town Hall to engage the " Royal Pavilion" Banqueting Room for that purpose : but, on hearing the application, a well-known Alderman and an Ex-Mayor, who happened to be present, suggested to him that the Town Hall would do as well, at the same time intimating that he thought it was not strictly *etiquette* " *to abuse a man in his own house*." The hint was taken, and the Town Hall, instead of the Pavilion, was engaged for the purposes intended.

which ought not to have been overlooked or passed over
slightingly, traits that will stand out in bold contradiction
to Mr Thackeray's assertion *that he was the very personifi-
cation of vices*. In Mrs Matthews' memoirs of her husband
is an anecdote showing conclusively a very great deal of
good nature in the King. The old Polish dwarf, Count
Boruwlaski, was, through Matthews' exertions, brought
to Carlton House to see the King, who had known him
many years before. The two visitors, a dwarf and a player,
were treated by the King with great kindness, and more
than this with much considerate delicacy. It was in
July, 1821, when the approaching coronation and some
less pleasant matters were greatly occupying the Royal
mind. When Boruwlaski came away, Matthews found
him in tears, and learned it was entirely owing to the
kindness the King had manifested towards him. While
the two were for a little time apart, the King had taken
the opportunity to enquire if the Count required any
pecuniary help to make his latter days comfortable, avowing the desire to supply whatever was necessary.

The King had also offered to show his Coronation
robes to the dwarf, and further asked him if he retained
any recollection of a favorite valet of his whom he named.
The Count professing a perfect remembrance of the man,
the King said, "He is now, poor fellow, on his death-bed,
I saw him this morning, and mentioned your expected
visit. He expressed a great desire to see you, which I
ventured to promise he should do, for I have such a
regard for him that I would gratify his last hours as much
as possible. Will you, Count, do me the favor of paying
my poor faithful servant a short visit? He is even now
expecting you. I hope you will not refuse a poor, suffering,
dying man." The Count, of course, expressed his readiness
to obey the King's wishes. Boruwlaski was first shewn
the robes, and then conducted to the chamber of the sick

man, which was fitted up with every comfort and care, a
nurse and another attendant being in waiting upon the
sufferer. When the Count was announced, the poor
invalid had to be propped up in his bed. He was so
changed by time and sickness that the Count no longer
recognized the face with which his memory was familiar.
The nurse and attendant having retired into an
adjoining room, the dying man (for such he was and felt
himself to be) expressed his great obligation at such
a visit, and spoke most gratefully of the King, whom
he designated *the best of masters;* told the Count of all
his goodness to him, and indeed of uniform benevolence to all who depended upon him ; mentioned that his
Majesty, during the long course of his poor servant's
illness, notwithstanding the circumstances that had
agitated himself so long,—his numerous duties and cares,
his present anxieties and forthcoming ceremonies,—had
never omitted to visit his bed-side twice a day, not for a
moment merely, but long enough to soothe and comfort
him, and to see that he had everything necessary and
comfortable, telling him of all particulars of himself that
were interesting to an old and attached servant and
humble friend. This account was so genuine in its style,
and so affecting in its relation, that it deeply touched the
heart of the listener. The dying man, feeling exhaustion,
put an end to this interview by telling the Count that he
only prayed to live long enough to greet his dear master
after his coronation, to hear that the ceremony had been
performed with due honour and without any interruption
to his dignity,—and that he was *then ready to die in
peace.*

Mrs Matthews adds, "Poor Boruwlaski returned to
the Royal presence, as I have related, utterly subdued by
the foregoing scene, upon which every feeling heart will,
I am persuaded, make its own comment, unmixed with
party spirit or prejudice."

We know the faults of character belonging to George IV. have, of late years, been largely insisted on, and perhaps it is not possible to extenuate them in any great degree. It is, however, a mistake to suppose that because a man is a voluptuary and more remarkable for good manners than good morals, he *therefore* is a person wholly bad. A human being is a mixture of various and often apparently incongruous elements, one relieving and redeeming another, sometimes assuming a predominance, sometimes the reverse, very much as the accidental provocations of external circumstances may determine. It was so with this Monarch, as with the humblest of his subjects. In his lifetime one often heard both of pleasant things said and of amiable things done by the King. His restoration of the forfeited Scotch Peerage in 1824 was a piece of pure generosity towards men who were suffering through no faults of their own. When that measure was determined on, the representative of a forfeited Baronetcy of 1715 applied for a like extension of the royal grace. Though equally suitable, from the fact of the family having purchased back their ancestral lands, it was refused by the Ministers : but the King, on hearing of it, insisted on the applicant being gratified. This is stated on the authority of one very nearly concerned in the matter. To prove the estimation and appreciation o character in which George IV. was held by the inhabitants generally of Brighton, in 1828, a subscription was entered into and a statue (by Chantrey) erected on the Steyne, at a cost of £8,000.

In the reminiscences of Michael Kelly his Majesty is thus spoken of :—

"I cannot here refrain from mentioning a circumstance which occurred to me at Brighton, on the 1st of January, 1822, and I sincerely trust there will not appear any impropriety in my doing so, since it records a trait of gracious goodness and consideration in his Majesty which, although but ono of hundreds, is but little known, and richly deserves to be universally so.

"On that evening, the King gave a splendid party at the Pavilion, and his Majesty was graciously pleased to command my attendance to hear a concert performed by his own fine band. His Majesty did me the honour to seat himself beside me, and asked me how I liked the music which I had that day heard in the chapel, amongst which, to my surprise, had been introduced the Chacoone of Jomelli, performed in the *Castle Spectre*, but which since has been called *the Sanctus of Jomelli, and is now used* under that title *in all the cathedrals* and churches in England and the Continent. His Majesty was all kindness and condescension in his manner towards me; but his kindness and condescension did not stop there.

"I had taken with me to Brighton that year a goddaughter of mine, Julia Walters, whom I have adopted, and whose mother has been, for years, my housekeeper and watchful attendant during my many severe illnesses. This little girl, at five years old, performed the part of the Child, in the opera of *L'Agnese*, under the name of Signora Julia. Ambrogetti was so struck with my little *protégée*, that he begged I would let her play the character, which she did, with grace and intelligence far beyond her years. This child asked me to procure her a sight of the King, and fixed upon the evening in question to press her request, when she might behold him in the midst of his Court, surrounded by all that was brilliant in the land, and in a palace whose splendour, when illuminated, rivalled the magnificence described in the *Arabian Nights*.

"I told my worthy friend Kramer, the excellent master and leader of His Majesty's private band, the earnest desire of little Julia, and prevailed upon him to admit her behind the organ, with a strict injunction not to let herself be seen; but female curiosity, even in one so young, prevailed, and after the first act of the concert, when the performers retired to take some refreshment, *Signora Julia* crept from her hiding place behind the organ, and seated herself between the kettle-drums. The King was sitting on a sofa, between the Princess Esterhazy and the Countess Lieven, and, though the orchestra was at a distance, His Majesty's quick eye in a moment caught a glimpse of the little intruder.

" ' Who is that beautiful little child ? ' said the King; ' Who brought her here ? ' and immediately walked to poor Julia, and asked her who she was.

" ' I belong to *K*,' said Julia.

" ' And who the deuce is *K* ? ' said His Majesty.

" I was seated quite at the farther end of the room, conversing with Sir William Keppell, and the moment I saw what was going on, I requested Sir William to go to the King, and say that the child belonged to me, which he, with great good nature, did.

" His Majesty kissed poor little Julia ; and taking her into his arms, threw her over his shoulder, and carried her across the room to me, and placed her in a chair by my side, saying, with the greatest condescension, ' Why did you leave the child in the cold ? Why not bring her into the room ? If she be fond of music, bring her here whenever you like.'

" This act of kindness, consideration, and goodness, was duly appreciated by all who witnessed it, and by me will ever be remembered with the most respectful gratitude. On the following evening, when I again had the honour of a command to the palace, His Majesty was pleased to inquire after my pretty little girl.

" My friend, Prince Hoare,° who was at Brighton

---

* This gentleman alluded to, will be remembered by many old "Brightonians," in having erected the house that formerly stood at the top, —the North side of Clarence Square : and the grounds attached to the same in front comprise the enclosure of it ; he was an eminent man of his day, an antiquarian, and the author of many musical and dramatic pieces.

at the time, wrote the following lines on the incident:—

"'ON JULIA, PEEPING

"'In the Music Room of the Pavilion, at Brighton, on the 1st of January, 1822, and discovered in the fact by His Most Gracious Majesty George the Fourth; who, with his never-failing kindness of heart and condescension, seized the little culprit in his arms, kissed and caressed her, and bore her in triumph, before the brilliant assembly, to her nearest and dearest friend, Michael Kelly, then present.

"'Behind the lofty organ's screen,
  One gala eve, sly Julia lay,
Intent to peep, at whiles, unseen,
  And all the glorious pomp survey.

"' O, little didst thou dream *that* eye
  Which wakes to guard Britannia's crown,
Would there thy tiny form espy,
  And give thee, Julia, to renown.'

" For many seasons past, upon my annual night, I have been regularly honoured with a munificent donation from my Sovereign; but, valuable to me as is that bounty in itself, the gift has scarcely been so gratifying to the feelings of his dutiful servant, as the manner of *presenting it,*—

    "' A delicacy, which anticipated wishes—
    A generosity, which exceeded hopes.'

" Were I to indulge my feelings, I should be diffuse upon this subject; but I check myself, lest I should offend in a quarter where displeasure would afflict me most.

" I therefore shall merely venture to add, that whenever my malady casts me upon a bed of suffering, I do not forget that the most august hand in the empire has condescended to place around it additional comforts; and that no sooner does my relenting star restore me to society than my benefactor's name blesses the first glass I carry to my

D

lips, and I say and sing, with heart and voice, devoutly and gratefully,

"God save the King!"

It must, indeed, be a dark cloud that has no silver lining, and many of the King's vices may be attributed to the age in which he lived, but let us hope from his charitable and benevolent disposition (as charity covereth a multitude of sins) that, when this earthly King shall stand before the awful tribunal before which we must all appear, to be judged by the great King of Kings, his virtues will be some atonement for the vices of which he was guilty.

In 1802 and 1803 further additions were made to the Pavilion by the purchase of shops in Castle Square, and in 1815 the Prince Regent purchased of the Lord of the Manor a piece of land to the north of Marlborough House, extending to the angle of the bottom of Church Street, and enclosed it with a flint wall ornamented with a long palisading. Marlborough House and the houses built on the western side of the road, recently closed, called Marlborough Row, were enclosed as far as the north gates (leaving outside the blacksmith's shop of Mr Coupeland, who would not sell his property under any consideration, although treble the value was offered for it). These purchases rendered the Prince's territory more compact, and made the extent of the same up to this period more than 7 acres.

The road being closed necessitated the making another, called the New Road. The property through which this road was made belonged to different persons, viz., Mr Furner, the father of our respected Judge of the County Court, and adjoining some property belonging to the Society of Friends, called "the Quaker's Croft," their original Meeting House standing on this property prior to its removal to the lanes. A portion of the property, formerly their burial place, situated in Church Street, adjoining the west entrance to the New Corn Exchange, has been rented for some years by the authorities of this town, the lessees entering into an agreement not to erect any building or to make any excavation whatever on the said spot.

The Corn Exchange, formerly the spacious Riding School,—200ft. long and 50ft. broad,—together with the Dome and Stables attached (these latter alone costing £70,000) were built under the direction of Mr Porden. They were commenced in the year 1805 and finished in 1808. Eastward of the Dome was a spacious Tennis Court, afterwards converted by William IV. into additional stabling for the horses of Queen Adelaide. There is likewise a subterraneous passage from the Pavilion to the Dome, which formerly had an outlet into Church Street, this, at one time, was used by the Prince of Wales and his associates for ingress and egress during the period of their indulgence in nocturnal rambles unknown to the occupants of the palace. The magnificent Dome, measuring 80ft. in circumference, and from its outward walls 120ft., is of the same size as that of the Church of the Invalides, at Paris. There are only a few domes larger in extent in the known world, as the following statement will show :—

	Feet in Diameter.		Feet in Height.
Pantheon, at Rome	142	...	143
Domo Sta Maria del Fiore, at Florence ...	139	...	310
St. Peter's, at Rome	139	...	330
Sta Sophia, at Constantinople	115	...	211
Baths of Caracalla (Ancient)	112	...	116
St. Paul's Cathedral, London	112	...	215
Mosque of Achmet	92	...	120
Chapel of the Media	91	...	199
Baptistry, at Florence	86	...	110
{ *Brighton Pavilion Dome*	80	...	60
{ *Brighton Pavilion Dome*, to the outward walls	120		
Church of the Invalides, at Paris...	80	...	173
Minerva Media, at Rome	78	...	97

	Feet in Diameter.		Feet in Height.
Madonna della Salnta, Venice	70	...	133
St. Généviève, at Paris (Pantheon)	67	...	190
Duomo, at Sienna	57	..	148
Duomo, at Milan	57	...	254
St. Vitalis, at Ravenna	55	...	94
Val de Grace, at Paris	54	...	133
San Marco, at Venice	44	...	

The outward circle of the Dome was used as the stables
for the horses of the Prince of Wales, and had a fountain in the centre. It was used likewise as the standing
place for the carriages belonging to the establishment, and
the upper circle, now termed the *Balcony*, was used as the
dwelling place (there being a number of small rooms) for
the servants and families belonging to the stable department. The whole of this has been converted by the
Corporation of Brighton into a vast Assembly Room, for
concerts, &c., and is capable of seating 3,500 persons, the
cost of the same being nearly £8,000. (The embellishments and decorations of the Dome and Pavilion have
been executed by Mr Tony Dury, of Warwick.) Since its
appropriation a magnificent organ has been added, replete
with every modern improvement, worked by hydraulic
power, and built by Willis of London, at the cost of £2,500.
The Dome has, likewise, fixed in the centre of the building, a splendid chandelier, fitted up by Green and Son, of
Pavilion Buildings, Brighton, its dimensions being as
follows : viz., diameter, 16ft.; height, 30ft.; and consisting
of 520 jets of gas, and its weight 1¾ tons. There are several
small chandeliers, likewise, around the circle. The alterations of this portion of the Pavilion Estate, as well as
the others, have been from plans of our talented Surveyor,
P. C. Lockwood, Esq., C.E., who has been indefatigable in
his exertions to develope its resources, and he is now preparing plans for a Public Museum and Library, at a cost
of £6,000, to be submitted to a Vestry Meeting for the
purpose of obtaining the sanction of the inhabitants for

the proposed outlay. If sanctioned it will be built on the eastern court, the site of the stables erected by William IV.

The Dome is a very conspicuous object when viewed from the hills near the town; on occasions of concerts, &c., when lit up, it presents a pretty appearance, from the different colors of the glass in its roof. It was used recently on the occasion of the town inviting the Hon. Reverdy Johnson to a sumptuous banquet (under the presidency of the then Mayor, Mr Alderman Lester), on his visit to this country in the endeavour to settle the differences caused by the Alabama claims made by our transatlantic brethren; and it is worthy of record that the first public manifesto on this subject was made at the Grand Hotel, to a deputation of the Corporation, by that functionary, and published in the public prints the following day, and which led to the town inviting him to the enter‑ tainment mentioned, afterwards followed by other large towns in the kingdom.*

The most memorable public event connected with the Royal Stables was that which took place on the 25th of October, 1809, on which occasion the Prince kindly granted the use of the Riding School to Mr Philip Mighell, for the purpose of feasting 2000 of the poorest inhabitants of this town to celebrate the Jubilee of King George III., he having ascended the throne in the year 1760, and this treat to the poor was further extended by a party of

---

* On the arrival in Brighton of the Hon. Reverdy Johnson, as a guest of the late eminent philanthropist, George Peabody, Esq., who was staying at the Grand Hotel, a deputation of the Corporation, consisting of the Mayor (Mr Alderman Lester), the Ex‑Mayor, Mr Alderman Hallett, Mr Alderman Alger, Mr Alderman Martin, Mr Alderman Brigden, Mr Alderman Abbey, Mr Alderman Ireland, and Councillors Fabian and Davey, waited on his Excellency and presented an address couched in congratulatory terms, and were afterwards invited by Mr Peabody to a sumptuous repast, being joined by several private friends,—Sir Emerson Tennant, Sir Curtis Lampson, Dr. Carter, and Mr Mayall, the eminent photographer, who, by instructions from Mr Peabody, executed a striking likeness of His Excellency, and at his request a copy of the same was forwarded to each member of the deputation.

gentlemen contributing a sum and feasting 1500 more poor persons in the barn and farm yard of Mr Scrase, at that time situated in the middle of Jubilee Street, the name of the same being taken from the event. The Freemasons dined in their Lodge Room at the Old Ship, where also the same evening there was a ball and supper in honor of the occasion.

The large chandelier formerly in the banqueting room was sent, in 1816, with Lord Amherst's embassy, as a present to his celestial majesty the "Emperor of China," in the endeavour to extend the commercial relations with that monarch, and his lordship travelled a considerable distance into the interior of that vast empire to the imperial palace, but the negociations were abruptly broken off, indignity being offered at Pekin on the 29th of August following. The embassy returned, their vessel was wrecked, but the presents were saved, and the chandelier was placed in the Pavilion by the Prince Regent's orders. It remained some time in its present position, till the third visit of King William and Queen Adelaide in 1834, when Her Majesty (in consequence of a dream that it would fall) caused it to be removed. It was re-modelled, and about 60 per cent. of the original material again used, when the Pavilion came into the hands of the Town Commissioners—at that period the governing body. The glass drops alone have been stated to have originally cost 1 guinea per lb. There was formerly in one of the rooms of the Pavilion a Chinese lanthorn, 12ft. by 8ft., and which, on all particular occasions, was brilliantly illuminated on the exterior, thus exhibiting its transparency and producing an effect too exquisite to be described. A small apartment adjacent, called Tippoo Saib's room, was fitted up with ivory chairs, sofas, &c., part of the spoils brought from Scringapatam, after the overthrow of that eastern potentate. All the fittings and embellishments were

of a gorgeous character, and in strict harmony
throughout the whole of this remarkable building;
on occasions, such as State Balls, &c., it must have been a
splendid spectacle, the uniforms of the Foreign Ambassa-
dors, General Officers, representatives of various orders,
all uniting to make the "coup d'œil" particularly striking.
King George IV. was a frequent visitor to Brighton (his
last visit was in the year 1824), and on his death, in 1830,
the Pavilion was inherited by William IV., who, on his
accession to the throne received an address from the town,
resolved on at a meeting convened for that purpose, under
the presidency of the High Constable (Mr. Thos. G.
Sarel), upon whom devolved the honor of presentation of
the same to King William, at Buckingham Palace. The
King's answer thereto was remarkably short, yet very
gratifying,—here are his words : "Tell the inhabitants of
Brighton I thank them, and shall soon be with them."
He kept his promise, a short time after. In the month of
July his Majesty paid a hasty visit, his object being the
removal of anything objectionable at the Palace prior to his
residence therein with Queen Adelaide, which took place on
the 30th of August, 1830. During the King's sojourn, he
gave instructions for important alterations to be effected,
notably the erection of the dormitories, the ivy-clad buildings to the westward of Carlisle House, at the southern
entrance of Pavilion grounds; the elegant northern entrance in Church Street; and a suitable entrance to the
south, in North Street. On this royal estate becoming
the property of the town, this latter building was
pulled down, and the present unpretentious entrance
substituted.

Their Majesties kept up festivities in the Pavilion in
a regal manner; the Royal invites to a County Ball
in the Palace on one occasion were accorded unto 1600 of
the nobility and gentry, and "the line" of carriages bearing
these numerous guests extended from the entrance of the

Pavilion, through East Street, to the Bedford Hotel, several hours elapsing before the last visitor was set down.

The decease of King William IV. took place in June, 1837; on the 4th of October, in the same year, Queen Victoria paid her first visit to Brighton, and in the autumn of the following year again honored our town by her presence. In February, 1842, the Queen and her royal consort, Prince Albert, arrived here, and sojourned four weeks; the following year, in the month of September, they landed from the royal yacht on to the Chain Pier,—on their return from a visit to Louis Phillipe, at Chateau d'Eu, near Dieppe.* The last royal residence here was in September, 1844; the Prince of Wales, Princess Royal, and Prince Alfred arriving here for the benefit of their health. Their stay was of short duration,—only a fortnight,—and hopes were entertained that Her Majesty would have joined the royal children during this marine visit, but these hopes were not realized, it being announced shortly afterwards that the Queen had purchased "Osborne," her favorite residence in the Isle of Wight, and from that period our beautiful marine palace has been forsaken by royalty. Yet let us indulge a sincere wish that the time is not far distant when we may be again honored by the residence among us of Royalty. The Prince of Wales and his illustrious Princess, the Princess Mary of Cambridge, the Duke of Cambridge and Prince Teck, Sir Hope Grant, Sir Richard Garrett and Colonel, now Sir William Knollys, paid us a visit on the Easter Review day in 1866, —a full length painting of the Mayor (Alderman Henry Martin), commemorative of the event, and presented by him

* A valuable and interesting painting, commemorative of the landing of the royal party, painted by our talented and honoured townsman, Mr R. H. Nibbs, and presented by him to the local authorities, is now on the walls of the picture gallery in the Pavilion.

to the town, is in the Pavilion ; Prince Arthur came down
on Easter Monday in the present year, 1871, and we trust
these visits to our attractive town are but the pre-
cursors of many such opportunities for rejoicing on the
part of the loyal inhabitants of this borough.

Gradually the Pavilion became despoiled of its costly
furniture and fittings, the royal servants were discharged
on the 27th December, 1847, and eventually it was
announced that the building was to be razed to the ground,
the materials sold, and the land disposed of for building
purposes. It further became publicly known in November,
1848, that the Royal Commissioners of Woods and Forests
intended to introduce into Parliament a Bill for the
sale of the property, the funds derivable therefrom to be
devoted to further improvements at Buckingham Palace ;
and from an estimate made of the value of the Pavilion, it
was thought worth £100,000. So much alarm was created
in the minds of the inhabitants at the idea of losing
this great local attraction, that our Town Commissioners
(the governing body prior to the incorporation of Brighton
in 1854) put in their claim for a restoration, by the Crown,
of the roadway which formerly existed through the Pavilion
from Church Street to Castle Square, also pointed out
that other portions of the ground which had been sold to
the Prince of Wales had restrictions against building, which
restrictions could not be removed without the consent of the
Lords of the Manor. The Bill for its sale, however, passed,
and on the 27th of July, 1849, a Vestry Meeting of the
rated inhabitants determined upon opening negociations
with the Crown authorities with a view to its purchase,
and the restrictions mentioned were urged with the
desire of obtaining it for a lesser sum than that
already named. Eventually, to avoid litigation, it
was arranged that the purchase money should be
£53,000, and an Act of Parliament was obtained to
give the Town authorities power to secure the estate. In

the meantime an opposition sprung up amongst some of the ratepayers, and at a Vestry Meeting called on the 20th day of December, 1849, an amendment was moved to the original resolution :—" That the report be received, and entered at the foot of the minutes, and that the Draft Bill to empower the purchase of the Pavilion be approved ;"—to the following effect,—" That the Bill now presented is disapproved of, and that a memorial be presented to the Honorable the Commissioners of Woods and Forests expressing the desire of the inhabitants that no further steps be taken in the matter." On this a poll was consequently taken on the 20th and 22nd with the following result : For the purchase, 1,343; against it, 1,307; majority for the motion, 36. It is now admitted by its most strenuous opponents that it would have been a suicidal act to have lost so eligible an opportunity for securing to the town such a valuable acquisition,—which has been not inaptly termed one of the lungs of Brighton, and its value has proved beyond price, affording, as it does, every facility for balls, concerts, lectures, religious and scientific meetings, flower shows, &c. The Bill founded on the resolution named was read, without opposition, on the 14th of February, 1850, and in the House of Lords the 2nd of May following. The money for the purchase, and £7,000 for the expenses of obtaining the Bill and restoration of the building,—amounting in the whole to £60,000,—was borrowed of the Bank of England. One arrangement in connection with the purchase was the demolition of the Royal Chapel, which stood upon a portion of the estate, ample compensation being allowed for the same. On the 13th of June following, the Commissioners of Woods and Forests were paid the required sum,· and a Ball in celebration of the opening took place January 21st, 1851. The inhabitants were first admitted to view the Pavilion (in its dismantled state) and grounds on the 28th June, 1850.

In a copy of the celebrated engraving of the Steyne, published in 1806, and presented, with many other valuable relics of Brighton, by Robert Furner, Esq., to the Town Museum, the Prince of Wales (as "the star of fashion") is represented on horseback, attended by Colonel Blomfield. Other notabilities are depicted in the picture, among whom are the Duke of Grafton, Earl Berkeley (Colonel of the South Glo'ster Militia), Mr Mellish, Bishop of St. Asaph, Earl Craven, Lord Coleraine, George Hanger, Colonel Lee, Sir John Lade, Mr Day (called "Gloomy Day"), Mr Treeves, sen., and Mr Treeves, jun., General Dalrymple (upwards of 22 stone in weight), Lord Sefton, Earl Clermont, Martha Gunn, of whom it is written :—

> See the fine rosy boy how he laughs at the fun,
> Of being douched in the sea by old Martha Gunn.

and Mr Cope (the "Green Man" so called), as he was universally attired in green, and of whom the following was penned :—

> A spruce little man in a doublet of *green*,
> Perambulates daily the streets and the Steyne,
> *Green* striped is his waistcoat, his small clothes are *green*,
> And oft round his neck a *green* 'kerchief is seen.
> *Green* watch string, *green* seals, and for certain I've heard,
> (Tho' they're powdered) *green* whiskers and eke a *green* beard ;
> *Green* garters, *green* hose, and deny it who can,
> The Brains too are *green* of this little *green man !*

Sir John Lade, who was in the receipt of an annual pension of £400, as driving tutor to the Prince of Wales, was an accomplished "whip," performing feats almost incredible in the "tooling" of his horses. One of the most daring was the driving, at full gallop, from Castle Square up

Market Street, passing to the west of Pear Tree House
(now the cloth establishment of Messrs Hannington and
Son) by the Knabb pump that at that period projected
on to the road at the bottom of the Lanes, then into
Brighton Place, then round the corner into Market
Street and back again to Castle Square. Sir John
was buried in Warbleton Church, and a splendid tomb
has been erected to his memory. Mr Mellish likewise
excelled as a four-in-hand coachman. Martha Gunn
was designated "the Queen of the Bath," and many are
the anecdotes related of her in the aboriginal vernacular.
This celebrity died May 2, 1815, at the age of 88, and
was followed to the grave by a very large assemblage.
Anecdotes of the most extravagant description are likewise
told of characters or loungers on the Steyne at that
period.

The houses on the west side of the Steyne, of some
note, comprise the Castle Tavern, Mrs Fitzherbert's,
and Lady Anne Murray's, afterwards Single-speech
Hamilton's, — Member for Haslemere, — so-called for
having essayed but one speech in his place in Parliament;
on the east side, Donaldson's library (formerly Thomas's);
and on the south side Crawford's* (with Post Office
attached), and a rival establishment called Dulot's Library,
afterwards Bowen's, the latter at that time allied to a
London establishment at 40, New Bond Street. Crawford
and Dulot issued two small editions of a work styled by
both, *A description of Brighthelmstone and the adjacent
country, or a new guide for ladies and gentlemen using
that place of health and amusement*, published about the
year 1794, and they are almost a *fac simile* of each
other.

---

* Kept by Mr Crawford, grandfather of the present Member for
the City of London of that name; and it will be remembered that his
father contested this Borough unsuccessfully at the first election of Members for Brighton, on its enfranchisement under the Reform Bill, on the
11th and 12th of December, 1832.

BRIGHTON CAMPS.

Of these there were several: the first formed
August 13, 1793. At three o'clock on the morning previous, the troops composing this camp struck their tents
in Ashdown Forest, and from thence, at five o'clock,
marched forwards, reaching Chailey Common at half-past
eleven, and tents were pitched for the night. The following morning at four they were again on the march,
and at noon arrived on the hills around Brighton. The
artificers and the heavy baggage came by way of Lewes;
but the route of the army in general, consisting of 7,000
men, was over the South Downs, the Prince of Wales
meeting them as they came over the hill. By two o'clock
the camp was formed, close to the town, in Belle Vue
Field, now known as Regency Square, and it stretched in
a direct line along the coast. This encampment, which
was increased to 10,000 troops, was composed of regulars
and militia, and continued till the 28th of October, on
account of some apprehension of an invasion by the " new
Republic of France." On the first Sunday after the
arrival of the army many of the soldiers attended the
Parish Church, and among them several officers of the
Surrey Militia, then quartered in the town. The
officiating Clergyman on the occasion was the Rev.
Dr. Vicesimus Knox, Master of Tunbridge School,
and late fellow of St. John's College, Oxford, who
had with his family taken up his residence here for a few
weeks at a house in North Street (west corner of Bond
Street, the property of Mr Alderman Henry Martin). He
had been solicited by the Vicar, the Rev. Thomas
Hudson, to preach on that Sunday, and, having
assented, he was assisted by the Curate, the Rev. J.
Mossop. The Doctor chose for his text the following
words, " Glory to God in the highest : on earth, peace,
good-will towards men." In the course of his narrative

of the event, chronicled in a work published by him (which must have created great interest as it passed through several editions), he observes that he was led to the choice of this subject from observing the extreme bitterness expressed, even in gay, good-humoured companies, against a great many of our fellow creatures ; from the almost daily accounts in the newspapers of slaughtered thousands, and the eagerness with which war had been adopted by all the nations concerned, when negociations might have effected every desirable purpose, without expense and without carnage. The first intimation received by him that he had given umbrage to any of the congregation was on his leaving the Church, when a lady, a perfect stranger, thus accosted him :—" I thank you for your sermon, I could have sat hours to have heard such with pleasure ; but, excuse me, I must tell you, from what I have observed in the pews among a certain description of persons, you have offended those who, I fear, have as little relish for the doctrine of forgiveness as they seem to have of peace. Many, like myself, were highly pleased with your discourse ; but there are those who are angry indeed."

From Erredge's *History of Brighthelmston* we quote the following further remarks of Dr. Knox (contributed thereto by the author of the present work), which will, we have no doubt, be read with much interest ; as showing the excited feelings of the military at that period :—

" My family, who stood around me, heard her observations, and were greatly alarmed. I was not in the least *alarmed*, though certainly concerned, to find that I had been misapprehended. Conscious of having meant nothing but what was humane, beneficent, and truly Christian, in all which I had delivered, I feared no ill. Having done no wrong, nor intended any thing but good, I felt a serene complacency, notwithstanding the alarm given by this unknown lady, in a tone of

voice, and with a look and manner, expressive of apprehension for my safety. I met with no molestation in the
church. I walked slowly through the church-yard.
Nothing but respect was shown me. I returned with my
family to my house with peculiar cheerfulness, flowing
from a faithful discharge of my duty, and the consequent
esteem of the parishioners, which, I believe, I possessed.

"I had friends to dine with me on that day, and the
church service in the afternoon began rather early. Under
these circumstances I might have been absent without
blame. But I rose from my table, acquainting my
company, that, as I understood the officers, who were at
church in the morning, were offended at me, I would
certainly walk to church, in the hope of meeting some of
them, of hearing what had given them offence, and of
coming immediately, before misrepresentation could take
place, to a full and amicable explanation. I wished
earnestly to meet the angry parties, that we might converse together, that I might acknowledge *my* fault, if I
had been in the wrong, and remove *their* mistake if they
thought me so, undeservedly. I had no resentments; I
only wished for reconciliation. I went therefore unaccom-
panied by my friends; for I sought not protection. I met
not a single officer. After hearing Mr Mossop, the Curate,
preach, I returned to my family to drink tea. In the evening
I proposed walking on the Steyne, still hoping to meet my
offended hearers in the military profession; many officers
were there, but I did not recognize any of those who were
at the church. No insult was offered me; for I can
hardly suppose that the speech above-mentioned, expres
sing a wish for a long, a bloody, nay an everlasting war,
could be intended as an insult to *me*, though it was repeated close to my ear, in a voice raised above the common
pitch, and with peculiar emphasis and *action*. My
sermon was talked of frequently in my hearing, but not
with disapprobation. I was pointed out as the preacher,

rather particularly indeed, but not rudely. I perceived a large party of the military assembled at the Castle Tavern, who were dining in a room which looked immediately on the Steyne, and I passed them unavoidably. I met with no insult on this public and crowded walk, though I purposely remained there till it was dark, and all the company began to retire. The inhabitants of Brighton, and the parishioners in general, behaved with their usual civility; not the least degree of rudeness did I on this occasion, or at any time, experience from *them*, or from any of the company resorting to that place, unconnected with the offended FEW, in the military line.

" On my return home a letter was brought to me, of which the following is a copy :—

" ' A stranger presents his compliments and sincere homage of thanks to Dr. Knox, for his most excellent sermon preached this morning, and earnestly requests him to publish it, as a means to promote the interests of humanity, and procure that great desideratum, 'Peace on Earth.'

" ' The ardour of Christian philanthropy it breathes should be diffused throughout the world, which is the object of this application. The writer wishes to distribute a number of copies in a distant county. A dissemination of such enlightening and convincing knowledge is only wanting to stop the effusion of human blood; for when mankind are well awakened, they will not permit the dignified human butchers, the insolent, unfeeling traffickers in blood, to lead them to destruction.

" ' Sunday, Aug. 18.'

" This anonymous letter, the honest effusion of philanthropy, I insert in this place, as it forms a part of my narrative. I have no suspicion whence it came. The servant, who delivered it at the door, went away in great haste. Several friends were present when the letter came, and read it as soon as it was opened.

"I beg leave to mention as I proceed, that from the pulpit, where I must have had a pretty good view of the whole Church, I saw VERY FEW OFFICERS ; and of those few, I knew not one even by name : I thought there were not twelve. Of common soldiers the number was also inconsiderable ; I thought there were scarcely twenty, and these *were not of the camp*, but of the Surrey Militia quartered in the town. There were indeed more of the same regiment in the porch or in the church yard : but too remote from the pulpit to hear a syllable of sedition, if there had been any to hear. I mention the paucity of officers and privates for the following reason : the public has been taught by mistaken prints to believe, that I was guilty of preaching peace and good-will before the *whole camp*, that the aisle was crowded with soldiers, and that all the officers of the camp attended. I appeal to the parishioners present, whether the number of military men, privates and officers included, was greater than I have conjectured. My sermon was not exclusively calculated for a congregation of persons in any particular profession. There was not a word addressed by an *apostrophe*, as I have heard it asserted, to the officers. I had no reason to suppose that any military men, but those of the Surrey Militia quartered at Brighton, would be at the church. I thought, and I believe it was so, that Divine service was performed by the chaplains in the camp, and that the *soldiers of the camp* would not be permitted to straggle to the town or the church, on a Sunday, during Divine service. The public has been much deceived in the exaggerated accounts of my preaching to the *whole army ;* but had the whole army been at the church, had it been allowed or been possible, I am certain they would have heard nothing from me but what was authorised by the Gospel, enforced by the law of man as well as of God, tending to promote their happiness in all events, and animating them to the discharge of every duty, on prin-

E

ciples of humanity and Christianity. I expressly asserted, while I was deploring the calamities of war, that the conductors of war were often men of SINGULAR HUMANITY AND HONOUR. I expressly commended the beautiful gradation of ranks in society. I enforced good order; I deprecated anarchy as much as despotism.

"I have already related the transactions of the Sunday. On Monday I went to the Downs, where the whole army was assembled. The beauty of the day attracted thither my friend and my family. I hoped also to meet those whom I had offended, that they might bring their charge against me face to face; and that I might explain what was misunderstood, or make a frank acknowledgment, if anything could be made appear on my part truly reprehensible. I hoped the explanation on both sides would be liberal, candid, and gentlemanlike. I cared not how many were present at it. Truth loves the light. I would not be protected by my company, or concealed in my carriage. I walked alone a great part of near four hours on the ground, amidst thousands; the rest I spent with my visitor, with my family, and the family of my friend, Mr Bridger, of Buckingham House, Shoreham. The military were indeed engaged in their evolutions; but they frequently passed me nearly, and might have spoken to me. The company of spectators was very numerous, and much of it connected with the army. My sermon, I have been since told, was a frequent topic of conversation on the ground, and I was pointed out as the preacher of it; but no insult was offered, and no personal application made to me. In the evening I went, as usual, to the Steyne, and the booksellers' shops on the Steyne, and met with nothing in either place, though crowded, but friendship and civility.

"The morning of Tuesday was spent on the Steyne, and in other places near Brighton. Even now I avoided not meeting those who, I had been recently told, were heard to *threaten* me severely, behind my back, on the preceding day. I preferred meeting them, and hearing the worst they could say, to SECRET CALUMNY; which, as it could not be encountered, could not be repelled. This fiend was busily at work, inflaming many against me who had never seen or heard me. Every one knows how things are unintentionally exaggerated when they become topics of conversation in the convivial hour, and when an emulation prevails of making a display of spirit or ingenuity. Saucer-eyed phantoms of sedition began to flit before disturbed imaginations. Old women, dreaming of *chimeras dire,* stimulated their husbands to buckle on the helmet and the shield, and take the spear, and go forth against the giant sedition, which appeared to their dim eyes in the form of a windmill.

" The important hour at length approached. · The anger of my enemies was nothing indeed in duration to the wrath of Achilles; but yet it appears to have been of a durable nature. The offence of Sunday morning was to be revenged on Tuesday evening. My friend, who was to return to London on the next day, proposed that some of my family and myself should accompany him to the Theatre. I had no desire to go ; but as I had determined to decline no opportunity of meeting those who now, it seems, expressed themselves with great RANCOUR against me, I consented immediately. Accordingly Mrs Knox, my eldest son (a boy of fourteen years), and my daughter (a year or two younger), set out with my friend for the Theatre. As we walked up North Street, several persons stopped and spoke to each other, in the hearing of myself and family, in terms of the highest approbation of the last Sunday's sermon. Near the door of the Theatre, Major Toraine and a young Lieutenant of the East Middlesex overtook me ; they were not going to the Theatre ; but they accompanied me a little way, and behaved with great politeness ; the Major inviting me to visit him in the camp, and expressing his concern that he had not seen me there before. They might not perhaps have heard of my offence; but, whether they had or not, it is certain that their behaviour was, as usual, friendly and gentleman-like. I have been since informed by a person, who had the opportunities of conversing in the camp, that, notwithstanding the misrepresentations of my sermon, a great part of the most *respectable** officers were far from expressing displeasure at its doctrine.

" On entering the Theatre, Mr Thomas, the box-keeper, accosted me by name, though I thought I was unknown to him; shewed uncommon attention, and begged leave to seat us all in a good place of his own choice. This place was the right hand side-box, next to the stage-box, where the Prince usually sits. He was not there. If he had been, I should have sought his protection, and have been safe in his justice.

"Soon after the curtain drew up a few officers entered the stage-box on the opposite side of the Theatre. They had not been there five minutes, before their whole attention seemed fixed on the box where my family, my friend, and myself were seated. They looked frequently at me, and then talked to each other with great apparent earnestness. Other officers, and several elderly ladies, soon appeared in the same box ; they also looked at us in a pointed manner, and then seemed to deliberate.† Their attention appeared to be engrossed by the consultation, and they seldom turned to the players on the stage. There were several other officers interspersed in other boxes. Messages were sent to some of them, and they removed into the stage box. A man whose looks were choleric, and who sat in the same box and on the same seat with

---

* Titles and riches do not make the most *respectable* officers.

CORPORAL TRUEMAN.

† Aliquid jamdudum invadere *magnum!*

me, was sent for, and I saw him taking his seat opposite
to me. He left his hat behind him, probably intending to
return when I should be excluded. They frequently went
in and out, and appeared extremely busy* and anxious in
concerting the plan of operations. This continued during
the whole of the play. My children observed it, and told
me that they expected some insult. I disregarded their
suggestions, and sat with perfect composure. Between the
play and the entertainment, the following note, directed to
me, was first handed from behind us, to Mrs Knox, who
gave it to me. My son had seen one of the officers
writing ; and there was no doubt but he was composing
this note, sent without a name, and couched in terms of
caution and subtlety. I must call it a *discreet note ;* and
as discretion is allowed to be the better part of valour,
I must add another epithet, and contend that it is a
courageous note :—

Copy of the MANDATORY NOTE *of Expulsion, dispatched by
a Confederacy of unknown Persons, styling themselves in
the said Note,* THE GENTLEMEN OF THIS THEATRE.
Superscribed on the back, Dr. KNOX.

"YOUR DISCOURSE LAST SUNDAY WAS SO OFFENSIVE
THAT THE GENTLEMEN OF THIS THEATRE DESIRE YOU WILL
QUIT IT IMMEDIATELY."

"It is so beautifully laconic that it might be taken
for the production of a Spartan Republican, if it were not
at the same time so authoritative as to resemble the edict
of a German despot. It is written with a pencil on a
scrap of torn paper. I intend to preserve it, that it may
supply documents to future historians, and hope to have
interest enough to get it deposited in the archives of the
Tower.

---

* Velut apes æstate novâ·

"I read the order, and gave it to Mrs. Knox. Immediately I rose, and addressing myself to the opposite boxes, which, however, were now nearly empty, *the military having accompanied their despatch*, requested to know who had sent me this impertinent paper without a name. The messenger, whoever he was, had disappeared. I turned back to look for him, and beheld a phalanx of military men, who had come round, and were drawn up behind me at the door of my box, and in the Lobby, through which I must pass in my retreat. While I was asking for the messenger, a clamour began, and finding the passage closed by the very persons who had ordered me to withdraw *immediately*, I stept a little forward, and endeavoured to say to the Theatre, which was not half filled, 'Ladies and gentlemen, I have this moment received an extraordinary paper, neither signed nor dated, containing a requisition that I should quit the Theatre immediately, on account of the sermon which I preached last Sunday morning in your parish church. I beg pardon for interrupting you; but under these circumstances, and surrounded, as you see I am, I humbly intreat the permission of the House, to ask aloud who sent me this note, and by what authority I am bound to obey it, in this place of public entertainment, where my family and myself have entitled ourselves to unmolested seats, by paying the price demanded at the doors. We have interrupted nobody. Will you authorize the arbitrary expulsion of us all? for my family and friend will certainly follow me. I beg leave, besieged as you see me by a considerable number of men behind me, who are at this moment expressing their anger by opprobrious names, to enter into a short explanation with them, to ask the particulars of my offence in *your presence*, and to declare, that if anything advanced in my sermon gave personal offence, it was unintentional, and that I am concerned at it. If any one of these gentlemen will prove to your satisfaction that he is justly offended, I will immediately beg his pardon. I beg *your* pardon, who are totally unconcerned in this attack, for this singular interruption, which I trust I shall obtain from you, as men and Englishmen; when you have before your eyes a defenceless individual, in a situation so singular, as will, I hope, justify my present address to you.'

"It was impossible to be heard distinctly. I could not find an interval of silence to utter half of the above, which I had conceived in my mind and wished to deliver. The clamour of the persons in uniforms behind me was loud and incessant. I heard myself called, in the first instance, *a democratical scoundrel that deserved to be* HANGED.* 'A Democrat, a Democrat, a d—d Democrat. Out with the Democrat—no Democrats.' Scoundrel and rascal were titles lavishly bestowed. It is needless to repeat the silly oaths and unmeaning expletives† which served those, who were too much enraged to be able to say any thing else, to add to the noise and drown my voice. I particularly remember hearing one man say, ' No speech—that won't do—he ought to be hanged--out with him :' and another call repeatedly for PERSONAL VIO-LENCE to be inflicted upon me before I should be suffered to depart. A grim and gaunt figure exclaimed, ' IRONS—IRONS, here; he ought to be put in IRONS directly.'

"I found it was impossible to be heard by the House at large, who could not know the cause of the disturb-ance. I thought my perseverance might create a riot. I

---

* I have been informed, since the publication of the former editions of this Narrative, that many of the assailants were of a different opinion, and thought DROWNING was to be preferred to HANGING me ; it having been proposed that I should be dragged to the SEA, which is near, and thrown into it. A person of veracity was told of this by a tradesman of Brighton; who added, that the presence of Mrs Knox and my children *alone* saved me from the WATERY GRAVE. I *laugh* at this; but there might be some danger, as these gentlemen were not of the HUMANE SOCIETY.

† Such as Bah! Boo! Boh! and other noisy sounds, of which I know not the meaning, not being in possession of the *St. Giles's Glossary*, or the *Scoundrel's Dictionary*.

said, therefore, to my terrified family, 'I will go, for the sake of peace. Fear not, they will not hurt WOMEN AND CHILDREN. I feel no anxiety for my own safety. There is no opposing so great a superiority of numbers. I hope for an explanation.'

"I entered the Lobby, and had a right to expect that the *passage would be clear*, and that I should be allowed to retire, as I was ordered, without molestation. But I found the narrow Lobby crowded by persons in regimentals, many of whom, as I passed, continued to use the same language which I had heard behind me, while in the House. No one, however, offered any *personal violence*, though ONE fellow in the next box to me, not *in uniform* (to the honour of the army), continued to call loudly and repeatedly for it. He did not think proper to approach me; for what reasons I know not. Probably for prudential ones; and discretion, it has already been observed, is a valuable ingredient in the composition of valour. He was VOX *et pretcrea* NIL. He did not begin to bray till the whole body of veterans stood around him. Conscious safety fired his TONGUE.

"When I had arrived—*per tot discrimina rerum*—at the opposite side of the House, I entered a box, and again attempted to speak to the *very few people in the Theatre*, who constituted the whole of the audience, except my pursuers, and were, I think, friendly. They were gazing in silence. They knew little of what was passing in the Lobby. They perhaps surmised that some French emissary or spy had been discovered, and was taken into lawful custody by the *defenders of our country*. I addressed them, and they would have heard me with attention. A few of them at last recognized me, and cried *Silence*; but the noise of my assailants continued. It was insisted that I should not speak to the people. 'Go,' said one who came up to me *much out of breath*, 'go directly—go you must;' while from behind resounded the cry, 'Out

with him—a Democrat, a Democrat, a Democrat—*da capo*
—a Democrat.—No Democrat, a d——d Democrat." I
wonder, in their patriotic zeal, they did not exclaim, *No
people! no people! no people for ever!*

"I now began to withdraw from the house; for the
poet says,

> ——*Parere necesse est —*
> *Nam quid agas? cum te furiosus cogat, et idem*
> "ARMATUS."

But I was determined, at all events, to find Mrs Knox
and the children, who had been separated from me in the
Lobby. On turning back, I saw Mrs Knox in tears very
near me, but without my daughter, and in great distress.
I then requested, and insisted, that I might be permitted
by the rushing phalanx to attend Mrs Knox, and fetch both
my son and daughter. While I was contending for this
indulgence, and received no other answer than, " Go—go
directly—go you must and shall, by God," my family and
friend came up to me, The generous victors shewed
clemency at last, and suffered us, children and all, on our
surrender, to march out unmolested. It is said, they
returned immediately to their post in the stage box; and
that *loyal tunes* were played by the band in celebration of
the triumph, by way of *Te Deum*, or, ' *The horse is thrown
and his rider*,' or some similar EPINIKION, sung while
Princes were dragged at their chariot-wheels, in honour
of the rivals of my assailants, the conquerors of
antiquity.

"On inquiring of Mrs Knox what passed in the
Lobby, while she and the children were separated from
me, she informed me, that a tall officer, on her turning
back to see for her daughter, pushed her violently by the
shoulder, and bid her go *along after her husband and be
d——d*. Another, who probably saw and was ashamed of
this behaviour, and to whom I am really obliged for this
tenderness, small as it was, to a woman in her situation,

did say to Mrs Knox, ' No personal violence shall be used; he should not have come among us. Had he stuck to peace, we should all have admired him.' Another, nodding his terrific plumes, exclaimed, ' It is well his wife and children are with him, or else——' here he used a fine *aposiopesis*. A student in rhetoric might indeed, on this occasion, have learned the use of many choice figures of speech; but he may succeed equally well in the ancient and celebrated school of Billingsgate. Mrs Knox, who was really anxious for my safety, not having perhaps remarked that barking dogs do not always bite, tried all her eloquence in expostulation, and in supplicating by the silent language of tears for clemency. But she was *hurried* along, and her gown and other parts of her dress *accidentally* torn in pieces. She has preserved them as TROPHIES in their lacerated state. Thus the only *personal violence* (which the *Knight of the terrible tongue* called for) was exercised on a defenceless female, weeping for her husband, and intreating to be permitted to return and conduct her daughter in safety, who had been forced in the crowd from the protection of both father and mother. Temporary rage got the better, not only of military politeness, and the unmeaning forms of decorum, but of common humanity.*

" My son, who was also separated from us in the Lobby, informed me that he ventured to say loudly, in an honest zeal for his father, ' What are you doing? is this fair ? so many against one ! Fie upon you !—near twenty against one: O for shame !' Upon this a tall officer, whether the same who assaulted his mother or not, he does not know, shook him violently, saying at the same time, ' Who are you, you dog? you ought to be hanged as well as your father, if it is your father; and all such as hold his democratical principles, you dog you !'

---

* VICIT AMOR PATRIÆ, LAUDUMQUE IMMENSA CUPIDO.—VIRG.

" To my *very young daughter*, who was left behind us all ; who, from a peculiar tenderness of disposition, was particularly distressed, and whom my friend was leading along with great difficulty, no other consolation was offered by MEN, who probably were themselves FATHERS, than a rough address, ' Don't fret—what do you fret for ?''—A little kindness to my daughter in such distress would have taught me to forget my own ill-usage in my gratitude. But we were a family of *Democrats*, I suppose ; and it was PURE PATRIOTISM that taught the defenders of our peace and liberties to treat us ALL with indiscriminate indignity, to forget, in their COUNTRY's cause, what was due to themselves, due to me and mine, and due to PUBLIC ORDER.

" The world has been told that they were a parcel of *drunken* boys who committed this outrage. There were some young men among the brawlers ; but the RING-LEADERS were, if I may judge from appearance, *veterans* in age, if not in service, and of high rank, if I may believe report, in their profession and in society. They did it in SOBER sadness.

" One circumstance I must beg leave to point out as particularly worthy of notice.—Of the assailants in the Theatre, *very few* (I believe) were my *hearers in the church :* so that the rest were probably influenced by the false representations of gossips, and the dreams of old ladies, to whom I have above attributed some of the ill-grounded alarm and offence. Whether anything which they *thought* glanced at the *finery* of their old beaux, hurt the pride of the elderly gentlewomen, I cannot ascertain ; but their instigations seemed to have considerable effect in stimulating the *corps*, who came into action *in the straits of the Lobby*, to the most valorous exertion.

" After the defeat, our little family-party walked home, arm in arm, with our good friend, to our house in North Street. In the terrified condition of the ladies, a carriage and the attendance of a servant were desirable ;

but we were not suffered to wait for them. None of those polite gentlemen expressed any concern, lest the ladies, heated by the crowd in the Lobby, should catch cold; or offered to send for our accommodations from home. True politeness, that politeness which arises from a polished understanding and an humane and good heart, would have shown some solicitude about *ladies*, thus singularly frightened, who could not possibly be involved in the atrocious guilt of my horrible democratical discourse. But no—the tall officer had said, ' Go along after your husband, and be d—d ;' and perhaps humanity or common civility from any of the shorter officers, after that order, might have been construed *mutiny*.

"As we passed along the street musing on the *Agreeable Surprise* (the drama we went to see), a gentleman, who purposely followed us from the Theatre, came up to me in North Street ; and after expressing his indignation at what he termed, in the warmth of first impressions, the *cowardly* treatment we had received, offered to be a witness, if I chose to bring an action against the offenders. I knew him not. He appeared to be a gentleman, a man of sense, and was of a *liberal profession*. I thanked him very sincerely ; and told him, what was strictly true, that I did not know the name of any of the persons in uniform who had caused the outrage ; and that it was too soon at present to come to any determination. He gave me his address, and left me politely ; with an assurance that, if called upon, he should come forward with zeal, in the cause of truth and justice, to bear witness against such unmerited insult, injury, and oppression. He felt hurt, as a man, for the ill-usage of me and my family ; and, as a Briton, for violated law and liberty. He told me he had been in the camp ; and I was mistaken if I thought that ALL the officers disapproved my sermon, or would justify the insult that had been offered this night, to punish me for the zeal it

displayed in promoting the happiness of human nature.
As he was much in the camp, and did not wish to be
personally embroiled in disputes, he desired his name
might not be mentioned, unless I should determine to
prosecute. He is still ready to come forward and give his
testimony in a court of justice.

"On the day following, that is, on Wednesday, the
21st of August, I had resided at Brighton just four weeks,
the term for which I had hired my house. My friend was
to leave the town on to-morrow. It was therefore determined that I should accompany him, and hasten, with all
my baggage-waggons of sedition and treason, to London.
I know not whether the Tower was fortified with additional works on my intention being discovered; but to
London I went, and Brighton Camp, I suppose, felt itself
relieved; like Rome when it had vomited out CATILINE."

The camp of 1794 was formed, early in the summer,
at about a mile and a half to the west of the town. It
at first consisted of 7,000 men; when the harvest had
been got in it was increased to nearly 15,000, owing to the
Militia regiments not being called out until the crops were
cleared, the men then composing the Militia corps being
principally agricultural laborers. On the breaking up of
this camp many of the regiments remained in barracks in
Brighton. These barracks were situated in West Street
(corner of Little Russell Street, afterwards the Custom
House); in North Street, property now known as Unicorn
Yard, Windsor Street; Jew Street; and in Church Street—
the late Infantry Barracks, now used as stores, and belonging to the Corporation of Brighton. Nothing of
importance took place during this camp, but that of the
following year will ever be memorable in the history of
Brighton, inasmuch as it is connected with the trial and
execution of two men, and flogging of several others for
mutiny, not that the mutiny took place here, but Brighton

was the military head-quarters of the troops, hence the court martial was held in this town, at the Castle Tavern.

Here is an interesting quotation with reference to this camp, extracted from *Erredge's History of Brighthelmston*:—

"East Blatchington, near Newhaven, was the theatre of the disaffection, arising from the shortness and bad quality of the bread and flour supplied to the troops; in consequence of which, some men of the Oxford Militia broke into the mill in the vicinity of the barracks, and also, in a rebellious mood, emptied the contents of a vessel laden with corn, into the river, at Newhaven. The Court Martial was held at the Castle Tavern, which occupied the site whereon now stand the buildings which formed the north-east corner of Castle Square. The trial occupied eight days; and ended in Edward Cooke,—termed Captain Cooke, from his taking the lead in the mutiny,—and Henry Parish being found guilty and sentenced to be shot. Six others were also convicted, but their sentence was only that they should be flogged. Much sympathy was shown by the inhabitants to the poor fellows, who were each day marched under a strong escort, from the guard house of the Battery, Artillery Place, to the Castle Tavern and back. Many of the residents in Russell Street, every night and morning, took them provisions, which they were able to pass through the bars of their airing ground; and on the morning of the execution of the sentence upon them the wretched men were unable, from their emotion, to express their thanks for the kindness the people showed them.

"From the hour of four in the morning of the day appointed for them to suffer, the whole lines of encampment were ordered to hold themselves in readiness; at five, however, in the evening, the officers were given to understand that the execution was countermanded for that day. The cause of this short respite was attributed to the absence of the Prince of Wales's 10th Regiment of Light Dragoons. afterwards the 10th Hussars, which did not march into Brighton till nine o'clock on the following morning, and of course could not pitch their tents till late in the evening. When this regiment was seen on the march to their station, all hopes of an expected reprieve seemed entirely to vanish. The most respectable people, however, of Brighton took this opportunity of one day's delay, to repeat their petition in favour of the two men ; but all proved ineffectual, for early on the 13th June, 1795, the Oxford Militia—the regiment to which the mutineers belonged,—began their march from the Barracks at Blatchington to Brighton, to be made awful spectators of their unhappy comrades' punishment, and to be their executioners. At four o'clock the whole were ordered to accompany them from the ground to Goldstone Bottom, at which place they arrived about five. The six men—for there were thirteen mutineers—that were sentenced to be flogged, proceeded afterwards in a covered waggon, guarded by a strong escort, which was composed of select men, picked from every regiment of the line. The two condemned to be shot followed in the rear in an open cart, attended by the Rev. Mr. Dring, and guarded by a second escort, under the command of Captain Leigh, of the 10th Regiment of Light Dragoons, and one of the Captains belonging to the Lancashire Fencibles. When they arrived, however, at the winding road which leads to Goldstone Bottom—or Vale—which is surrounded by an eminence, both the escorts were commanded to halt. The six men sentenced to be flogged were then taken from the covered waggon, and, having been marched through the entire line, which was under arms to receive them, they were brought back to a whipping-post, that was fixed in the centre of the different regiments. The drummers selected to flog them were men belonging to their own corps. To three of them were given three hundred lashes each. This was the number they then received, as, from their long durance, and consequent weakness, the surgeon pronounced that they could suffer no more. The fourth was then stripped, and, after being tied to the flogging-post, was reprieved, as were also his two other comrades.

"This part of the distressing ceremony being gone through, the two unfortunate men condemned to be shot were taken from the cart and marched, as the others had been, up the line, with this difference only, of being conducted also through part of the outer line, which was composed of the Prince's Regiment, and the Lancashire and Cinque Port Fencibles. They were then marched to the front of the Oxfordshire Militia, where the coffins stood to receive their bodies, the Artillery being planted on the right, with lighted matches, in the rear of the Oxfordshire, to prevent any mutiny, if attempted, and the whole height commanded by two thousand cavalry.

"Cooke and Parish being conducted to the fatal spot, exchanged a few words with the clergyman, and then kneeled, with the greatest composure and firmness, on their coffins: the first time, however, they kneeled, it was done the wrong way, but being placed in a proper situation they received their death from a delinquent platoon of twelve of their own regiment, at the distance only of six paces. One of them was not quite dead when he fell, and was therefore shot through the head with a pistol. This, however, was not the last awful ceremony the line had to experience; for, to conclude the dreadful tragedy, every regiment on the ground was ordered to file off past the bodies before they were suffered to be enclosed in their coffins. The whole scene was impressibly awful beyond any spectacle of the kind ever exhibited.

"No disturbance whatever resulted from the melancholy affair; everything was conducted with the greatest solemnity and order: the awe and silence that reigned on the occasion infused a terror, mingled with an equal degree of pity, that was distressing beyond conception. The Oxfordshire Militia naturally experienced more conflicting sensations than any other regiment on the ground.

" Cooke and Parish were both young men, and behaved with uncommon firmness and resignation; they marched through the lines with a steady step, and regarded their coffins with an undaunted eye.

" On the morning of his execution Cooke wrote to his brother a letter, the original of which is in the possession of the author of this book. It is written in a free and bold style, very different to what might be expected from a man under sentence and at the point of an ignominious death. The following is a correct copy, *verbatim et literatim,* of the original :—

" ' Brighton, 13th of June, 1795.

" ' Dear Brother,—This comes with my kind Love to you, and I hope you be well. I am brought very low and weak by long confinement and been in great trouble. Dear Brother,—I am sentenced Death, and must Die on Saturday, the 13th of June; and I hope God Almighty will forgive me my Sins. I never was no body's foe but my own, and that was in Drinking and breaking the Sabbath, and that is a great Sin. I have prayed night and Day to the Almighty God to forgive me and take me to Heaven, and I hope my prayers be not in vain. I am going to die for what the Redgment done; I am not afraid to meet Death, for I have done no harm to no person, and that is a great comfort to me: there is a just God in heaven that knows I am going to suffer innocently. Dear Brother,—I should be very glad to see you before I Depart this Life. I hope God Almighty will be a Guardian over you and all my relations, and I hope we shall meet in heaven, where we shall be ever happy without End. So no more from the hand of your ever loving and Dying Brother,

" ' EDWARD COOKE.' "

" A print extant of the execution of these misguided men is in the possession of Mr. George Shelley, Church-warden. It is thus inscribed :—

" ' The Awful Scene or Ceremony of the Two Soldiers belonging to the Oxfordshire Militia, which were shot on June 13th, 1795, in a Vale, while in Camp at Brighton, by a party of the Oxfordshire Militia which were very Active in the late riots, the men appeared very composed and resigned, the party which shot them were much affected, Infantry and Artillery, were drawn up in lines on the occasion.' "

F

"The engraving, which is about 18 inches by 15 ditto, represents the men kneeling on their coffins, the figure signifying Cooke being in the attitude of prayer, with clasped hands and a firm countenance; while Parish, though with his hands clasped denoting his devotion, is dejected in his general position and has downcast looks. Three lines of four men each are at 'present!' the front rank kneeling, while at each side of the men to be executed is a man at 'ready!' The Rev. Mr Dring, who is in his clerical robes, is departing from the scene towards the rising ground to the right, at the foot of which is an infantry regiment at 'attention,' with the 10th Regiment of Light Dragoons at their rear. On the crown of the hill are the civilians, male and female; in front of whom, to the right, are soldiers formed in a circle, within which, at a triangle, is a man undergoing the punishment of the lash, an officer, evidently the surgeon, superintending the proceedings. Immediately in the rear are the tents of the encampment.

"Thirteen regiments were present at the execution, which for nearly fifty years was pointed out by the form of the coffins, the positions of the men firing, and other incidents of the scene, being cut out in the turf by the shepherd, whose innocent flocks browsed where so tragic an affair occurred. The plough has since obliterated all traces of the tragedy from the spot.

"A singular instance of the effect of nervous excitement is connected with the execution. The Rev. Mr Dring, the Chaplain of the regiment, who attended the culprits in their last moments, being a nervous man, and having a great horror of the duty which he had to perform, made a special request that after he had administered to them the last religious consolation, he should have sufficient time to get beyond the sound of the report of the fatal muskets before the order to fire was given. Promise of compliance with his request was made; but either from his tardy progress in leaving the spot, or a miscalculation of time, the word of command was given, and the firing took place while he yet was within hearing. The effect upon him was that he fell to the ground, and never after recovered the shock upon his nerves.

" The bodies of the two mutineers were interred in Hove churchyard, contiguous to the centre of the old north boundary wall, where their remains continued undisturbed till the restoration of the Church, in 1834, when a saw-pit was dug at the actual spot, and a few of their bones were exhumed. The burying party was under Sergeant-Major Masters, who afterwards was a publican at Witney. The receipt for the burial fees on the inter- ment of the bodies is still retained by his family. A few years since, Mr Samuel Thorncroft, the Assistant- Overseer of Brighton, being at Witney, by chance called at Masters' house, when, the subject of the execution of the two men being introduced, the receipt referred to was shown him, and Masters stated that so infamously con- structed were the coffins in which the corpses were put that, notwithstanding they were buried in their regimental attire, their blood oozed through the coffins and ran down the backs of their comrades who conveyed them to their grave."

Several of the Militia regiments were here for some time after the breaking up of the Camp; the South Glo'ster Militia, commanded by Earl Berkeley, remaining with others many years, and had one of the principal bands attached to it. The Band Master, Mr Wœrth, was the author of several musical pieces, among others, " Brighton Camp, or the girl I left behind me " (music which seems inherent to fifes and drums); and the " Nightingale," a military rondo, dedicated to the Prince of Wales, first performed before him at the Royal Pavilion, in 1803.

On Sept. 23, 1805, a grand review of the Inniskillings, Queen's Dragoons, Artillery, and South Gloucester,

Dorset, Monmouth, Brecon, and South Hants Militia took place near Rottingdean; and on the 13th August, 1810, a sham fight took place on the Race Hill, at which there were present the Prince of Wales, the Dukes of York, Cumberland, Clarence, Sussex, and Cambridge; 30,000 spectators assembled. Several persons descendants of members of the above-named Militia regiments are resident in Brighton, and occupying good positions.

THE AMUSEMENTS OF BRIGHTON AND THE THEATRES.

The Assemblies were held every Monday from August to March. In the season only, promenade concerts were given at the Castle Tavern, Castle Square, corner of the Old Steine, looking eastward. This tavern was opened in 1755, and pulled down in May, 1822. These concerts were given three times a week, under the superintendence of Mr Forth, who was elected M.C. in 1808, as successor to Colonel Wade.

In removing the hotel portion of this building it was anticipated that it would greatly improve the Pavilion. The Ball and Assembly Room was converted into the Royal Chapel and consecrated, remaining as such till the Royal property came into the possession of the town,— when, in 1850, in accordance with arrangement, it was razed to the ground and the materials sold to Miss Wagner (sister of the Vicar), and re-erected in Montpelier Place, known as St. Stephen's Church, the Rev. George Wagner receiving the appointment as officiating clergyman, and now held by the Rev. C. E. Douglas.

The other ball and assembly rooms were those known as the Old Ship Rooms, situate at the rear of the Old Ship Hotel, and erected in the year 1650; from this establishment arose the name Ship Street. Masonic meetings and banquets took place in these fashionable rooms prior to the holding of the same in the Pavilion. The Old Ship Hotel is of long established reputation, and is renowned for the admirable manner in which its visitors are catered for. Under the able proprietorship and superintendence of Mr. Robert Bacon, who is assisted by his brother, Mr. Arthur Bacon, this hotel must continue to enjoy its popularity.

The amusements at this period were numerous,— comprising tea parties, and fireworks at Promenade Grove, the entrance to which was in Prince's Place, North Street. Bull-baiting and cock-fighting were also in vogue, the original printed bills announcing them are now in the author's possession. Here are copies of them:—

A BULL BAIT

AT HOVE,

On *MONDAY, JUNE* 11*th*,

1810.

A DINNER will be provided, and on Table at Two o'clock.

COCKING,

To be fought at the Cock Pit,

WHITE LION, NORTH STREET,

BRIGHTON,

On *THURSDAY, the* 18*th APRIL,* 1811,

A Main of Cocks, for TWENTY GUINEAS a Battle, and FIFTY GUINEAS the Main; between the Gentlemen of the Isle of Wight, and the Gentlemen of Sussex.

Feeders { POLLARD, Isle of Wight.
{ HOLDEN, Sussex.

N.B. A pair of Cocks to be on the Pit at Eleven o'clock.

At this period the Theatre was in great favour, and very fashionably patronized. Situated in North Street, at the back of premises now occupied by Messrs. Cunditt, jewellers, its erection dating back to the year 1774. Owing to the rapid increase of the population, a theatre was erected, in 1778, at the upper part of Duke Street, and later, in 1807, on the completion of the New Road, another, on a more extensive scale, was erected by Hewitt Cobb, Esq., of Clement's Inn, London, on the site of the present one. The first stone of this building was laid by Mr. Brunton, sen., on the 24th September, 1806, and the theatre opened on the 6th of June, 1807. The tragedy of *Hamlet* was selected for the opening play, the celebrated artistes Mr. and Mrs. Charles Kemble sustaining the principal characters. In the month of August, in the year 1809, Mrs. Siddons, "the queen of tragedy" (sister of Mr. Charles Kemble), appeared as "Mrs. Beverley" in the play of *The Gamester;* her farewell performance on the stage.

Appended is a copy of the "bill of the play":—

THEATRE, BRIGHTON.

The MANAGERS feel happy, in most respectfully announcing to the Public, that

Mrs.   SIDDONS,

Previously to her FINAL Retirement from the stage, has consented to appear in
Two or Three of her

PRINCIPAL CHARACTERS.

On TUESDAY, August 8, 1809,

Will be acted the Tragedy of

THE GAMESTER.

Beverly *(for that Night only),* Mr BARRYMORE,

(Of the late Theatre Royal, Drury Lane.)

Lewson..	.. Mr. BRUNTON,	Bates ..	.. Mr. JAMES
Stukely..	.. Mr. CRESSWELL.	Dawson ..	.. Mr. STANLEY.
Jarvis ..	.. Mr. MURRAY	Waiter ..	.. Mr. PHILLIPS.

Mrs. BEVERLY,

By Mrs. SIDDONS.

| Charlotte .. | .. Miss BOYCE. | Lucy | .. .. Miss SHARP. |

To which will be added the Farce

OF AGE TO-MORROW.

Frederick .. .. .. Mr BRUNTON.
Piffberg .. .. Mr LOVEDAY. | Friz .. .. .. Mr TURNER.
Malkus .. .. Mr RUSSELL. | Waiter .. .. Mr PHILLIPS.
Lady Lumbrack .. .. .. Mrs LOVEDAY.
Sophia .. .. Miss CHAPMAN. | Maria .. .. Mrs BRUNTON.

Doors to bo opened at Half-past Six o'clock, and to begin at Half-past Seven precisely ; no places can bo kept after the End of tho First Act.

BOXES, 5s.—PIT, 2s.—GALLERY, 1s.

Tickets to bo had, and Places in tho Boxes to bo taken, of Mr PHILLIPS, at the Theatre, from Eleven till Three.

Here is an interesting description of Mrs Siddons' farewell of the public, a short time after, at Covent Garden Theatre :—

"COVENT GARDEN THEATRE.

"This celebrated actress last night closed her professional career at this Theatre, in the part of 'Lady Macbeth,' for her own benefit. So early as three o'clock in the afternoon the people began to assemble about the pit and gallery doors, and at half-past four the pressure was so very great, that those who had attended early, in the hope of getting a good situation, were driven from the doors by the rush of those who were under the arches. Several persons who had attempted to get in, became overpowered by the heat, and in endeavouring to retrace their steps, created great confusion. So formidable was the crowd, not more than twenty ladies obtained places in the pit, and the house was crammed in every part. When Mrs Siddons made her appearance, she was received with the loudest acclamations. She appeared much affected, and shed tears, which seemed to relieve her, and she went through her part with her usual excellence. At the end of the sleeping scene, the plaudits continued from the time of her going off till she again appeared to speak her address, which was nearly a quarter of an hour, which she delivered in a very impressive manner; and at the conclusion of which Mr Kemble came and led her off by the hand. She then, as well as himself, appeared much affected; for the audience, not satisfied with the usual method of shewing their approbation, stood up upon the seats and cheered her, waving their hats for several minutes. It having appeared to be the wish of the majority of the audience that the play should conclude with her scene, the curtain was dropped; but Mr Kemble came forward and announced, that if it was the wish of the house, the play should proceed. The audience were divided, and the Farce of *The Spoil'd Child* commenced, amidst loud acclamations from one side, and disappointed from the other. This continued during the whole of the first act, there being a constant cry from pit and gallery of 'The fifth act! the fifth act!' It was then found in vain to proceed any further, as the house was all noise and confusion, and the voices on the stage were totally inaudible; it was therefore deemed advisable to drop the curtain, and the audience, in some short time after, quietly dispersed.

The following is a copy of the Address spoken by Mrs Siddons :—

Who has not felt, how growing use endears
The fond remembrance of our former years?
Who has not sigh'd, when doom'd to leave at last
The hopes of youth, the habits of the past,
The thousand ties and interests, that impart
A second nature to the human heart,
And, wreathing round it close, like tendrils, climb,
Blooming in age, and sanctified by time?

Yes! at this moment crowd upon my mind
Scenes of bright days for ever left behind,
Bewildering visions of enraptured youth,
When hope and fancy wore the hues of truth,
And long-forgotten years, that almost seem
The faded traces of a morning dream!
Sweet are those mournful thoughts: for they renew
The pleasing sence of all I owe to you,
For each inspiring smile, and soothing tear—
For those full honours of my long career,
That cheer'd my earliest hopes, and chased my latest fear!

And though, for me, those tears shall flow no more,
And the warm sunshine of your smile is o'er—
Though the bright beams are fading fast away,
That shone unclouded through my summer-day,—
Yet grateful Memory shall reflect their light
O'er the dim shadows of the coming night,
And lend to later life a softer tone,
A moonlight tint, a lustre of her own.

Judges and Friends! to whom the tragic strain
Of nature's feeling never spoke in vain,
Perhaps your hearts, when years have glided by,
And past emotions wake a fleeting sigh,
May think on her, whose lips have pour'd so long
The charmed sorrows of your Shakspeare's song ;—
On her, who, parting to return no more,
Is now the mourner she but *seem'd* before,—
Herself subdued, resigns the melting spell,
And breathes, with swelling heart, her long, her last farewell!

Mrs Siddons first appeared in the Theatre Royal, Drury Lane, in 1775, under an engagement,—made with Mr Siddons, at Cheltenham, that summer,—for Mr Garrick. Her salary was £6 per week, and that of Mr Siddons, 40s. Her first appearance was in "Portia" in the *Merchant of Venice*, a character not best suited to her powers; and afterwards she made a more unfortunate attempt in comedy, in Mrs Cowley's *Runaway;* soon after which her admirers had the mortification to see her descend at the close of the season to peronate the walking Venus in the revived pageant of the *Jubilee*. She returned to the Bath Theatre in 1776, and, as is well known, returned a few years afterwards to re-illumine the London Theatre, with a splendour of talents which continued with undiminished lustre to the present hour.

MR. LISTON.

MR. KELLY

Begs leave to inform the Nobility, Gentry, and Inhabitants of Brighton that his
BENEFIT IS FIXED for
SATURDAY, 14th *OCTOBER*, 1809,
When will be acted
A FAVORITE PLAY,
IN WHICH
MR. LISTON,
Of the Theatre Royal, Covent Garden, will Perform.

To which will be added, the Burlesque Tragedy of
TOM THUMB.
The part of Lord Grizzle, by MR. LISTON.

Tickets to be had of Mr. KELLY, at Mr. PARSONS, Shoe Maker, 25, Ship Street, and of Mr. PHILLIPS, at the Theatre, where places for the Boxes may be obtained.

Here is proof that the boards of Brighton Theatre were trodden by principal actors in the kingdom in bygone days. About the year 1814, there was a tragic actor performing at this Theatre of the name of William Cory, playing the second parts to one of the Kembles. On one occasion Kemble was engaged for the part of "Rolla," in *Pizarro*, but from some unavoidable cause was

absent, and the character was undertaken by the actor
spoken of at a very short notice, he achieving a great
success in his impersonation of the same, and which, in
consequence, excited the jealousy and ire of the absentee,
leading to Cory's dismissal. He then, in conjunction with
his wife, likewise a member of the *corps dramatique*,
established two schools at the top of Mulberry Square, in
North Street, opposite Ship Street (now extinct and at
present forming a portion of the business premises of Messrs.
Palmer and Co.), where they resided for many years. He
was the composer of " Will Watch, the Bold Smuggler,"
a celebrated song of world-wide renown, the authorship
of which has been erroneously attributed to others,
but the author of this work vouches for the accuracy
of this statement. Eventually this leading place of
amusement became the property of George Cobb, Esq.,
and by him, a few years since, was disposed of to the present
owner, Mr. Henry Nye Chart, who has recently re-
erected and beautified the same, and, in conjunction with
his worthy partner,—a much-esteemed lady, cater for the
public requirements in a manner beyond all praise, en-
gaging the first talent on the boards in their desire to
gratify the frequenters of their establishment.

In 1808 a permanent Circus was erected on the Grand
Parade, near the spot occupied by the Grand Parade
Chapel. It was opened in August of the same year, under
the lesseeship of Mr Brunton, had a frontage of 100ft.,
and was of the same depth. As adjunct thereto, there
was a brilliant lounge, also confectionary department and
a Coffee House and hotel, the latter occupying a wing to
the south of the Circus. From want of support the Circus
had but a short existence, closing in 1812 ; the premises
for some years after were used as a Bazaar, and above the
stall of Mrs Richardson there was suspended an immense
painting. Since the demolition of the Grand Parade
Circus, various equestrian troupes have visited Brighton,

notably those of Batty, Franconi, Cooke, Sanger, and Bell. Batty's Circus was situate in Mighell Street, and much frequented. Franconi converted the Riding School of the Pavilion into a Cirque, and certainly presented the best artistes of the day, both English and Continental. Cooke and Franconi's troupes had, respectively, the honour of performing in the Riding School, in an impromptu ring, before their Majesties King William and Queen Adelaide; also, a few years after, Queen Victoria, the Prince Consort, and royal family,—the gallery on the eastern side being converted into "the royal box" on each occasion. The school was admirably adapted for a Circus, but local requirements were paramount, and it has now been converted into a Corn Exchange, the want of a suitable building for that purpose having for long been seriously felt.

In 1818, posts and rails were erected around; the Northern Enclosure, opposite the King and Queen, and shrubs and trees planted therein,—a vast improvement upon its prior appearance and condition,—it having been, previously, the resort of all comers, and the receptacle of filth and refuse. Here Brighton Fair was celebrated, at which showmen, toy vendors, pedlars, and "Cheap Jacks" mustered numerously, and at that time the fair was one of the festivals of the inhabitants,—held annually on Holy Thursday and succeeding day, and on the 4th and 5th September. Numerous have been its *locus in quo:* for many years it was held on the Cliff, between Black Lion Street and Ship Street, afterwards in Belle Vue Field,—now covered by the Regency Square property, —from thence transferred to the Northern Enclosure; next held on St. Peter's Green, whereon St. Peter's Church stands; then upon the Level; afterwards upon the Royal Cricket Ground, known as Ireland's Tea Gardens, where it was established for several years; subsequently recovered its old quarters, the Level; again was held north of the Level, in Blaker's and Tilly's Fields, on the Lewes Road; and finally the remnant of this ancient custom ekes out its miserable existence in a field near the Queen's Park. It is evident that this, like other kindred institutions, has outlived its original uses.

At the south-western portion of Belle Vue Field, before spoken of, stood Streeter's Mill, which was removed by 86 oxen to the top of Preston Drove, on the Dyke Road, on Sept. 20, 1792. Under the Cliff at the south-east corner of Belle Vue Field was a contrivance, protected by walls east and west, called by the inhabitants at that time "Smith's Folly," the real object of which was to draw up, in stress of weather, into a place of shelter and security, fishing boats and smacks ; but not answering the intended purpose it was pulled down. Recently, on excavating for the erection of the Sailing Club Room, the foundation of the old walls were found. The original intention was to have called Regency Square Waterloo Square, but it was abandoned for the present name.

In 1807, the principal flock masters of Brighton and neighbourhood sought to establish upon the Level an annual sheep and lamb fair, to take place upon the 4th of September,—they entering into a guarantee to contribute to the fair none but the purest Southdown breed. Near 20,000 animals were penned on the first occasion, and met with a ready sale, buyers being plentiful. The following year the fair was equally well attended, but, notwithstanding the exertions of its most strenuous promoters, the fair lapsed after seven years' existence.

In 1832 another ineffectual attempt was made to establish a Cattle Market,—a portion of the Workhouse property abutting on to the Dyke Road, and near to the Old Manor Pound, being selected for the purpose : but the market existed only for a few years,—and the natural deduction formed as to the cause of these failures was the absence of pasturage and grazing land in the neighbourhood,

—so extremely essential to all Stock Markets,—and to this want can be traced the abortive efforts to establish two valuable local institutions.

At various periods the Level has been the scene for celebration of festivals and important national events by the inhabitants,—and many of these rejoicings in modern times are in the recollection of persons living in Brighton. On the coronation of George IV.—July 19th, 1821, two bullocks were roasted and distributed,—also an abundant supply of bread and beer, by the Committee formed for the purpose of managing the celebration of this auspicious event. The inhabitants turned out *en masse* to witness the festivities, all shops were closed and business of every description suspended in the desire to manifest the loyalty and devotedness of the inhabitants to their royal patron; and so intent were they upon the Level rejoicings, that barely a person could be met in the streets. This opportunity was seized on by a party of smugglers, who, at mid-day, landed a cargo of contraband goods at the bottom of Black Lion Street, in the very centre of the town, their only opponent a solitary coast-guardsman, who was impotent to stay their escape, hence they got off successfully with their booty.

On this day of rejoicing Osborne's Lewes coach, which usually ran, from the Blue Coach Office, Castle Square, to and from that ancient town but once per day, did a double journey.

The Level was again the scene of revelry on her present Majesty's Coronation Day, June 28th, 1838. The carcases of an ox and some sheep were roasted; thousands of children dined on the Steyne in honor of the event, and much merriment prevailed.

Later, June 4th, 1856, we had the memorable "Peace Celebration,"—during the Mayoralty of the late Mr Alderman Hallett. Brighton was gay with bunting,—house fronts were decorated, and illuminations at night time were beautiful and countless. Children, on this day, dined in the avenues of the Level,—tables being fitted up for their accommodation beneath the trees around this delightfully cool retreat. In order that the juveniles should have all the convenience possible and unalloyed enjoyment of the good things provided for them, a fence was erected to exclude the general public. It may be here observed that, by resolution of the Town Commissioners, of 21st November, 1844, the trees around the Level were planted, — and their present appearance con- tributes very materially to the beauty of the people's play-ground and neighbourhood surrounding. A great drawback to this spot is the number of paths permitted to intersect the same,—but we trust our local authorities will soon remedy this defect.

BRIGHTON RACES: THEIR RISE AND DECLINE.—WHITE HAWK FAIR.

The first mention made of Brighton assisting in racing matters is met with in the *Racing Calendar* of 1777. On the 31st July of this year the Brighthelmstone Plate— of the value of £50, a four-mile heat,was run for at Lewes, and won by Sir Jno. Shelley's Hudibras, beating six others. This race continued for a few years.

In 1788 a race course was formed in this town and a stand erected. This event is described by Wigstead and Rowlandson, in an embellished work, entitled *An Excursion to Brighthelmstone made in the year* 1789, from which we quote as follows :—" The race ground is exceedingly well adapted to the purposes for which it was intended ; and is one of the most beautifully situated spots in the world, The prospect is wonderfully extensive and magnificent. The races are in July, and there are always three fifties besides several sweepstakes, matches, &c. A handsome

and convenient stand, sufficiently capacious to receive a
great number of spectators, is erected on the Course."
This stand was burnt down on the 23rd of August, 1808,
—a misfortune attributed to the carelessness of the
occupant, he having, unknown to the Proprietors, who had
allowed him to take up his residence therein,—erected a
temporary fireplace of bricks upon the basement floor.
Having occasion to leave the building, he neglected a
large fire then burning in the above named grate : in his
absence the flames communicated to the woodwork of the
structure (which was principally of timber), and before any
attempt could be made to stay their progress, the building
was nearly destroyed. Notwithstanding this occurrence took
place at mid-day, it was distinctly seen for nearly 20 miles.
People from various parts of the neighbourhood came to
the scene of conflagration : some on horseback and many on
foot entered the town during the day and night to make
enquiries respecting it, apprehensions prevailing that the
enemy had made a descent on that part of the coast,
and (as formerly) evincing *a love* (!) for the natives by
setting fire to their dwellings. The congregating of persons
from afar is not remarkable when it is considered how few
buildings intercepted the view of the Grand Stand at that
time. One other fire, at noon, occurred in August, 1820,
—the total destruction of the Southwick Brewery,—which
was distinctly seen from the Old Church Yard : a number
of persons assembling at that spot to witness the same.
The brewery, however, was not rebuilt ; but its business
connection was transferred to extensive premises erected
at the northern part of Brighton, by Richard Tamplin, Esq.,
and called " The Phœnix Brewery" (from the ashes of the
old one), and from that time to the present the firm has
been successfully carried on under the name of
Tamplin and Son.

A singular circumstance occurred during the Race
Stand fire before alluded to. An officer of the Prince'

regiment, attracted to the spot by the volumes of flames and smoke, was reviewing the terrific encroachment of the devouring element, when a cat, dreadfully singed and terrified, sprung through the blaze and alighted on his shoulder. The officer, somewhat surprised at first, endeavoured to shake her off; but poor puss, firmly fixing her claws in his jacket, was not so easily got rid off. Perceiving her reluctance to leave him, he at length humanely determined that, as she had in the moment of danger and fear flown to him for protection, she should accompany him to the Barracks, and here she was well taken care of by her new master and his comrades.

At a small distance from the Race Ground there was formerly a Roman Station, called White Hawk, some vestiges of which, in a circular shape, are still visible. The Prince of Wales, the officers of the various militia regiments quartered here, and several of the county gentry were the chief supporters of the races at their commencement. This meeting extended over four days,—Friday, Saturday, Monday, and Tuesday,—and in 1791 the dates were respectively July 29th and 30th, August 1st and 2nd, (a Sunday intervening, on which day a fair was held, called White Hawk Fair), and the "running hours" of the races were so apportioned as to admit of the races being run before and after dinner. Connected with this fair, the *Morning Herald* of Monday, Aug. 3, 1807, makes the following allusion to the preceding day :—

" BRIGHTON.

" White Hawk Fair, as it is termed, has attracted much company to the Race Down to-day, though but few individuals of fashionable note were to be seen in the throng."

These races attained such a degree of excellence under the auspices named that few provincial meetings could rival them, some of the most celebrated horses in the king-

G

dom being engaged here, viz. : Waxy, Pot 8-O's., Smolenski Pavilion, Sancho, &c. In 1804 there were 19 horses entered for the Pavilion Stakes p.p. of 100 Guineas, and a majority of them accepted and started.

The following *bona-fide* match for 2,000 guineas, h. f., between the celebrated horses Sancho and Pavilion, arranged to be run for over the Lewes Race Course, on July 24th, 1806, excited the greatest interest in Brighton, as the appended quotation will show : —

" Brighton, July 26th.—This place is all hurry and bustle with preparations for the great match at Lewes to-morrow, between Sancho and Pavilion. A report was circulated yesterday that Sancho was not well, and that bets were 7 to 4 in favour of Pavilion. It was, however, entitled to no credit, Sancho continues to be the favorite. Every carriage is taken to convey the company to Lewes to-morrow."

The following description of the race, &c., is also of great interest :—

Yesterday, the 27th, the long-expected match between the Earl of Darlington's famous horse Pavilion and Mr Mellish's no less famous horse Sancho, was decided upon Lewes Race Ground. The distance was four miles, equal weight, each horse carrying eight stone seven pounds. No match has taken place for a long time that excited so much interest. The people of Brighton, Worthing, and all other neighbouring towns and villages, at an early hour, began to put themselves in motion. About twelve o'clock the company upon the ground amounted to about 1,000 ; but in less than an hour they exceeded 3,000, and many bets were made. Sancho had been always the favourite, and for some days past the odds were 7 to 4 in his favour. On Wednesday, however, they varied a little, and came down to 5 to 4 ; but yesterday morning public opinion declared in favor of Pavilion, the odds completely changed

sides, and 6 to 4 were frequently laid upon him. This
revolution was produced by a report that Sancho was not
well. At a quarter to two, his Royal Highness the Prince
of Wales arrived upon the ground in his barouche and six
beautiful greys. His Royal Highness sat upon the barouche
seat, and was driven by Sir John Lade. The company
inside were the Earl of Darlington, Mr Smith, and three
other gentlemen. The barouche drove up towards the
judge's box, and took its station at a distance of about
twenty yards from it. Mr Mellish, the owner of Sancho
drove up soon after, in his barouche and four beautiful
greys, with the Countess of Barrymore and three other
ladies inside. At two o'clock the two horses came upon
the ground. Pavilion was the first. He was walked the
length of the railing, and was surrounded by the company,
who were greatly pleased with his fine appearance. Great
activity was now used to clear the course, no person being
suffered inside the railing. In this business Mr Mellish
shewed great anxiety and exerted himself very much. At
five minutes past two the horses were saddled, and Mr
Mellish went up to Sancho, and led him about ten yards
before the start. Buckle rode Sancho, in a white jacket and
crimson sleeves. Pavilion was ridden by young Chiffney,
in a light orange jacket with gold lace stripes. Expectation was now raised to its extreme height. The moment
of trial at length arrived, and the horses started at ten
minutes past two. Pavilion took the lead and kept it
about four lengths for the first two miles. Sancho now
began to fetch up the distance, and gained about a length
in the third mile. Five minutes had now elapsed, and
the two horses had turned the post, Pavilion maintaining
his last mentioned distance a-head of Sancho. The bets
now ran 2 to 1 upon Pavilion. Just in the flat, at the
commencement of the last mile, the grand struggle and
display of speed and jockeyship commenced. In running
home this last mile, Sancho felt himself upon the ground

where he usually made his pushes against the hill, and Buckle now pursued the same system. Sancho ran in a fine style up to Pavilion, passed him, and for a moment victory appeared doubtful. This arduous and anxious struggle lasted until the horses came up to the distance post, when, to the great sorrow and disappointment of everyone who did not gain by the event, Sancho suddenly broke completely down. Pavilion ran home and won easy. It was in his near fore foot that Sancho failed. He was so lame, it was with difficulty he carried his weight to the winning post.

Just at the moment Sancho broke down, the odds had changed greatly in his favour, and 5 to 1 was betted upon him. Pavilion did not appear in the least distressed. Mr Mellish, it is said, had £20,000 depending upon this match, including the £2,000 for which the match was made. It was stated he would be obliged to forfeit half of the two matches which Sancho was to run; that is, a mile at Brighton, for the same sum, between the same horses; and the match for £1,000 against His Royal Highness the Prince of Wales's famous horse Haphazard.

Among the company present were, the Duchess of St. Albans, in a curricle; her Grace was in mourning, and looked very interesting. The Marchioness of Clanri-carde, in a barouche and four fine greys; the beautiful Countess Berkeley and four other Ladies, in a landau; Mr Potts and family, in a barouche and four bays; the Earl of Barrymore was on horseback, in company with the Hon. Capt. Stanhope; Lord Monson, Lord G. Cavendish, Mr Dalton, Col. Graham (from Worthing), Lord Stawell, and several officers of the 6th Light Dragoons, from Lewes, were among the fashionable equestrians. The Prince and his party, and Mr Mellish and his party, after the race, went to the Star Inn, Lewes, where they alighted, and partook of some refreshment; and, at half-past three, they returned to Brighton. Thus ended this busy scene.

The above-named "crack" horse, Pavilion, at the Brighton Races on July 28th, a week afterwards, won the Gold Cup given by His Royal Highness the Prince of Wales, added to a subscription of ten guineas each, beating Mr Mellish's Headley and two others. Headley having bolted and ran towards the sea. At the conclusion of the race Mr Mellish came up to the Prince and said he was never so vexed at losing money as on this occasion, and it could not be called a race. He had lost £2,000 upon it, but observed that he had won £2,600 the preceding night. The race day, &c., is ‘thus described :—

" The morning was very fine, and the race-ground, at twelve o'clock, crowded. His Royal Highness the Prince of Wales was in his barouche, with six bays, his postilion in a new livery, black velvet sleeves, covered with gold lace, and scarlet body, with gold stripes. At a quarter to one the Prince arrived. The Duke and Duchess of St. Albans were in a curricle and pair. Sir John Lade in his barouche and four. Mrs Fitzherbert in her barouche with three ladies. His Royal Highness left the race-ground at five o'clock. A grand cricket match was to have taken place after the race, between some of the Brighton gentlemen and some of the sporting visitors, but the rain prevented it, to the great disappointment of three thousand spectators.

" The Ball, at the Castle Assembly Rooms, last night, was numerously attended. His Royal Highness the Prince of Wales was present. The Countess of Jersey looked divinely. Her Ladyship wore a point dress. The Earl and Countess of Barrymore, Mrs Fitzherbert, and the whole of the Prince's party were present. The Prince left the Ball Room at one o'clock. The Duchess

of St. Alban's was prevented, by a slight indisposition,
from being there. Her Grace and the Duke intend leaving
Brighton to-morow.

"The Earl of Barrymore gave a grand dinner to
the Earl of Darlington, Sir John Lade, Mr Mellish,
and several other gentlemen. The Theatre is crowded.

"*Nine o'Clock.*

"His Royal Highness the Prince of Wales left
Brighton at half-past seven this evening, for London. It
is said, in consequence of an express he received at two
o'clock this day."

This state of matters relative to racing continued
for some years, but the races eventually declined;
in the year 1816 they were suspended, and remained
in abeyance till 1819, when means were taken to
resuscitate them. The *Brighton Herald* of July 31st,
of that year, thus speaks of the same: — "The
town is in the meridian blaze of gaiety; would that
every town in the kingdom exhibited such emblems
of joy and pleasure as Brighton. The Race Hill
at this moment is covered by an immense assemblage of
persons. The equipages are numerous, dazzling and
elegant. The equestrians, for the most part, are all well
mounted, and those on foot include a very considerable
portion of respectable individuals. The scene is truly
enlivening; the Duke of York, who, accompanied by
Colonel Cooke and Mr Dighton, arrived here on Sunday, is
among the spectators. There is also a long list of noblemen and gentlemen of sporting celebrity. The common
observation is that Brighton never shone in such splendour.
Those who have so spiritedly come forward to re-establish
the races have now the gratification to perceive that their
efforts have proved decidedly successful. The sports
yesterday were exceedingly good and consisted of a
sweepstakes of twenty guineas each, won by Lord

A Perspective View of FRESHWATER in the Isle of Wight, 1795, and the Sea Coast as far as the ISLE of WIGHT

Egremont's Snowdon, and a gold cup given by the Prince Regent, added to a sweepstakes of ten guineas each, won by Mr Turner's Anglesea, and a plate of one hundred guineas won by Mr Turner's Rhoda. The sports of this day and Monday are expected to be equally good. The course is in excellent order and the weather could not be more favorable. A new judge's stand has been erected and is admirably adapted for the purpose. Mr Paul Hewitt, wine merchant, of German Place, who, as Chairman of the Committee of Subscribers to the racing fund, has shewn an ardent zeal and devoted a great deal of his time in promoting the success of the races, officiated as judge in the most impartial and satisfactory manner. It is with pleasure we here observe that the Duke of York warmly interested himself in the cause, and on Thursday last called at Mr Hewitt's house* to ascertain how the entries were getting on. The town generally will, we are sure, applaud the style in which the measures for securing this desideratum to the town have been carried out, the success has been complete, and we sincerely hope that what has been so well begun will be kept up by a corresponding spirit, for we are sure that annual races will prove of the highest advantage to the town. The Race Ball, under the patronage of the Stewards of the Races, viz., the Earl of Egremont and J. Douglas, Esq., M.P., will take place on Monday next, August 2nd, at the Old Ship Hotel, under the superintendence of W. S. Forth, Esq., M.C." The same journal, in its first publication after the races, mentions :—" It is with much pleasure we state that measures have already been adopted which will cause more *éclat* to the races next year. The Pavilion Stakes are revised and to which there are several subscribers ; and to the Regent's gold cup are eight subscribers ; and no less

---

* This house was *the first erected eastward of the Steyne,*—nothing intervening between it and Donaldson's Library. It is now in the occupation of Mr Casher.

than fifteen to a sweepstakes of ten guineas each with sixty to be added by the town. Besides the above, Mr Harrington and other gentlemen have subscribed one hundred guineas to be called the Brighton Club Stakes."

The Races again progressed smoothly and satisfactorily for some years, then again they were on the wane, and the journal spoken of had the following remarks connected with them on August 12th, 1837 :—"These races commenced on Thursday last, and perhaps within the memory of the present inhabitants they have never proved so significant a failure. The attractions presented were of the meanest sort, the attendance, hitherto so numerous on such occasions, has been, on the present, the most trifling possible, scarcely anything remained to remind us of what they once were but the erection of some booths for the sale of articles of refreshment, and a tolerable sprinkling of the usual attendants at such scenes. The whole of the affair was 'flat, stale, and unprofitable'; each day afforded, by advertisement, but one race. The first for the Brighton Stakes was won by Mr Jno. Day's Airy, beating his horse, the Drummer, and Lord Chesterfield's Hornsea. The second day Her Majesty's Cup was won by the last horse mentioned walking over the course, being the only one placed. Unless something be done to restore our Races to their former state and vigour they will shortly become extinct. Thus ended this very dull affair to the disappointment of all. Time was when these Races bore a very different complexion, and if they were of any use to the town, now is the moment to prevent their total extinction. A ball with fireworks has been given each evening at Brown's Royal Gardens."

The Races continued for a few years longer, but the Committee felt their efforts were paralysed by not having any interest in the Stand, as all the money received for admission went into the pockets of the shareholders, who rendered no account whatever of their receipts and disbursements. Matters were consequently drawing to a climax between them and the then Race Committee, inasmuch as at this period,—1848,—the Committee had not sufficient funds to discharge one-half of their obligations, involving the vital principle of winners of races remaining unpaid, the greatest creditor being that noble sportsman, Lord George Bentinck. The death of the Earl of Egremont, one of the principal supporters of the Races, added to their decline, and the Duke of Richmond withdrew his support in favour of Goodwood, which Races had been fixed to take precedence of Brighton, and the withdrawal of the Royal gift of 100 guineas for a gold cup helped forward this result.

At this juncture a movement was made by the Town Commissioners to obtain the Race Stand on behalf of the inhabitants, and a Committee was appointed for that purpose, who took possession of the same, which act was repudiated by the general body at one of their meetings, who threw the responsibility of it on the members of the committee individually,—actions for trespass being served on them by Mr Thomas Attree on behalf of himself and co-trustees ; but these proceedings were withdrawn, the *amende honorable* having been made. The Trustees afterwards offered to sell the interest they held in the same for £400 to the Race Committee. This offer was declined by the existing Race Committee, but afterwards a public meeting was called at which a new Committee was formed, and the subject re-opened, the result being the purchase of the Stand for £380 (the Railway Company contributing £100 towards the amount, irrespective of their annual subscription to the Races of £100), Mr Lewis Slight, jun., acting as Honorary Secretary, and it was evident that unless a great effort was made the sports would have to be abandoned and the beautiful gallop over the breezy downs be lost to the public.

This property being acquired, gave the new *regime* a freedom of action to improve the management of the Races. The annual public money given at this period to be run for was £350, and the public money has gradually increased up to the present time, and is now upwards of £2000.

The first step taken was to raise subscriptions to pay all debts owing; and assurances of support were given by the Chairman, Mr Samuel Laing, of the London and Brighton Railway Company (which had recently come into existence), and its Traffic Manager, Mr George Hawkins, and by dint of great efforts the required sum needed to pay off the obligations was obtained. The Races again assumed a more healthy aspect, and the following notice of the same appeared in the *Brighton Herald* of the period:—

"It is with great satisfaction we announce that in consequence of the spirited steps taken by a party of gentlemen interested in the welfare of Brighton, not only has the credit of the town been relieved from the unworthy stigma that has been attached to it, but after satisfying Lord George Bentinck's claim and others, a considerable sum remains towards carrying out the Races for the ensuing year in a proper and sportsmanlike manner. We may now hope for a revival on a new footing. Lord George Bentinck has been paid, and under the direction of a Committee, consisting of a party of gentlemen to whom the greatest thanks are due, we have no doubt but funds will be raised that will enable the town to offer such prizes as will ensure the attendance of the best horses. However, a conscientious feeling will prevent, as we know it has done, many worthy and influential inhabitants of the town from lending their support and countenance to racing; still we do not think it ought to be concealed that under proper directions these sports must prove highly beneficial to the town and their offensive features become much modified. However we may incline to respect the conscientious feeling that withholds the support of our Dissenting brethren, still we cannot disguise the fact that the amusement of the visitors has not been fully considered, and that the interests of the town have suffered in consequence. To use a homely phrase, 'We all row together in the same boat,' and we are bound to sacrifice something towards supporting the character and prosperity of Brighton."

The next step taken was the erection of a new Grand Stand in the place of the shabby wooden building of 1803. The Town Surveyor of the period, Mr Allan Stickney, was requested to furnish the designs, and the present handsome and commodious structure was commenced May 1st, 1851, and opened in August following at a cost of £5000. The southern wing has since been added, and was first occupied on the occasion of the Easter Monday Review of 1866, by the Princess of Wales, Princess Mary of Cambridge, the Hon. Mrs Stonor, and the Mayoress, the Mayor of Brighton (Mr Alderman Henry Martin), Sir William Knollys and Colonel Tyrwhitt. The Prince of Wales marched past at the head of his corps, The Honourable Artillery Company, and in the presence likewise of H.R.H. the Duke of Cambridge, Prince Teck, Sir Hope Grant, Sir Hugh Rose, and other distinguished Officers. The Royal party and suite were, after the Review, entertained by the Mayor and Corporation to a sumptuous repast in the Banqueting Room at the Royal Pavilion. The Prince of Wales, in responding to the toast of "The Prince and Princess of Wales,"—proposed by the Mayor,—thanked the Mayor and Corporation for the hospitality and cordial welcome accorded to them, remarking that "He had been highly pleased with his visit to Brighton, and the proceedings throughout the day had given him entire satisfaction."

Since that period the northern wing has been added, making the sum of £10,000 expended on the Stand, Course, &c. The Trustees appointed by the Race Committee, and in whom the property is vested, are Mr Alderman Burrows, Mr Alderman Henry Martin, Mr Robert Williams, Mr H. F. Stocken, Mr Lewis Slight, and Mr Lewis Slight, jun., and under the able superintendence of Mr Henry Dorling, of Epsom, (Clerk of the Course), and the Race Committee, together with the Honorary Secretary, Mr H. F. Stocken (the successor of Mr Lewis Slight, jun.), who has been indefatigable in carrying out the onerous duties of his office, the Races have proved very attractive.

The Brighton Season commences with their advent (and those of Goodwood the week prior)—they occupy three days ; the last one being devoted to those of the Brighton Club, and it was an old saying amongst the inhabitants, " That the last horse at the Races brought winter on his tail."

The Race Ground consists of 105 acres and 30 perches, over which the right of pasturage has been vested in the Marquis of Bristol, by its purchase from the late Mr Thomas Read Kemp, subject to the public rights, —viz., the erection thereon, by the inhabitants, of booths and stalls, &c., for the accommodation and recreation of the public during the Races.

The booths, &c., were erected formerly on the west side of the Grand Stand and near to the wall of the New Workhouse premises, but about 20 years ago were removed to a more convenient position on the north side of the Stand, parallel to the Course.

The height of the Stand at the Race-ground is 384ft. above the level of the sea at low water. Hence the distance which you can observe at sea from the same is about 24 miles. The Isle of Wight is visible from this spot, and, as the distance to which you can see

towards it, upon the sea there, is rather more than half-
way, any land which is lower than this hill may be seen
in a direct line; but on account of the refraction of the
air, it would appear more elevated than it is in reality,
and the refraction varying in different states of the air,
the island will at times appear at varied elevations above
the sea, when the sea is at the same altitude. If we
admit the breadth of the Channel to be 70 miles, it would
require land on the other side to be about 1452ft. high,
to be seen in a straight line from this hill; but as there
is no land on the opposite coast the height of which is
nearly equal to this, it can neither be seen directly, nor
can the refraction elevate it sufficiently to render it visible
from hence.

The following is the description of the Course, viz. :—
" The Old Course," on which the Cup and Stakes are run,
forms a figure like three sides of a square, with very easy
turns, and is one mile and three-quarters and 265 yards
in length. The first quarter of a mile is level, with a
slight dip at the end of it; the next half mile is on the
ascent, and from the mile post there is a descent until
about one-third of a mile from the finish, where there is a
sharp hill up to the " Winning Post." " The New
Course" is one mile and three-quarters and 144 yards,
and is formed by starting from " The Winning Post,"
and running about three quarters of a mile from home
to the right, round an elbow and turning into " The
Old Course " again about midways between the " T.Y.C."
and the mile post. The " T.Y.C." is three-quarters of a
mile ; " The New Ovingdean Course" is about five furlongs.

A large portion of the Course is out of the parish of
Brighton, and held by an arrangement with the owner.
Formerly it was customary to give a quantity of wine
annually for the use thereof, but the custom having been
broken on one occasion, and notice having been served on
the Race Committee to discontinue racing over that portion,

they were then compelled to alter the Course from the top
of the same near the Windmill, turning westward, and
finishing southward to the Grand Stand. But this state
of affairs only lasted one year, an arrangement having been
made with W. C. Mabbott, Esq., the owner, to pay 10
guineas for its use annually. The property was afterwards
purchased by the late Charles Beard, Esq., of Rottingdean,
who, in the true spirit of a sportsman, returned it in the
shape of his yearly contribution to the Race Fund, and
his nephew, Stenning Beard, Esq., the present possessor,
has likewise acted in the same liberal spirit, so also the
tenant, W. J. Green, Esq., of Ovingdean : both gentlemen
at all times afford every facility to the Race Committee,
in the carrying out of their arrangements to secure sport
on the occasion of the annual gatherings.

The Course extends over a part of the Hill called
Whitehawk Hill, where are the remains of an ancient
triple entrenchment, which by some is supposed to be a
Roman, and by others a Celtic fortification, though it is
probable that it was the resort of the distressed Britons in
the time of danger and trouble.

HUNTING IN THE NEIGHBOURHOOD.

Having treated of racing matters to some extent, we
will next allude to that of a kindred character,—Hunting,
which extends over the Downs, &c., to a distance of some
20 miles—a country so diversified, and, indeed, so well
suited for hunting, that we are not surprised at the large
number of sportsmen and others attending at the various
" meets" to take part in the invigorating exercise thus
offered. The district is well supplied with sport, both
hares and foxes being abundant. Sportsmen seldom meet
with a blank day ; but even in such case a gallop or a
walk over the South Downs is alike as beneficial to the

robust as to the valetudinarian. There has been a pack of "Harriers" kept in this town or immediate neighbourhood for the last century and a half, the kennel, about a century ago, being situated in the old chalk pit that formerly existed between Regent Row and Upper North Street. The huntsman's name was Parr. About half a century since the kennels were on the spot now covered by the present entrance to Longhurst's brewery, on the London Road. The huntsman was familiarly called Harry Mitchell, he succeeding one by the name of Austen. The management of the Hunt devolved upon a committee, the leading members of which being Mr William Chapman (the then proprietor of Chapman's brewery, of this town), and Messrs. Scrase, Tanner, Chatfield, Blaker, &c., the Treasurer being Mr Buckman. It was then removed to its present position in Hollingdean Road, the owner of the land in that neighbourhood (Thomas Read Kemp, Esq., the projector of Kemp Town), generously giving the site of the same, and the committee constructing the house and kennel,—the condition of the gift being "that it should belong exclusively to the 'Brighton Hunt.'" The same donor also gave a piece of ground in the same neighbourhood for the Jews' burial place. The Hunt has been carried on from that time to the present with varied success, under the management of a committee principally consisting of the holders of the land over which the sport takes place, and during the period has been represented by different Masters, who have recently been Messrs. Willard, Hudson, Bridger Stent,* Dewe, the present Master, Peter Thorpe being the Huntsman. A few years ago there was another

---

* This gentleman undertook the Mastership, on an emergency, at the unanimous request of a large number of persons interested in its management, and, after two or three successful seasons, was suddenly snatched away by death, to the great grief of a large number of friends, to whom he was endeared by his amiable and unassuming manners.

pack of Harriers, belonging to Jno. Brooker Vallance, Esq., called the "Hove Harriers," and the Huntsman's name Seal. After some little time, however, it became amalgamated with the Brighton pack, the hounds being generously given by that gentleman to further its prosperity. Also another pack in the neighbourhood called the Brookside Harriers, — the kennels of which are at Iford, — confining their sphere of action to the South Downs in the immediate vicinity of the west side of Lewes river. They afford excellent sport, are exceedingly well-managed, and have been for a considerable time under the joint superintendence of Messrs. Beard, Saxby, &c. This hunt, like that of the Brighton, afford the means of enjoyment for a large number of our visitors and residents, and the town is under a deep obligation to those gentlemen who so kindly grant the use of their respective lands for the purpose, adding thereby to its prosperity. The inhabitants should, therefore, requite such kindness by liberally subscribing to the funds raised for their support.

There is, also, a pack of Foxhounds, the kennels being situate at Ringmer,—a most delightful and pleasant village, about twelve miles from Brighton and four eastward of Lewes; it has a large share of fashionable patrons from Brighton, during the season, at its respective "meets," which take place in this neighbourhood once in each week, and it not unfrequently happens that from 400 to 500 equestrians, of both sexes, assemble to witness the same. We have been assured by the hospitable land-holder, Thomas Pearson, Esq., of Erringham, near Shoreham (one of the favourite "meets" of this popular pack of hounds), that the attendance of equestrians and pedestrians has in instances reached double and treble the above numbers, an irrefutable proof of the high estimation in which it is held. Another favourite meet takes place at Poynings Cross Ways, and we find that in 1812 there was a pack of hounds located in the neighbourhood, called "The Newtimber Foxhounds" and the Findon Foxhounds frequently met in this locality. At this period there were two days' racing over the Findon Race Course (then in existence) for Cups and Stakes. These races were mainly supported by Mr Walker, of Michelgrove ; Newnham of Findon, and others in the vicinity. It may not be uninteresting to our readers to trace the South Down Foxhounds' Hunt to its origin, inasmuch as it will be found that about the year 1820 there was quartered in the Barracks that existed at that time a troop of Royal Artillery. An interesting sight at the time for the villagers of Ringmer was the Church parade of the Artillery, preceded by its band. The Officers of the corps, thinking doubtless that as they were stationed in a locality of numerous covers well stocked with foxes (which the constant depredations of these nocturnal ramblers on the chicken-houses amply testified), and in order, moreover, to destroy the monotony of a country district, came to the resolution of purchasing a small pack of hounds, which was designated "The East-Sussex Foxhounds," the senior officer in command, Major Cator, undertaking their management. The gentlemen in the neighbourhood having assisted the funds of the Hunt by their subscriptions, &c., the kennel was erected on the Barrack property, and matters progressed favourably for some time (the Huntsman's name being Perkins), until an order came down from the Board of Ordnance with peremptory instructions at once to remove the pack from Government property, which was accordingly done. They were then taken to Broyle Gate, formerly the entrance to Broyle Park ⁰ (very near the spot that the Hunt Steeple-chases

---

* This park was of an extensive character, consisting of 2,000 acres, and formerly belonged to the Archbishop of Canterbury, who resided in the mansion, (standing at that time on the domain), when his clerical duties in this neighbourhood required his personal attendance. It afterwards became the residence of Sir William Springett, who at the siege of Arundel,

H

annually take place at the conclusion of the season).
Matters thus progressed till the year 1827, when the
Barracks were taken down (except the officers' quarters),
and the materials sold. At this time Lord Gage came forward and liberally assisted the fallen fortunes of the Hunt,
by allowing the stud belonging to the same to be taken
to his stables at Firle. He also purchased some cottage
property at Rushy Green, Ringmer, and built kennels and
stables thereon (using a considerable quantity of the old
Barrack materials in their erection). C. J. Craven, Esq., of
Kemp Town, was then Master of the Hunt; Press, the
Huntsman,—and for a short time, Hennessey. A few years
later, upon Mr Craven relinquishing the Mastership, Capt.
Green undertook the management, but after some time the
Hunt totally collapsed, and the hounds, kennels, stables, &c.,
were sold. It remained in abeyance for a time, and was then
resuscitated by Freeman Thomas, Esq., of Ratton, near
Eastbourne (Brooker being the Huntsman), under the name
of "The Southdown Foxhounds." It was afterwards thought
desirable by many that an attempt should be made to bring
them back to their old locality, it being within easy reach
of Brighton, and its funds would thereby be enriched by
the numbers that would consequently attend its meets in
the neighbourhood.   It was finally resolved that, if possible, this should be done, and means adopted to bring about
so desirable an end. The first step taken was to find
suitable premises for its requirements, and efforts were
made to induce the Government to grant a lease of that
portion of the Barracks that had not been demolished, for
the purposes of the Hunt, which for many years had
been used as a Lunatic Asylum ; but these proved

---

by the Parliamentarians, contracted a cold and died therefrom in 1643.
He was buried in Ringmer Church, wherein a tablet is erected to his
memory.   It is likewise on record that, the roads being so extremely
bad, his family, to attend Divine Service, had to be drawn to Church by
eight oxen.

unsuccessful. Application was then made to Mr Henry
Martin, of Brighton, by Mr Thomas Ellman, of Bedingham'
and Mr Withers, of Ringmer (steward to Sir James
Langham, of Glyndbourne), for premises belonging to him
that were suitable for its requirements at Ashton Green in the
same parish, and within a quarter of a mile of the former
kennels: he concurred in the view that it was very desirable
that the hounds should be brought nearer Brighton, and at
once entered into a preliminary agreement in furtherance of
the object sought. This property formerly belonged to
Mr Henry Martin, a farmer and miller (great grandfather
of the above),—a man of some note in his time and excessively found of hunting with the pack of harriers that
existed at that period in the neighbourhood,—and whose
ancestor, of the same name, it is supposed, left this parish,
or the adjacent one of Isfield or Ripe, with Colonel
Morley,* of Glynde, and Sir William Springett (already
spoken of) to join the Parliamentarians to oppose King
Charles I. and the Royalists. To show the respect this
person was held in, Sir Ferdinando Poole, of Lewes (a
renowned sportsman and breeder of horses, whose stables
were in this parish), stood sponsor to his youngest son,
who was named after him, also made him a present of a
hunter on the occasion.

This Sussex worthy is made the subject of a tale,
called "My Grandfather's Hat," in an interesting work by

---

* Colonel Herbert Morley, soldier and politician, was elected M.P. for
Lewes in 1641, and the year after he undertook to raise men and gun-
powder for its defence against the Royalists, and at the siege of Chichester
held a prominent command. After the dissolution of the long Parliament
he was elected for Rye; but excused himself from serving, "from an
intolerable fit of gout." After Cromwell's death he was returned both for
Lewes and Sussex; he elected to sit for the county. On the restoration of
Charles II. he escaped the severer punishment of the regicides by the payment of £1000, and by his not having signed the death warrant of
Charles I., although he was present at the trial and condemnation of that
monarch. He died at Glynde, in 1667, in the fifty-second year of his age,
and was buried there amongst his numerous ancestors.—*M. A. Lower's*
"*Worthies of Sussex.*"

Mr Charles Fleet, entitled "*Tales and Sketches for Fireside Reading*," and the following remarkable instance of longevity connected with his family appeared in the *Brighton Herald*, of November 26th, 1831 :—"There are now living four sons and three daughters of the late Mr Henry Martin, of Ringmer, whose united ages amount to 500 years, and all in the enjoyment of perfect health."

In order to show the enthusiasm with which the subject of our memoir entered into matters relative to hunting, the following anecdote may be mentioned, —"On riding past a cottage in the parish, he was called to account by the house-wife in consequence of her not being able to obtain the weekly grist at the mill, and he gave the following laconic answer, 'Odd, zounds, dame! how can you expect it, for there hasn't been sufficient wind this week to grind meal enough for the puppies.'" He died January 12th, 1798, in his 81th year. One of his sons alluded to hunted with and capped for the Brighton Harriers for nearly a quarter of a century, and died November 23rd, 1846, in his 85th year.

It may here be mentioned—as being somewhat re-markable,—that there has been six or seven, probably more of this family of the same name,—eldest sons of eldest sons, —for some generations. It may be also stated that the village of Ringmer is particularly healthy, and many instances of the longevity of its inhabitants are recorded : an inscription can be seen near the sun-dial in the Church-yard to the memory of Elizabeth Imms, who attained to the great age of 102 years.

The arrangements for the premises, before alluded to, were not carried out, in consequence of a communication from the War Office received a short time afterwards, to the effect that on a re-consideration of the application, they were disposed to let the Barrack property for the purposes of the Hunt; matters were consequently arranged, and the kennels, &c., erected, the hounds again taking up their old quarters in the parish from which they had been removed for many years, Mr Henry Martin expressing himself satisfied, and absolving the gentlemen who applied to him for his premises from all liability in respect of the same, the object sought having been accomplished. Alexander Donovan, Esq., of Framfield, became the Master, and Champion, the Huntsman. After a few years Mr Donovan was succeeded by William Langham Christie, Esq., of Glyndbourne, who, at the conclusion of the season of 1871, relinquished the same, and was followed by the present master, R. J. Streatfield, Esq., of the Rocks, Uckfield, who, we hope, will enjoy the sport for many years, and successfully conduct the fortunes of the Hunt. There are other packs of hounds in the county, but our object has been to give a short history of those more immediately connected with the town of Brighton.

ROUTES AND TRANSIT TO THE METROPOLIS.

There have been, from time to time, several distinct routes from Brighton to the Metropolis, although of late years some of them have been in disuse. One road (prior to the making of the present one to Falmer and Lewes) proceeded by way of Elm Grove crossing the hills above Bevendean and Falmer, and onwards to Lewes, Offham, Chailey, Witch Cross, East Grinstead, Godstone, Croydon, &c., to London, the distance being 57 miles ; or, if after leaving Lewes, the road traversed being by way of Uckfield, Forest Row, and East Grinstead to Godstone and Croydon, the distance was two miles longer.

Another route was by way of Ditchling Hill, passing the upper end of Lord Chichester's park and the Beacon, down the Bosthill, through the Village of Ditchling to

Lindfield, &c., into the main road at Reigate; and another road by way of Saddlescombe, Poynings, Henfield, Horsham, &c.; but the one most frequented at this period was by way of the upper road leading to Old Shoreham, passing Goldstone Bottom, and onward to Bramber Gorge, as it was then termed, the main road leading to Beeding Hill, diverting from the Old Shoreham Road some little distance westward of Southwick Mill, and crossing the river at Bramber Bridge, through Steyning, Horsham, Dorking, Epsom, &c., to London; the distance being 56 miles.

Subsequently a new and more direct road was made — reducing the distance to 54 miles, — via Preston, Cuckfield, Crawley, Reigate, Tooting, Clapham, &c., and, before the cutting of Clayton Hill, ran close by the east side of Piecombe Church; and the outlay for this improvement caused a serious diversity of opinion amongst the trustees for its management which led to the formation of a new road from Piecombe, through Albourne, Hickstead, &c., to avoid hills, and shortening the distance to London by two miles—lessening the distance to 52 miles,—the same was opened on the 28th of June, 1810.

In 1745, "The Flying Machine," as it was termed, left the Old Ship Inn (in summer) at 5.30 a.m., and reached London the same evening; and, if we take into consideration the then state of the roads, which were, generally speaking,—especially in the winter, almost impassable, it must have been a great achievement. The general mode of travelling was by pack-horses, consequently the summer was the only period available to the visitors.

The high roads of Sussex had an unenviable notoriety for their inferiority. It is recorded that on one occasion Charles II. paid a visit to the Duke of Northumberland, at Petworth House (then the residence of the Percys): the vehicle in which he rode was capsized no less than a dozen times, and had it not been for the worthy boors of Sussex, who supported the carriage on each side on their shoulders, the number would have been greater.

It was not until the latter portion of the last century that any great improvement was effected in the method of travelling to the Metropolis. At this period a vehicle left Brighton for London, called "Wessin's Coach," by way of Bramber, Steyning, Horsham, &c., and, *with the consent of the majority of the passengers*, arrived at its destination in about 12 hours. Afterwards a new "Post Coach," to carry 4 insides and no outsides on the top, set out from the Old Ship, at 6.30 a.m., on Mondays, Wednesdays, and Fridays, in the summer, to the Golden Cross, Charing Cross, returning the alternate days at 6 a.m.,—and from the limited number of passengers that this vehicle carried the price charged must have been extremely high. Another coach running to London on alternate days at 6 a.m., at a cheaper rate, through Reigate and Cuckfield, the fares being, insides 18s., outsides and *children on lap*, 7s., allowed 14lbs. luggage, all weight above to pay 1d. per lb. Since this period and the commencement of the present century great improvements in time and speed in the performance of the journey to the metropolis have been introduced, consequent on the influx of visitors being greater; and it is recorded that in August, 1809, "neither a house or lodging could be obtained for love or money." On May 21st, 1810, the first mail coaches were put on the road between Brighton and London, and a coach called the "Regent" commenced running September 6th, 1813, and in less than a week, on Sunday 12th, it overturned at Merstham, causing great injury to the passengers. The traffic increased so rapidly, that in October, 1822, there were no less than forty-two coaches running daily between Brighton and London alone. The first coach that performed the journey from Brighton to London, returning the same day, belonged to Mr J. Whitchurch, and ran from the office corner of Prince's Place, North Street, adjoining the Chapel Royal, and afterwards a very few of the coaches occupied more than five or six hours on their journey,— and on important occasions, such as the delivery of the Queen's speech on commencement of the Session, or the prorogation of Parliament, the information has been brought down in less than four hours and a half.

The road waggons of the past and present centuries belonged respectively to Messrs. Davis, E. Mighell, Bradford, Orton, Hope, Patching, Weller, Gander, Durtnall, &c. There were also three four-horse vans leaving this town every evening, at five o'clock, for the conveyance of goods, parcels, &c., called the "Blue" (belonging to Messrs. Crossweller, Blaber, & Chalk), the "Red" (belonging to Messrs. Pocock and Winch), the "Red Rover" (from the Clarence Hotel, belonging to Messrs. Wilde, Holmes and Co.),—all these latter succumbing to the modern leviathan, "the railway," and the well-appointed stage coaches gradually shared the same fate after its introduction. The railway was commenced March 19th, 1838, and, on the 9th of July, 1841, opened to Hayward's Heath: on the 21st September following it was opened from Brighton to London.

ROUTE TO FRANCE & MODES OF TRANSIT.

The route from London to Paris, *viâ* Brighton and Dieppe, was performed by sailing vessels, and it will be found there were nine so occupied in the year 1817, viz :

The Nancy	Capt. Blaber.
The Unity	" Clear.
Ann and Elizabeth ...	" Daniels.

The Nautilus	Capt.	Wingfield.
Elizabeth	"	Lind.
Lord Wellington	"	Cheesman.
Prince Regent	"	Bulbeck.
Duke of Wellington ...	"	Cole.
Neptune	"	Wallis.

The time occupied by these vessels on their voyage (wind and weather permitting) was from 10 to 12 hours. The journey from Dieppe to Paris was performed by diligence in 14 hours, through the beautiful valleys of Arques and Rouen, and this route being 90 miles shorter than by way of Dover and Calais, gave it a decided advantage over the other.

During this year, 1817, the Customs House returns of passengers were as follows : from Brighton to Dieppe, 2481 persons ; returning from thence 1947. If it be considered that it was the summer season only, and the small number of travellers, as compared with the present time, between the two ports, it will be seen this route was extensively patronized.

The following summary account of Dieppe may not be uninteresting to the reader, particularly as the general manners and customs of the place present a striking contrast to those of its English neighbours, only a few hours distant therefrom.

The appearance of Dieppe from the sea is very striking, not so much from the size of the place as from the contrast of the surrounding scenery. The cliffs on either side of the town though not high, are steep and rugged, and the ancient chateau, which is built on an acclivity east of the town, adds to the wildness of the appearance. The country, however, round about, is far from being barren or uninteresting ; on the contrary, it is both woody and fertile, and the glimpses of it that are caught from the sea show it to be highly diversified. The town is situated on a declivity formed by the shelving of the cliff, and to the west is the river, the mouth of which forms the harbour. Immediately facing the shore is an elegant building called the Caroline Baths, which was finished in the beginning of the year 1828, but as the name does not convey the purposes of the erection, we will describe it more particularly. In the centre is an archway supported by Ionic columns and adorned with statues of marine deities, where are small rooms in which the people live who look after the place: on each side of this is a covered walk about fifteen feet wide, and at the end of each walk is a handsome and spacious room, the one on the last side fitted up as a reading and the other as a billiard-room. This constitutes the whole of the building, and the process of immersion is carried on in the sea. The bathing machines, which are not on wheels, are stationed before the building in two divisions, that on the east being allotted to the ladies, and that on the west to the gentlemen. The former, when attired in their bathing-gowns, are carried into the sea by men appointed for that purpose, and generally remain there a considerable time, continually jumping up and sinking down with each wave in the most *original* manner! In the evening the gardens belonging to the baths and the building itself form the fashionable promenade of the town.

The Pier is situated west of the town and at the east side of the river. When the packets arrive this place is generally crowded; and the costume of the Norman inhabitants, with their high conical caps and brilliant coloured garments, presents a very striking contrast to that of the English peasantry.

No sooner is the vessel moored along the quay than the Custom-house officers take possession of the gangway, and scrutinize the passport of every passenger previous to landing: the ordeal is very moderate as regards the gentlemen, but ladies are examined in an apartment by females appointed by Government, the excess of whose tyranny is only to be equalled by its occasionally ludicrous result.

The greatest annoyance on landing is from people dispatched from the respective hotels, whose urgent solicitations for the welfare of their employers are anything but agreeable to the visitants.

The Hotels are capacious and neat, and although mostly conducted on rather different principles from the English, are still very comfortable. The bedrooms are large, but without carpets, and paved with red tiles, which are kept in a high state of polish. The beds are usually filled with wool instead of feathers. The female servants have a very slovenly appearance: they wear wooden shoes, and make no scruple of divesting themselves of their gown when the heat of the summer renders such garments inconvenient.

The houses (excepting the modern buildings) present an unseemly appearance; many are in a decayed state, untenanted, and seemingly in a most precarious condition. They have very high roofs, indeed so much so, that many contain two or three attic stories, and are finished in a careless and rough style. The Cathedral and church are very old buildings, and bear on their exterior evident traces of a popular revolution: the interior, however, of both are simple and bold. The organs are very handsome, and well toned: it would, perhaps, be useless to go more into their details: every person who reflects upon religious subjects will form his own estimate thereon, and most will duly appreciate the peculiarities of their tenets, as well as their many ostentatious forms and ceremonies of worship.

The English Protestant Chapel is a plain building, and was formerly a concert-room. There is service every Sunday at one p.m.

The Theatre is small, but very elegant; and the Public Ball Room, situated near it, is capacious and handsomely decorated.

The Castle is a massive old building with round turrets and slated roofs: admission to it is only to be obtained by an order from one of the Corporation of the town.

The trade of Dieppe is inconsiderable, consisting principally in turnery, laces and toys, It is, however, famous for its ivory carving, which is carried to an exquisite state of perfection; large vessels are modelled in a most beautiful manner, the rigging and sails are made of threads and shavings of ivory, and the countenances and attitudes of the various groups of figures are wonderfully expressive.

Trains to Rouen start several times daily, and the view of the town from a neighbouring eminence on the road to the capital of Normandy is very beautiful, commanding a fine prospect of the adjacent countries, as well as of the expanse of ocean skirting the horizon.

The roads about Dieppe are tolerably good; they are wide and unpaved, and are in many places bordered by apple-trees, which produce in autumn an immense quantity of fruit, which is manufactured into cider. The chateaux, or villas, are built near the roads, with high old-fashioned roofs, and in many places surrounded with the former paraphernalia of ancient gardening, although very many are situated in pleasure-grounds laid out in a most tasteful manner, and themselves elegantly decorated.

The Norman peasantry are usually agreeable in person, short in stature, and generally quick and shrewd. The women dress in a remarkable, though not altogether unbecoming costume, with extravagantly high caps (like towers of linen) on their heads. But these even the young children have, not even in miniature, the head-dress being often at least half the size of the whole person of the wearer. The men generally use shoes made from solid timber.

The French vehicles are not among the least curious part of continental peculiarities. The diligences have been imitated in London by the omnibuses, but the former can only be drawn up very steep hills by the exertion of nine horses. The horses are harnessed in a most irregular manner, and the driver is seated on the near wheel horse, and in this manner drives usually from four to seven horses. He places little dependence on his reins, which are made of rope, but encourages his cattle by the most vehement gesticulations.

The table d'hote presents to a stranger a novel and interesting scene ; novel, because the order of things seems completely reversed ; and interesting, because any thing in the eating or drinking way must prove so to a hungry man. The master and mistress take the two opposite sides of the table, instead of the top and bottom ; this plan affords a facility of communication, which would be impossible from the extreme ends of a long table. The company, generally consisting of all nations, range themselves promiscuously on either side ; although it is considered the privilege of the lady who has made the longest stay in the house to take the top. Amongst Parisians who resort to watering places in France during the summer, many take up their residence at the hotels at so much per diem. They generally retain the same places at the table d'hote during their stay. This will explain to strangers the cause of so many long-necked bottles ranged along the table, to each of which is affixed a napkin, tied with a peculiar knot ; some containing the remains of half-a-pint of *vin ordinaire ;* others the remains of a bottle of small beer—the stranger must by no means place himself before any of these luxuries. The appearance of the guests is also deserving notice. Some are

dressed in the most elegant dinner style, others with large
bonnets and shawls; while some from the recent effects
of sea sickness, look more dead than alive; gentlemen in
black silk stockings and shoes, some in gaiters, and others
in boots, covered with mud or dust; and to finish the
picture, in come one or two officers of the garrison, whom
a sudden shower has not only well drenched, but delayed
till dinner is nearly over, which prevents the possibility
of their shifting, should they be in possession of a second
wardrobe.

The dinner is generally protracted to an unusual
length, in consequence of the host carving and helping
everything himself. He begins with soup, then bouilli
(meat from which the soup is made); then is divided in
small portions and handed round, larded veal, or some
other made dish; fish follows, then poultry; after which,
mutton cutlets; French beans, brocoli, or other vegetables
are then served separately; pastry follows. The table is
then cleared, with the exception of the cloth, for the
dessert, which generally consists of apples, pears, biscuits,
&c., with *butter and cheese*. After which, coffee and liqueurs
are introduced—but be it understood, this last is an *extra*
charge. It is not the custom among the French to have
their knife and fork changed with their plate.

Those who go to France for the purpose of seeing
everything strange, should invariably take up their abode
at a French hotel.

In rewarding servants, at hotels in France, the best
plan when paying your bill, is to add at the bottom,
with your pencil,—servants so much, which is to include
them all.

One franc and a half, or two francs from travellers
who sleep at the house, is as much as is expected for the
waiter, chambermaid, and boots. If you are staying any
length of time at an hotel, one franc per diem is always
expected.

The mode of communication between the two countries by sailing vessels shared the same fate as the transit by coaches, &c., both being superseded by steam, inasmuch as in the year 1822, on Saturday morning, May 25th, at eight o'clock, a steam packet, called the " Swift," 80 horse power, commenced running between this town and Dieppe, and continued on Wednesdays and Saturdays during the season, commanded by Captain Hugh MacGregor; the fares of the same being respectively, cabin, £1 15s, and steerage, £1 5s ; the same vessel proceeding every Monday morning, at eight o'clock, for Ryde and Southampton, and returning the following day at the same hour for Brighton.

It may be easily imagined with what consternation these proceedings were viewed by the owners and parties interested in the sailing vessels, to see, in all probability, in a short time, a lucrative occupation lost. The owner of the " Elizabeth," Captain George Lind, came to the conclusion that the best plan, under the circumstances, was to bow to the new order of things, consequently he advertised that the " Royal George," steam vessel, of 800 tons burthen and 80-horse power, would commence running under the patronage of George IV. on October 19th, 1822.

A season or two following the General Steam Navigation Company put on two vessels, the time occupied on the journey being about ten hours ; some time after another Captain of the nearly defunct sailing vessels, of the name of Cheesman, of the " Lord Wellington," was taken into the employ of the Company, continued for many years in the same capacity, and was highly respected.

The Consul at Dieppe is a gentleman of the name of Chapman, and grandson of one of that name who was a resident of Brighton some years ago, and left to occupy the same position at this Port.

After the opening of the Railway to Newhaven, December 6th, 1847, these Packets were superseded by others in connection with the Railway Company, built expressly for this traffic, with all the modern improvements, to accelerate their speed from this port to Dieppe, generally accomplishing the journey in five or six hours, and a tidal service in the summer; but the communication with the opposite coast continued throughout the year, and with this increased facility and accommodation the traffic has increased to an enormous extent, there having been upwards of a thousand passengers embarked and disembarked in a day from the port of Newhaven. The railway trains run in conjunction with the packets on both sides of the Channel, and the whole distance from London to Paris and vice-versa may be accomplished in twelve hours. This route, from the subjoined letter written by Lord Buckhurst,* the Lord High Treasurer, to Mr Secretary Cecil, in 1600, evidently shews it has been in use for centuries, and will be interesting, as exhibiting the contrast between the locomotion of the time of Queen Elizabeth and that of the present day, inasmuch as the journey between the two ports then occupied as many days as it now does hours :—

"Sir,—This enclosed letter came to me this forenone, about xi of the clock. By this you may see that the Governour of Diepe landed at Newhaven in Sussex yesterday being thursday in the afternone, having wth him a 100 persons, and lodged the same night at Lewis and purposed to be gon the next day, being this friday morning by 5 of the clock. This Gentleman, Mr Shurley† being a Justis of peace I dout not but will do his best to

---

* Unquestionably the Lord Buckhurst who was one of the Commissioners to settle the differences between the seamen and landsmen in this town many years before, and alluded to in the chapter on " Ancient Customs."

† Probably J. Shirely, Esq., of the Friars, in Lewes.

acomodate him, but I fear he will be forced to tary at
Lewis longer than his apointed time of departure before a
100 horse can be there upon such a sodain provided for
him. I have therefore sent away now presently my
messenger wth on letter to Sir Walter Covert, who is the
next deputy lieftenant dwelling nere Lewis, to assemble as
many of the Gentlemen as he can & to repair unto him
& do him all the honor he can by attending upon him
and seeing him furnished wth all his desieres as much as
he can performe for him. And I have sent one other
letter to Grinsted Town in Sussex wch is 14 miles from
Lewis & is the next Town in which he must either renew
his horses or lodge all night—written to the Constables
there, (for there is no justice nere by 7 miles) to se him
and his trains furnished wth horses and all things he shall
desier fit for him. This is all that can be doon by me
upon this sodain. What farder is to be doon by any to
mete him from thens or in Surrey, where my lord admirall
comandes onlie, you ar to consider. His way from Lewis
to London is thus :

    Sussex. From Lewis to Est Grinsted,
        a very good towne, able to
        receive him   ... 14 miles.
    Surrey. From Est Grinsted to God-
        stone, therein are only two
        innes and not above 5 or 6
        houses besides   ... 7 miles.
    Surrey. From Godstone to Croydon.. 7 miles.
    Surrey. From Croidon to London ... 7 miles.*
      " In hast, this 18 of April, 1600.
      " Your very loving freund
             " T. BUCHURST.
    *   *   *   *
" To the right honourable Mr Secretary Cecil
    be thease geven."

Here let us express a hope, as the blessings of peace

---

* Sussex miles were of old proverbially "long and narrow," and the
Lord-Treasurer's estimate of the distance between Lewes and London
would be confirmatory of that notion. The real distance is fifty miles, not
thirty-five.—*M. A. Lower's Sussex Worthies.*

have now dawned on our continental neighbours, that the
intercourse between the two nations will be greatly
augmented, and bonds of amity and friendship will be
cemented by such means for a very long period to come.

LOYAL REJOICINGS IN THE OLDEN TIME.

It will be seen, from the following very interesting
description of the manner of celebrating the Prince of
Wales' birth-day; August 12th, 1809, with what enthusiasm
all classes participated in the enjoyments of the day :—

Half-past Eight p.m.

His Royal Highness the Duke of Sussex has just
arrived at the Pavilion—the bells are ringing for the
arrival of the Royal Dukes—bands of music are heard in
every direction—the Steyne is crowded with company—
the front of the Pavilion is surrounded with ladies and
gentlemen.   Mrs Heseltine has a concert at her house on
the Steyne—her melodious notes attract numerous groups
round the house, who are very liberal of their *bravos* and
encores.   In addition to the numerous party at the Pavilion
are Sir R. and Lady Cunningham, Count Palfy, Mrs Orby
Hunter, Mr Sheridan, Mr A. Davison, and Mr W. Porter.
    The morning was ushered in by the ringing of bells,
and the flag was hoisted upon the Church ; since five
o'clock the town has been all in motion ; at ten the Otter
and Gallant fired a salute ; at eleven o'clock the Eclipse
came in, and also fired a salute—the Otter, Gallant,
Eclipse, and Griffin, had all the national colours flying.
The flag was also hoisted on the west batteries, and every
demonstration of joy appeared—two oxen were roasted ;
at nine o'clock they were put down to the fire ; in a

hollow to the left of the Prince's Cricket Ground. By
half-past eleven the brigade was formed on the Race
Course (at the four-mile heat), and consisted of the Royal
Horse Artillery, the detachment of Royal Artillery at
Ringmer, the King's Dragoon Guards, the 6th Dragoon
Guards, and 4th Dragoons; the Royal South Gloucester,
the Royal Cheshire, Nottingham, and South Hants, which
met in review order, on the Downs, near to the Race
Course, near the town, at half-past eleven, and fired a
feu de joie, in honour of the Prince of Wales's birth-day.
The King's Dragoon Guards took the left, fronting the
south, the Infantry occupied the ground on the left of the
King's Dragoon Guards, and the 6th Dragoon Guards
took post on the left of the Infantry; the Royal Artillery,
from Ringmer, took the left, flanking the whole. The
troops were in open column, and wheeled into line on the
approach of His Royal Highness the Prince of Wales,
which was announced by a salute of 21 guns. The troops
marched in slow time, and resumed their ground; they
then opened their ranks, a *feu de joie* was fired, beginning
with seven guns, from the Royal Horse Artillery, which
was taken up from right to left, when the 6th Dragoon
Guards fired; and the Royal Artillery fired seven guns.
The Royal Horse Artillery then re-commenced their fire,
and so on; after the third fire, the ranks were opened, and
a general salute took place. At one o'clock the Royal
Party arrived on the ground. Their Royal Highnesses the
Dukes of Clarence and Cambridge mounted on dark bay
horses, and dressed in crimson jackets, and trousers, and
helmet caps, rode first; then Major Bloomfield and Colonel
Lee; then His Royal Highness the Prince of Wales,
mounted on a beautiful bright grey charger, richly
caparisoned, the *shabadake*, or housing trappings were of
gold, richly embroidered; the bridle and stirrup leathers
were also richly ornamented with gold; the stirrups were
of solid gold; the rosettes at the sides of the horse's head

134

were of gold, and the head-stall in front was also of gold net. The *tout ensemble* had the most splendid appearance the imagination can conceive.

His Royal Highness was dressed in his state uniform, with gold tassels to his boots, and appeared in high spirits, casting a beneficent smile on every person he passed. The Duke of York was on his right, and the Duke of Kent on the left of the Duke of York—they were both mounted on iron-grey chargers; then followed Earl Berkeley, and Earl Moira, who was dressed in a Highland uniform, mounted on a grey charger; next General Lennox, Colonel Savary, Colonel Smith, and the Duke of Orleans, and several officers and noblemen. There never was a grander staff. Earl Craven was not present, on account of indisposition.

As soon as the Royal Party arrived on the ground, the signal guns from right to left were fired, then the whole line presented arms, the different bands playing "God save the King." The Royal group and suite passed in front of the line, and took their station in the centre, when the whole passed before the Prince in review order, marching in ordinary and quick time; after the troops had passed the Prince they formed in line again, and fired a *feu de joie*, and gave their beloved Prince three cheers, the bands playing "God save the King." The Royal party expressed their approbation at the fine appearance of the men. As soon as the Royal salute was given, a signal gun was fired, and a signal hoisted at the signal post, when the ships fired a Royal salute, the Royal party placed themselves at the top of the hill to see it. The fineness of the day contributed to this grand military spectacle. The Royal Party left the ground at four o'clock. The cavalry were commanded by Major-General Hugonin. The infantry was to have been commanded by Earl Craven; and the whole brigade by Lieut.-General Lennox. There were about 7,000 troopers on the ground.

The Masters Fitz-Clarence were on the box of the Prince's landau. Mr Sheridan was on the box of the Prince's barouche (there being two of the Prince's carriages), and Miss Seymour was in the inside. The Marchioness of Downshire and all the surrounding nobility were present.

At three o'clock the Lord Chancellor arrived on the ground, and, alighting from his carriage, went up to the Prince, who, the moment he espied his Lordship, went forward to meet him ; and, taking him by the hand, said, " My good Lord, how do you do ?" It is allowed to have been one of the grandest sights ever witnessed. The only disappointment was the absence of Lord Keith, whom the wind would not permit to come round.

His Royal Highness the Duke of York will, to-morrow morning, review, at the Devil's Dyke, the Royal Horse Artillery, the King's Dragoon Guards, the 6th Dragoon Guards, the 4th Dragoons, and the 17th Light Dragoons.

Eight o'Clock p.m.

Nearly five thousand people are assembled near the camp, scrambling for the roast beef, which flies in every direction. Eight hogsheads of ale are on the ground. " Long live the Prince !" echoes from every quarter. A proportionate quantity of bread is also distributed to the multitude. The Pavilion is surrounded with gentlemen and ladies ; the Masters Fitz-Clarence are at Mrs Fitz-herbert's, where they have a juvenile party ; they are lovely boys, and, for their age, highly accomplished ; the Prince is extremely fond of them.

The Steyne is crowded, and a refreshing shower we have had this afternoon, has added to the pleasure of the scene. Several tar barrels are just brought to the front of the Pavilion, for a bonfire. The illuminations are very splendid ; among the most conspicuous are—Mr Donaldson's Library: over the Colonnade, in variegated lamps, is the Prince's plume with the star underneath, and the initials, G. P., on each side; along the Colonnade, there is a festoon of variegated lamps. Mr Pollard's Library, on the Marine Parade, displaying the plume, and initials, G. P. The Theatre, the plume, richly encircled with a festoon of variegated lamps. Mr Pearson's china warehouse, the corner of Prince's Place, the crown, the plume, and the initials, G. P., with festoons of variegated lamps. The Castle, the plume, and the portico, encircled with festoons of lamps. Mr Thunder's, in North Street. All the Coach-offices are brilliant; and, in differents parts of the town "Long live the Prince!" is placed at several windows.

Ten o'Clock.

The whole town is a blaze of light, from the illuminations and the bonfires, the flames of which reach above the tops of the houses, and are surrounded by near three thousand people. The fireworks are to be seen in every direction. The South Gloucester and Nottingham Bands are playing on the lawn, in front of the Pavilion, and the Prince's Band is playing in the left wing. The Nottingham Militia are at present scrambling with the townspeople for the remainder of the carcase of the oxen, and have succeeded in carrying them off to their camp, spits and all.

Above one hundred persons of distinction, and the Commanding Officer of each regiment that was on the ground, dined at the Pavilion this evening. Among other additions to the Royal Party, this day, are the Duke of Argyle, the Marquis of Hertford, Lord Petersham, the Lord Chancellor, and Mr Cavendish Bradshaw. The ball, at the Castle, is well attended.

ROYAL & FASHIONABLE MOVEMENTS.

The following copious selections from metropolitan journals of the year 1806, relating to Brighton, will be read with great interest : as affording an insight into the period when Royalty was at its zenith among us,—the year in which the celebrated picture of the Steyne originated, wherein is pourtrayed living "characters," then in existence. The year, also, of the celebrated fête in commemoration of the Earl of Delawarr attaining his majority (he having been left a minor at the age of nine years). He was succeeded a short time since by his son, who, as Lord West, saw much military service in India and elsewhere,—a much esteemed nobleman, and who represents one of our most ancient county families. Other quotations in relation to subsequent years are also appended :—

BRIGHTON, JULY 7, 1806.

The arrivals during the last week were very numerous, among them are the following :—

Earl of Kenmare, Countess of Kenmare, Lady Huntingfield, Mrs M. Cleverly, Mr J. Joseph, Mr Yellowly, Mrs M. Edmunds, Mrs Waiting, Mr and Mrs Aylmer Haley, Mr G. Favene, Mr Brown, Mr Fitzjohn, Mr Price, Mrs Albin, Rev. Mr Tutte, Mr Beard, Rev. Mr Richards, Mr D. Sattin, &c.

The Steyne is now very gay, and enlivened every evening by bands of Savoyards with hand organs, tamborines, &c., &c. The spacious new Library is nearly completed, and is decorated in a style of elegance, suitable to its situation and the quality of its subscribers.

At a general Meeting of the inhabitants, held at the Old Ship, on Wednesday, on the subject of incorporating our town, it was resolved, "that the adoption of such a measure would be inexpedient, on account of the expense that must necessarily attend it. The meeting, neverthe-less, entertained a high sense of the honour conferred by the Prince's Message on the subject, to the Parish Officers, previously communicated by Mr Rycroft."

Our Managers, ever assiduous to please, have engaged Mr Richer, the famous performer on the tight rope, for a few evenings.

The good behaviour and exemplary conduct of the Monmouth and Brecon Militia, commanded by the Duke of Beaufort, who marched lately from Steyning, rendered their departure very much regretted at that place. The second division marched under the command of Sir Samuel Fludyer, Bart.

Captain Hutton has matched his brown pony, Mark Spratt, 5 years old, against Captain Fletcher's chestnut pony, 6 years old, for 200 guineas, two miles, to run at our ensuing races, to carry 7st. each.

BRIGHTON, JULY 20, 1806.

Company increases every day. The Prince of Wales, it is said, again honours us with his presence on Wednesday next.

The Theatre here is the most fashionable lounge of an evening. Richer's benefit produced nearly £90 on Tuesday. On Wednesday it was full again, under the patronage of Lieutenant-General Lennox. On Friday it was crowded too; the Earl of Kenmare bespoke. And last night it overflowed, under the patronage of the Marchioness of Clanricarde. The performance was the comedy of *The Soldier's Daughter*. On Tuesday, Earl Craven will patronise the performances.

On Friday was played here the match of cricket, between General Lennox and Major Ready against Captains Burrel and Shum, which has been a long time spoken of; which was won by the General, who is a first rate player. A vast deal of company is expected to the races.

The match between Sancho and Pavilion, on the 24th, at Lewes, will be numerously attended from this place. Sancho yet continues to be the favourite, though the odds are not more than 5 to 4.

The foot race against time, twenty miles in two hours and a quarter, against which 100 guineas to 60 are betted, and which it was agreed on should be decided here, between the Brighton and Lewes races, is now postponed to the 18th of September.

BRIGHTON, JULY 23, 1806.

Towards seven o'clock, last evening, the carriage, with Mrs Fitzherbert, the Hon. Miss Seymour, and Mrs Fitzherbert's favourite female attendant, Mrs Strickland, at a brisk rate, passed the numerous inhabitants, who were in waiting to receive Mrs Fitzherbert, who kindly saluted them as she passed, and appeared in good health and spirits. The bells rang a merry peal, both last night and this morning. The most beautiful stands of flowers were placed round the Pavilion, and every preparation made for the reception of the Prince. At three o'clock a detachment of the South Gloucester Militia, with their band, colours flying, &c., were ordered out to receive His Royal Highness. At half-past four Earl Berkeley desired them to withdraw, which has caused a report that he will first go to Lewes. Twenty-one horses belonging to His Royal Highness arrived this morning. It rained violently this morning, but cleared up about two, when the Steyne was enlivened by the presence of the Earl of Darlington, Sir John Lade, Mr Mellish, and Mr Dalton. The Earl and Countess of Barrymore, Mr Johnston and family, and Lord Stawell arrived yesterday. Mr Mellish will give a grand dinner this day at the Castle, to the Earl of Darlington, Sir John Lade, &c.

BRIGHTON, JULY 24, 1806.

Earl Berkeley inspected the South Gloucester Militia, last evening, on the North Parade, which was crowded with spectators. The Steyne was crowded until eleven o'clock, in expectation of the Prince's arrival. The Colonnade before Donaldson's Library was filled with Ladies, who seemed to take a lively interest in the bets; Sancho, the favourite; 5 to 4 on him. In the afternoon the report of his illness gained ground, and produced 7 to 4 against him. The celebrated Buckle, who is to ride Sancho, was on the Steyne, and did not appear in "tip-top" spirits.

Robert Potts, Esq., and family and Mrs Wilgrasse arrived yesterday at their elegant house on the Marine Parade. Dr. Wilgrasse is expected this day. *The Heir at Law* and *Three Weeks after Marriage* were performed last night, by desire of Mrs G. Torrane.

At two o'clock this morning His Royal Highness the Prince of Wales arrived at the Pavilion; and since five the town is in a bustle, preparing for Lewes. It is said, the match will take place at twelve o'clock. At the Castle Tavern, last night, bets ran even.

BRIGHTON, JULY 31, 1806.

The Steyne, last night, was fuller than at any preceding time this season. Mr Mellish, Mr Burke, Mr Derby, and Mr Crampton laid bets on leaping over handkerchiefs, rails, &c. Mr Crampton was the hero; but much as he excelled, it was nothing to the leap he made at Harrogate, from the ball-room into the very high orchestra. Mr Hawke made a match to run a given distance with Mr Mellish, giving Mr Mellish five yards, and Mr Hawke won. There were many matches between boys, supported by gentlemen. The Earl and Countess Berkeley, the Earl and Countess of Barrymore, and Sir John and Lady Lade, were among the spectators. The entertainments at the Theatre to-night are, *The Heir at Law*, the wonderful Richer on the Tight Rope, and *The Turnpike Gate*.

BRIGHTON, AUGUST 3, 1806.

Such was the fury of the wind and tide last night that three of the bathing machines that were lashed to the Marine Parade have been carried out to sea, and the boats that were sent in search of them have returned unsuccessful. Mr Mellish's establishment went to London this morning; the absence of this gentleman will be much regretted. The Countess of Sefton is expected, in a few days, to honour Brighton with her presence.

The 2nd battalion of the 40th Regiment of Foot marched into this town last night, from Bexhill barracks, and paraded this morning at the top of North Street; they are to be joined, next Tuesday, by the 1st battalion, which are now on their march from Bexhill; then the whole will proceed to Portsmouth, where they are under orders for embarkation. Mr Bradford left the Castle this morning, at half past twelve, in his barouche and four, for Petworth, the seat of the Earl of Egremont. Earl Berkeley attended divine service on the parade this morning, at eleven o'clock, which was read by the Chaplain of the South Gloucester Militia. An excellent sermon was preached at the Chapel Royal, by the Rev. Dr. Portis, from St. Luke vi. 46 ; the congregation was numerous ; Lady Lade, Mr and Mrs Potts, Dr. and Mrs Wilgrasse, the Misses Metcalf, and the Misses Walpole were present.

At four o'clock the Steyne was most brilliant. The Prince, dressed in a plum-coloured coat and a brown hat, accompanied by Colonel Bloomfield, the Countess of Jersey, elegantly dressed in white, on her head, a gold *bandeau*, from which was suspended a most beautiful veil, the Earl and Countess Berkeley, the Misses Walpole, and many other Nobility honoured it with their presence. Now that the Races are over, we expect the Nobility will crowd to this delightful place. It is said His Royal Highness the Duke of Clarence is expected this or the ensuing week, on a visit to His Royal Brother. The Duke is a great favourite here, his good nature and suavity of manners endear him to every person, and the Prince never is so happy as when he is with him. The coaches have come down to-day, loaded with company within and without.

BRIGHTON, AUGUST 4, 1806.

The Steyne, this evening, is crowded with company The Duke and Duchess De Castries, the Countess of Barrymore, Mrs Fitzherbert, and Miss Seymour, walked for an hour at the front of Donaldson's Library together. The Countess of Jersey, the Earl and Countess of Kenmare, the Earl and Countess Berkeley, Lady F. Osborne, Lady Charlotte Lennox, Sir John and Lady Lade, were amongst the company that graced the Steyne. The prevailing dress was the Gipsey-hat, and pink, lilac, and white mantles; brown parasols, trimmed with white lace; some of the first-rate *elegantes* wore dove-coloured stockings and shoes. His Royal Highness the Prince of Wales had a large party at the Pavilion this evening, including most of the Nobility here. The Ball at the Castle Tavern was not crowded.

BRIGHTON, AUGUST 5, 1806.

Miss Johnston, who has been indisposed for some days, was so much worse yesterday, that Dr. Blane was sent for express, and arrived at twelve o'clock last night; the fever is said to have taken a favourable turn, and that there are some hopes of her recovery. This morning is extremely fine; numerous parties are going on the water. The Gallant gun-brig is again come to anchor.

Numerous donkey parties are gone towards the Downs and Rottingdean.

Earl Craven, Earl Berkeley, General Lennox, Major Whatley, and several other Field Officers arrived, at

eleven o'clock, on the Brighton Hills; and the South
Gloucester, the North Hants, and Nottingham Militia,
were formed into a line ; the South Gloucester took the
right of the line, and the North Hants the left. They
marched in slow and quick time, the bands playing ; then
formed into close columns ; and at half-past one were
dismissed.   There was no company present, it being
preparatory to a grand review, which will soon take place,
at which his Royal Highness the Duke of York is expected
to be present.   The ground was very slippery; Earl
Berkeley and Major Whatley received each a fall from his
horse, but received no other injury than the left knee of
their pantaloons being torn.

The Steyne has been very dull to-day : we have not
been gratified with the presence of His Royal Highness
the Prince of Wales.   The Duke and Duchess of
Marlborough are expected here in a few days ; their house
is getting in readiness for their reception.   The Earl and
Countess of Clermont arrived at four o'clock this afternoon from London.   The Earl of Barrymore will entertan
a select party to dinner this evening.

The sporting Mr Clark is still here ; he has taken
lodgings in George Street, and on going up to view the
ante-chamber got jammed in the staircase, which is very
narrow, and it was with much difficulty he could be
extricated, to the great amusement of his brother
sportsmen.

The play this night is, by desire of Mrs Cooper,
The Honeymoon, with the ballet of *The Savage;* and,
for the first time, *The Weathercock:* and to-morrow, by
desire of Colonel Fane and the officers of the 1st Regiment
of Dragoon Guards, will be performed, *The School for
Scandal*, *The Drunkard*, and *The Liar*.

At six o'clock His Royal Highness the Prince of
Wales walked on the Steyne, in company with Sir John
Lade, the Earl of Barrymore, and Mr Crampton, who

jumped over the rails, over the Earl of Barrymore's horse, and finished with a somerset, in which he hurt his ankle.

Brighton, August 7, 1806.

His Royal Highness the Prince of Wales left Brighton, in his travelling carringe and four, at half-past six this morning, for London, in consequence of an express he received, at half-past ten last night. He is expected to return to-morrow. All the Royal Dukes are expected at the Pavilion on Monday night or Tuesday morning. We expect one of the grandest reviews that has been seen for many years. Earl Berkeley at seven o'clock this morning was on the parade, and the whole of the South Gloucester regiment mustered, each man with twelve rounds of blank cartridge, which they fired with great correctness. The Prince's party was augmented last night by the arrival of the Marquis and Marchioness of Downshire, who arrived at Belle Vue House, West Cliff, at half-past eight, and immediately proceeded to the Pavilion. The Prince's band, belonging to the 10th Dragoons, practised this morning at the Pavilion, the South Gloucester band having officiated for them till they came. At ten o'clock, the marines on board the Gallant sloop of war were mustered on deck, and went through their exercise with their small arms, and afterwards fired their larboard and starboard guns, to the great alarm of the ladies who were bathing.

The first division of the Nottingham Militia, from Steyning, are expected here on Sunday morning, and the second division on Monday; they will form a camp by the cricket ground; this is done to be ready for the grand review, which, it is said, will take place on the 13th. At two o'clock the Otter and Gallant sailed on a cruise, in company with Earl Craven's brig, who was on board her with a party, to amuse themselves with fishing. At two

o'clock the South Gloucester Militia were inspected by
Earl Berkeley on the parade.

Lady Emily Best, Captain Crampton, and Mr Dalton
breakfasted this morning with the Earl and Countess of
Barrymore ; the Duke and Duchess De Castries were also
there. Mr Crampton seemed to be recovered from the
accident he received in his ankle, as he danced in great
style. After breakfast he was to have gone to town with
Mr Dalton, and the post-chaise was waiting at the door,
when the Countess of Barrymore prevailed on him and
Mr Dalton to stop a few days longer, and to join their
party at dinner to-day, which they accepted.

There is a gentleman here of much eccentricity of
dress and manners. He wears a green coat, very short,
and very full-plaited sleeves, green pantaloons, boots, and
a whip in his hand. His whiskers meet under his chin,
his hair very highly powdered, and a round hat fixed on
the side of his head ; and with the dress I have described,
sometimes wears a large cocked hat, bound with broad
gold lace. He appears about thirty years of age, his name
is said to be Cope, and with all his eccentricity of appearance, looks like a gentleman ; he is always alone ; walks
slow ; and stops and looks at every lady he passes. We
cannot call him the courteous stranger, as he never
honours us even with a smile. If notoriety be his object,
he has fully succeeded, as the windows are filled with
ladies whenever he passes. Even Mr Townsend does not
know what to make of him.

The Earl of Clermont went out in his carriage this
day towards Rottingdean. There will be a ball at the
Castle Tavern this evening. The play for to-morrow night
is, by desire of Lady Charlotte Lennox, *The School for
Scandal*, the first time of its being performed here, and
the Ballet of *The Black Forest*: and on Saturday, by
command of His Royal Highness the Prince of Wales,
for the benefit of Miss Brunton, *The Soldier's Daughter*, in

which Miss Brunton will play the "Widow Cheerly;" followed by a new Scotch Dance, called "Jamie and Peggy," and Mr Kenny's farce of *Matrimony*. Every box is already taken.

There will be a private review to-morrow morning on the Race Ground, consisting of the South Hants, the Cheshire, and the South Gloucester. The men will be out every day preparatory to the Grand Review.

A most distressing accident has happened to a Mrs Bullock, who resided on the West Cliff; she was looking out of her window, when the sash fell, and caught both her hands; she might have remained some time in this dreadful situation, had not one of the sentinels heard her shrieks, and alarmed the house; her hands are most seriously injured.

BRIGHTON, AUGUST 10, 1806.

Earl Berkeley attended divine service at eleven o'clock, on the parade, with his regiment. The Marchioness of Downshire, Mrs E. Palmer and family, Mr Potts and family, and Dr. Wilgrasse, attended at the Chapel Royal. Mr Goldsmid and his beautiful daughter took an airing in their elegant landau. The Earl and Countess Berkeley walked on the Steine after Church. At half-past three His Royal Highness the Prince of Wales took an airing on horseback up Church Hill, in company with Major Bloomfield and Colonel Lee. Count Palfy arrived at the Earl of Barrymore's this morning from London. To-morrow morning it is expected the encampment will take place; the ground marked out yesterday opposite Carlton Place not being thought large enough, it is determined that it shall be at the left of the Prince's Cricket Ground.

His Royal Highness the Duke of Clarence and two Masters Fitz-Clarence arrived at five o'clock this afternoon, at the Pavilion. Some of the Duke of York's suite have arrived; and His Royal Highness the Duke of Orleans, and Dennis Bowles Daley, Esq., M.P., for Galway, are expected to-morrow. Lord Keith is also expected from "the Downs" with several men-of-war, in honour of the Prince's birth-day.

At the Parish Church, this morning, while the banns were publishing between a young couple, the father of the lady, a Sergeant in the South Gloucester Militia, forbade the banns, the fair candidate to enter the Hymeneal Temple being only sixteen years old.

BRIGHTON, AUGUST 13, 1806.

The Grand Ball at the Castle Tavern last night was one of the most splendid which was ever witnessed; never was seen a greater assemblage of beauty and fashion, and the arrangements were in the greatest style of elegance and splendour; the tables were laid out for four hundred persons, and abounded with every delicacy; the wines were excellent, and the whole conferred the greatest credit on the managers. By ten o'clock the Castle Tavern was surrounded with spectators, and carriages from the adjacent neighbourhood began to arrive. At eleven o'clock His Royal Highness the Prince of Wales, and their Royal Highnesses the Dukes of York, Kent, Cambridge, Sussex, and their suite, entered the Ball Room. Amongst the company present were—

The Duke of Argyle, the Duke of Orleans, the Duke and Duchess De Castries, the Marquis of Headfort, the Marquis and Marchioness of Downshire, the Marchioness of Clanricarde, the Earl and Countess Berkeley, Lord Dursley, Earl and Countess of Kenmare, Earl Moira, Earl and Countess Barrymore, and Countess Lauderdale, Viscount and Viscountess Gage. Ladies—E. Best, Charlotte Lennox, Honeywood, Smith, and Daly. Lords—Erskine, Arthur Somerset, and Petersham. Generals—Hulse, Lennox, and White. Colonels—Kington, Lee, Gould, Fane, Smith, and Savary. Majors—Bloomfield, Watley, and Onley. The Hon. Mrs Walpole. Mesdames—Fitzherbert and E. Palmer. Masters—Pott and Brown. Messrs.—Sheridan, Walsh Porter, Alexander Davison, Goldsmid, and E. Palmer. The Misses Goldsmid, Smith, and Metcalf.

J

The Ball was opened by Lord Petersham and the beautiful Miss Goldsmid. The ladies were most elegantly dressed. The prevailing costume was silver tissue, and the head dresses folded in the Grecian style. The Marchioness of Clanricarde wore a pearl tiara, with a diamond cornet comb. The Misses Goldsmid also wore a profusion of diamonds. The comb, with the Prince's plume, and the motto, *Ich Dien*, was universal.

Mr Brookman displayed uncommon taste in his arrangement of the ladies' head dresses.

At two o'clock His Royal Highness the Prince of Wales, his Royal Brothers, and the whole Prince's party, returned to the Pavilion, where much mirth and good humour continued until a late hour this morning. The remainder of the company sat down to supper, and did not separate until five o'clock.

Lord Erskine left Brighton at half-past twelve last night, for London.

At seven o'clock this morning Admiral Lord Keith, with two 74 gun ships, hove in sight, but could not make way, the weather being unfavourable. His Lordship came on shore at eleven o'clock, and dines this day at the Pavilion. The wind has blown so very hard towards the shore, that the ships could not come near enough for a full view of them to be obtained; his Lordship came ashore in a cutter.

It has rained the entire night, and this morning is most unfavourable for the Grand Review at the Devil's Dyke.

Six o'clock p.m.

At ten o'clock the troops consisting of the Royal Horse Artillery, the King's Dragoon Guards, the Carabineers, and 4th Dragoons, began to move towards the ground; and by half-past twelve were formed. At half-past one His Royal Highness the Prince of Wales, mounted on his grey charger, their Royal Highnesses the Dukes of York, Clarence, Kent, and Sussex, the Duke of Argyle, Duke of Orleans, Count Beaujolais, Earl Berkeley, Generals Lennox and White, Major Bloomfield, Colonels Lee and Savary, and several other officers, arrived on the ground; they were received by a salute of 21 guns from the Artillery; the whole marched past in single files, after which the cavalry charged in regiments, and deployed in a column of divisions, and, after forming the line, the rain coming on very heavy, the whole were obliged to quit the field. The troops were an hour and a half passing in single files, their bands playing. The Royal party left the ground at half-past three; it rained very hard the whole time. There were very few persons present. The weather thus prevented one of the most beautiful sights. Thousands of people were prepared to attend the review, but the torrents of rain that fell made it impossible. The Prince gives a grand dinner at the Pavilion this day, and a grand ball afterwards.

Mr Sheridan, yesterday, presented Aaron Graham, Esq., one of His Majesty's principal Police Magistrates, to the Prince of Wales, who received him most graciously, and invited him to His Royal Highness's Ball, to be given this night; Mr Goldsmid's family are also invited. Miss Johnston continues extremely ill, which is the subject of universal regret. The Theatre was crowded last night, and will be the same this evening. There were several men to have been flogged yesterday, but, by desire of the Prince, they were pardoned.

Their Royal Highnesses the Dukes of York and Clarendon left the Pavilion at half-past twelve for Windsor, the Earl of Moira for London, and Lord Keith for Portsmouth.

The ball at the Pavilion was one of the most brilliant that was ever witnessed; never did the Pavilion present a greater assemblage of beauty and fashion. Every apartment was brilliantly lighted by magnificent Grecian and Egyptian lamps; three supper tables, for 150, were laid out in the apartment in the left wing; they were covered with every delicacy that could be procured. At eleven o'clock the ball was opened by His Royal Highness the Duke of Cambridge and the Countess Berkeley. At two o'clock the company sat down to supper. His Royal Highness the Prince of Wales sat at the middle of the upper table; His Royal Highness the Duke of Clarence sat on the right of the Prince, and His Royal Highness the Duke of Sussex on the left; then the Duke of Orleans, and the Count Beaujolais. In the brilliant assemblage were,—

The Duke of Argyle, the Duke and Duchess De Castries, the Marquis and Marchioness of Downshire, the Marchioness of Clanricarde, Earl and Countess of Berkeley, the Earl and Countess of Barrymore, Lord Dursley, the Marquis of Headfort, Lord Petersham, Lord Arthur Somerset, Lady Angerstein, Lady E. Best, the Hon. Mrs Walpole, Aaron Graham, Esq., Mrs Masters, Sir Wm. and Lady Jerningham, Mr Alexander Davison, Mr Sheridan, Mr, Mrs and the Misses Goldsmid, Lady Honeywood, Major Bloomfield, Capt. Davies, Mrs Fitzherbert, General and Lady Charlotte Lennox, Mrs Brown, the Earl and Countess of Kenmare, Count Palfy, Sir William and Lady Smith, Mr Walsh Porter, Mr Burke, Mr Crampton, Mr Dalton, Earl of Clermont, Major Watley, Colonel Lee, and most of the neighbouring nobility, and several military officers.

After supper His Royal Highness the Prince of Wales's health was drank with three times three. The company returned to the ball room, and it was half-past four this morning when this brilliant party separated. The Masters Fitz-Clarence danced all night. The Prince was delighted with their dancing. At one o'clock they took leave of the company. His Royal Highness shook them by the hand at parting.

At eleven o'clock a bonfire was lighted opposite the Pavilion, and every demonstration of joy was manifested by the inhabitants for their beloved Prince. The new organ was placed at the bottom of the room, where the company supped, and played several melodious airs during supper.

His Royal Highness the Duke of Sussex left the Pavilion at two o'clock this afternoon, for Kensington Palace. We are sorry to say His Royal Highness is indisposed.

The Duke of Clarence and the Master Fitz-Clarences will leave the Pavilion at ten o'clock to-morrow morning, for Bushey Park. His Royal Highness's birthday is on the 21st, which will be kept with great splendour at Bushey Park. It is expected that the Prince and all the Royal Dukes will be present. Mrs Fitzherbert will give a private ball this night.

Lady Fortescue and the Hon. Miss Fortescue arrived at six o'clock this evening, at their house. Her Ladyship's illness prevented her arrival before.

At eleven o'clock this morning the bells rang merrily for the marriage of Mrs Bÿthesra to Captain Sober, of 1st Regiment of King's Dragoon Guards. The ceremony was performed at Brighton Church, and at half-past twelve the newly-married pair set off in a new and elegant chariot and four, for Arundel, to pass the honeymoon.

It is said the Prince will leave to-morrow, but it is not determined on.

Sir W. and Lady Jerningham left at twelve o'clock this morning in their carriage and four for London. At two o'clock their Royal Highnesses the Prince of Wales, and Duke of Clarence, the Duke of Argyle, Duke of Orleans, Count Beaujolais, Major Bloomfield, and Colonel Lee, took a ride towards the Downs. At half-past three a thunder storm came on, which was accompanied with several flashes of lightning, and severe claps of thunder; the atmosphere was on a sudden as dark as night, but blew off in the course of an hour.

Tuesday morning a deputation of the inhabitants of this town presented the following address to the Prince, to

which every householder of note had previously most
cheerfully subscribed his name :—

"To His Royal Highness the Prince of Wales,

"We, the Ministers, High Constable, Churchwardens, Overseers, and
principal Inhabitants of the Town of Brighthelmstone, with the most
grateful recollection of the many gracious instances of Your Royal Highness's patronage conferred upon us, to which alone are to be attributed
that prosperity and those advantages unfelt by, and unknown to, any other
Provincial Town, most humbly approach Your Royal Highness, to express
the dutiful and thankful sentiments which this recollection inspires, and
more particularly calls forth on the anniversary of this day. While we
entreat Your Royal Highness to accept these our humble acknowledgments
and congratulations, we devoutly implore the Supreme Disposer of all
events long to preserve a life so invaluable to us, to whom your immediate
protection is so liberally dispensed, and so dear and important in its
general consequences to the nation at large."

His Royal Highness received the address with that
urbanity and polite condescension which so happily mark
his character, accompanied with a gracious intimation
that he would still continue to honour the port of
Brighton with his august presence, patronage, and
regard.

Brighton, August 17, 1806.

This morning is very fine and there are numerous
bathers. The Colonnade of Donaldson's Library is surrounded with gentlemen, reading the newspapers. The
Earl and Countess Berkeley set out for London at ten
o'clock. The Chapel Royal was fully attended; in the
congregation were—the Marchionesses of Downshire and
Clanricarde, the Countesses of Kenmare and Albemarle,
the Hon. Miss Fortescue, Mrs Brown, the Misses Metcalfe,
Dr. Hunter, and, indeed, almost all the fashionables here.
Dr. Blane has arrived this morning, from London, and
has given hopes of Miss Johnston's recovery, to the great
joy of her family and friends. The Duke and Duchess of
Marlborough, the Marquis of Winchester, the Marchioness

of Clanricarde, the Marquis and Marchioness of Downshire, the Earl and Countess of Kenmare, the Earl
and Countess of Albemarle, the Earl and Countess of
Clermont, Mr E. Palmer and family, Lord and Lady
Frances Spencer, Lady Honywood, and General and
Lady Charlotte Lennox, took an airing round the town
in their elegant carriages.

Mr Cope, at four o'clock, walked on the Steyne; he
wore a huge cocked hat, with gold tassels. He was surrounded with company, who expressed their surprise at
the size of his hat; when he answered, that he was
then performing a different character from that of the
preceding day. He is the gaze of Brighton. An artist
yesterday took a sketch of Brighton, and intends making
him and Martha Gunn the prominent figures on the canvas.

The South Gloucester Militia mustered in the barrack
yard at eleven o'clock this day; prayers were read by
Major Watley. At two o'clock the whole of the South
Gloucester Militia mustered, with their side arms only,
and the officers with crape round their arms, consisting
of Major Watley, Major Onley, Capt. Crawley, Capt.
Goodyer, Capt. Merryweather, Capt. Merchant, Capt.
Scudamore, and Capt. Jones, and proceeded, in funeral
procession, with the body of Lieut. Bourke, to Brighton
Church-yard, for interment. Mr Herbert, Lieut. and
Paymaster; Mr Harris, Lieut. and Quarter-Master;
Lieut. Hudson and Lieut. Longford were pall-bearers.
There was a double guard on the occasion, which fired
three volleys over the grave. It is only when an officer
is much respected that they have a double guard. A
new piece of music was performed, composed for the
occasion. Lieut. Bourke was a native of Ireland; but
there is nothing in his letters or papers to shew
what family he belonged to; he constantly received
remittances from Ireland, but even his confidential
servant never knew the source from which they were

drawn. He was seven years in the regiment, and had been repeatedly offered promotion, which he always declined. No man was ever more beloved by his corps.

BRIGHTON, AUGUST 25, 1806.

This morning we have had a most interesting view ; 100 sail of the Jamaica homeward-bound fleet, under convoy, have passed by for the Downs. A Captain Campbell, and a Mr Campbell, (the latter gentleman has been resident in Jamaica seventeen years,) have landed, and intend setting off in a post chaise for London. From them we learn that 80 sail had parted from them on Thursday last, for their different desti-nations—all well—Ireland, Liverpool, Bristol, &c. There are 24 sail missing ; the fate of one only known—the Will, of Liverpool, which was upset, and went down by a sudden squall of wind ; it is not supposed there were more than five or six lives lost on board her, one a gentle-man passenger, who was sick in bed.

Five o'Clock.

More of the fleet are now passing, and some more boats coming on shore. A lady and gentleman,. some children, and black servants have landed, and are gone to the Custom House. More boats appear to be coming in.

They have had a quick, but tempestuous passage, being *only nine weeks* since they left the Island.

Amongst our last arrivals are—

Viscount Ossulston, Lady Morris Gore, Lord and Lady Tara, Sir Frederick Eden, Bart., Mr G. Yates, Misses Gower, Mr J. Gibbons, Mr Chollet, Mr C. Palmer, Mrs C. Cole, Mr Jutting, Mr Wilson, Mr and Mrs Grill, Mr How, Miss Call, Mr Williams, and Sir John Bridger.

The Prince's magnificent stables are now so far finished that the Royal stud, at least such of His Royal Highness's as are left at Brighton, are stabled there. These elegant buildings comprise sixty-one stalls, in-cluding loose stables, viz., thirty-eight for hunters and other saddle horses, with doors opening into the area beneath the Dome; and twenty-three for coach-horses, opening into a square yard of the eastern wing. The western wing, not yet finished, will comprise a spacious riding house, with appropriate apartments; and the whole, when completed, will form the grandest pile of buildings, for equestrian accommodation, in Europe.

Mr Thunder is erecting an elegant Music Room, for the exhibition of his improved pianofortes, and for the performance of concerts, &c. The situation is the most eligible that could have been chosen, being near the New Inn,* in North Street.

This night the entertainments at the Theatre are for the benefit of Mr J. Brunton, under the patronage of the Duchess of Marlborough. His own merits would procure him a bumper, but the patronage of her Grace will insure him all the adjacent nobility; so that we expect not only a crowded but brilliant audience. The performances are, *The Wife of Two Husbands*, the dance of *Goody Two Shoes*, and *Catherine and Petruchio*. Miss Brunton plays the high-spirited "Kate;" "Petruchio" may, with great truth, call her his bonny "Kate." Powell, at Lewes, has very wisely engaged her for his benefit; also Mr J. Brunton, Mr Murray, and Mr Bennet. *George Barnwell* will be performed at Lewes, to-night, for the joint benefit of Mr and Mrs Dormer, and Mr and Mrs Whaley.

BRIGHTON, OCT. 2, 1806.

Notwithstanding the season is so far advanced, this town is fuller of company now than it has been at any period during the summer. Houses are so scarce that several families have been compelled to go away for want of accommodation. The Prince is expected here daily,

* Now the Clarence Hotel, of which Mr Thomas Rose is the much-respected owner and proprietor, and the Music Room named was erected on the ground whereon the present model lodging-houses stand.

which, in some measure, may account for the late numerous arrivals.

Last night the *elegantes*, attracted by the serenity of the weather, and the beams of the moon, which played beautifully bright on the undulating ocean, promenaded the Steyne to a very late hour. The calmness of to-day, and the dulcet notes of the military bands, bid fair to hold out a similar invitation for the present evening. The Jerusalem ponies have been in high requisition all the morning; not only the young Misses, but the valetudinarians of the hardier sex seem to consider it no degradation to take their airings on those patient quadrupeds.

The South Gloucester Militia have just returned from their exercising ground, having had a field day. Colonel Wall, who commands the regiment in the absence of Earl Berkeley, fell from his horse, but happily sustained no injury by the accident.

Hamlet and *The Waterman* are announced (by particular desire) for to-morrow evening. Mrs Fitzherbert patronises Miss Lamb's Concert at the Old Ship the same night. The Green Man had lately the honour of supping at the house of that lady, and, by his eccentricities, afforded the party much amusement.

BRIGHTON, OCT. 19, 1806.

The rides and promenades have been unusually crowded for several days past. The uncommon fineness of the weather induces the *elegantes* to display their pretty persons, regardless of old Boreas, to whose blustering rudeness we are sometimes indebted for an accidental display of a graceful leg and a well-turned ankle. The arrivals still continue to be very numerous, and nearly in proportion to the number of departures. Mrs. Fitzherbert and her little *protege* (Miss Seymour) are here, and daily perambulate the Steyne, which is constantly thronged with beauty and fashion.

A very grand review took place yesterday, about two miles from hence, on the Shoreham Road, of all the regiments quartered in the neighbourhood. Upwards of 4,000 troops were supposed to be present ; and, from its being generally understood that it would probably be the last for the season, an immense concourse of visitors attended to witness the exhibition.

The Green Man, who has entertained us so long with innocent absurdities, has effectually confirmed what before, from the singularity of his costume, and the incoherence of his conversation, could be scarcely doubted. It seems this harmless, though unfortunate maniac, for so he really proves to be, leaped yesterday out of a window, and soon afterwards over the cliff. The rumour is that, in a fit of phrenzy, he fancied there was a serious riot, and that his immediate presence was essentially necessary to quell the disturbance ; acting under the influence of such worthy motives, his derangement, and the consequences are the more to be deplored. He is reported to have sustained some severe contusions, but his life is not considered in danger. It is said that the person in whose house he resides has laid an embargo on his papers, and has gone up to London for the laudable purpose of concerting measures with his friends to insure his future safety.

BRIGHTON, OCT. 26, 1806.

All this day the town has been one continued scene of bustle—the promenades have been crowded with elegance and fashion, and the rides have exhibited a greater number of carriages than we ever before witnessed, among which were several very splended equipages ; the cause of all this interesting and agreeable stir was the happy event of the

Earl of Delaware coming of age, in celebration of which a grand fete is to take place this evening at the Castle Rooms.

As many as 279 cards of invitation had been issued up to this morning, and more, we understand, were put in circulation this afternoon. The bells have rang merrily the whole of the day, and the Castle Tavern has been beset by hundreds of persons, anxious to obtain a sight of the magnificent preparations which have been made to celebrate the event.

Several waggon loads of laurel and olive, of orange and lemon-trees, have been devoted to the ornament and decorations of the superb suite of rooms belonging to the above Tavern, which, moreover, are appropriately illuminated with suitable transparencies and variegated lamps. The floors also are chalked in a tastefully and masterly style, and devices and inscriptions, emblematical of Britain's naval and military triumphs, at once arrest and please the eye, and warm and animate the heart of every one present.

The supper rooms display almost every luxury which either nature or art could supply; it would occupy too much space to particularize them. It is now half-past nine o'clock, and the company are fast assembling—carriages are everywhere in motion, all directing their course, as to one common centre, towards the Castle. It is expected that above 300 persons will be present. No expense, we understand, has been spared in rendering this one of the most splendid fetes that ever took place in England. First-rate cooks and table-deckers, and a numerous train of ornamental decorators have been procured from London, as well as (*mirabile dictu*) fashionable hair-dressers, and other appendages of the *beau monde*, too numerous to mention. The cost of all this, in all its various relations, will, it is calculated, amount to at least £2,000.

An immense concourse of persons are collected in Castle Square, and the confusion which reigns is beyond description. The High Constable and Headboroughs had been solicited by the Earl of Delaware to attend, and a room was to have been provided for them at the Castle, with every necessary entertainment; but just as those gentlemen were about to obey, with all possible cheerfulness and alacrity, his Lordship's wishes, a counter-order was sent intimating that their attendance would be unnecessary, in consequence of a company of soldiers having been engaged to preserve order !

Among the company invited were—

Marquis—Camden.

Marchionesses—Wellesley and Camden.

Earls—Bathurst, Chichester, Egremont, Abingdon, and Leitrim.

Countesses— Bathurst, Clonmell, Chichester, Galway ; Dowager Lonsdale, Leitrim, Abingdon, Sefton, Conyngham, and De Gouton.

Viscounts—Gage, Hawarden, and Ashbrook.

Viscountesses— Gage, Ashbrook, Templetown, Hawarden, and Dowager Hawarden.

Barons—Gustavus Nollekin and Montalembert.

Baroness—Montalembert.

Lords—Glenbervie and Arthur Hill.

Ladies—Perth, Hyde Parker, C. Howard, E. Pelham, Hariet Neville, Charlotte Scott, Pratt, Caroline Bertie Townshend, Collins, Asgill, and Baker.

Sirs—C. Asgill, R. Baker, C. Bishopp, James Bathe, H. Dashwood, Godfrey Webster, &c.

Generals—Hammond and St. John.

Hon. Lieutenant-Colonel and Mr Stapylton.

Colonel Duckett.

Major Graham.

At the Chapel Royal, on Sunday, a most excellent and animated discourse was preached by the Rev. Mr Dibdin, on behalf of the Brighthelmstone Dispensary and Sussex General Infirmary : on which occasion the efforts of the eloquent preacher were attended with all the desired success, the collection amounting to no less than £92.

BRIGHTON, OCT. 27, 1806.

The Grand Fete, given last evening by the Earl Delaware, has been the universal theme of conversation during the day, and we doubt not but it will so continue for some time, as it surpassed everything of the kind ever witnessed in this part of the kingdom. The following are a few additional particulars :—By eleven o'clock nearly the whole of the company, consisting of between 300 and 400 of the most distinguished fashionables, had assembled, at which hour dancing commenced, to the favourite tune " Mrs M'Cloud of Muir," led off by the Earl of Delaware and Miss Webster, sister to Sir Godfrey Webster, M.P. for this county, and followed by Baron de Montalembert and Miss Johnson, and upwards of 120 couple, forming two sets ; the succeeding dance was the " Prince Regent," led off by the same party. At one o'clock waltzing commenced, led off by Baron de Montalembert and Miss Johnson, followed by the Earl of Delaware and Miss Webster, which was kept up with great spirit till half-past two, at which time the supper-rooms were thrown open. It would be utterly impossible to do adequate justice to the taste and magnificence here displayed. This department was under the superintendence of Mr Ward, of Bond Street, who displayed his well-known talents to the best advantage ; the decorations of the table, in particular the sand work, were universally admired, nor was there anything deficient that could delight the eye, or please the palate. Upon the removal of the cloth, the health of the Earl of Delaware, with prosperity and long life, was drunk with three times three. His Lordship, in a very animated and eloquent speech, returned thanks. The following toasts were then drunk with the utmost enthusiasm :—

" The Prince Regent "—" The Marquis of Wellington "—" Prosperity to the House of Delaware "—" The Duke of York and the Army," &c., &c.

The excellent band of the 18th Hussars played several delightful airs during supper.

At the upper end of the room, at which his Lordship presided, was a brilliant transparency of Fame and Cupid, surmounted by a coronet in variegated lamps ; to the right was a transparency of the immortal Hero of Trafalgar; on the left a striking likeness of the Marquis of Wellington, appropriately ornamented with laurel.

Dancing recommenced at half-past three, and was continued, without intermission, till six this morning.

The decorative part of the ball-room, &c., was under the immediate direction of Mr Harrison, of the Opera House, and in which the utmost elegance and simplicity were united. The avenue leading to the rooms exhibited the appearance of an olive grove, and, illuminated as it was with variegated lamps, had an effect truly enchanting. The ball room was tastefully hung with laurel and artificial flowers, at the extremity of which were two figures on pedestals, supporting a scroll, with the word "Delaware" and the figures "21" in variegated lamps, surmounted by a coronet: in the centre the letter "D," embellished with roses surrounded by glory, underneath his Lordship's motto, *Jour de ma vie*,* and over the entrance door the date of the year.

His Lordship intends giving an entertainment at the Castle Tavern, consisting of a ball and supper, on Thursday next, to the upper domestics of his Lordship's establishment and their friends, at which, we understand, upwards of 100 will be present.

The weather during the whole of the day has been very boisterous, the rain falling in torrents, with a strong south wind and heavy sea; scarcely a carriage has been seen in the course of the day. Munden and Emery perform at our Theatre this evening, in the *Birth Day*, for the benefit of Mr Field, Stage Manager.

BRIGHTON, FEB. 6, 1808.

Owing to the excessively high wind of Monday last, the sea rose to a very unusual height, and beat violently

* Day of my life.

against the Cliff, but we are happy to state without doing
any considerable damage. A great many casks of foreign
brandy were driven on shore at the different parts of our
coast, and were picked up by the populace; but they were
afterwards generally taken possession of by the Revenue
officers, and secured in his Majesty's warehouses.

A pipe of excellent port wine, found on Tuesday last
near Blatchington, was drawn off in small casks by the
persons who found it, and who safely conveyed it to their
respective houses.

Repairs are actively applied to the different groynes,
which, from the heavy press of the late swelling tides,
have suffered considerably. On the Cliff leading to
Rottingdean new and substantial railings have been
placed, by which, though the pass is somewhat narrowed,
its comforts, on the score of safety, are considerably
increased.

BRIGHTON, AUGUST 6, 1808.

The Steyne last night was not very full of company,
the weather being unfavourable. His Royal Highness
the Prince of Wales entertained his usual party in the
evening; the Earl and Countess of Kenmare were in
the brilliant circle. At nine o'clock last evening Lord
Burghersh, eldest son of the Earl of Westmorland,
received an express at the Castle, from Portsmouth. His
Lordship immediately set off, the expedition at that place
being expected to sail at five o'clock this morning. There
has been very little company out to-day; Sir John Lade
drove His Royal Highness the Prince of Wales's barouche,
with four horses in hand, several times round the Steyne.
At one o'clock His Royal Highness the Prince of Wales
walked on the Steyne for near an hour, in company with
Colonel Lee; and, at half-past three, His Royal Highness
mounted his grey pony, and, with Colonel Lee, took an
airing towards Rottingdean; the Countess of Kenmare,

in her carriage ; the Earl of Barrymore, on horseback, accompanied by Mr Crampton ; the Earl and Countess of Berkeley, on horseback; and Sir John and Lady Lade took an airing towards the Downs ; Mrs Fitzherbert, in her barouche and pair, went towards Rottingdean ; the Honourable Miss Seymour, attended by her governess, walked along the Marine Parade. Miss Johnson is rather better this morning. His Royal Highness the Prince of Wales was among the numerous inquirers after her health. Lord Thurlow went to the New Baths at three o'clock. His Royal Highness the Duke of Sussex is expected here after the Prince's birthday, on which day great rejoicings are expected. Miss Brunton, as "Juliana," in *The Honeymoon*, last night received very great applause, and Mr J. Brunton, as "Tristram Fickle," in *The Weathercock*, kept the house in bursts of laughter. Mrs and Miss Meade sat in the Prince's box. Earl Craven, Colonel Searle, Mr and Mrs Pigou, Mr and Mrs Calvert, and Mr and Mrs Darley were among the company. There have been several donkey parties. The Duke and Duchess of St. Albans are gone to London. The Prince gives a grand dinner, at the Pavilion, this day, to the Duke and Duchess De Castries, the Earl and Countess Berkeley, the Earl and Countess of Barrymore, Lady E. Best, Colonel Lee, and General and Lady Charlotte Lennox. The company before dinner walked on the lawn of the Pavilion.

BRIGHTON, AUGUST 9, 1808.

The town this morning was enlivened by the arrival of His Royal Highness the Prince of Wales's Dragoons, the Sussex, the North Gloucester, and the Cheshire, who pitched their tents on Church Hill. His Grace the Duke of Norfolk, Lord Charles Somerset, and all the Staff Officers, repaired to Church Hill by eight o'clock in the morning, to view the ground for the encampment; after

K

which they returned to the Pavilion to breakfast. The fineness of the morning attracted a numerous company to Lewes ; every vehicle was in motion, and by eleven o'clock Brighton was entirely deserted.

BRIGHTON, Nov. 28, 1808.

The arrivals up to this day include :—

His Royal Highness the Prince of Wales, Admiral Douglas and family, Charles Pechell, Esq., Colonel and Lady Ann Digby, Hon. W. W. Pole, Hon. Miss Seymour, Colonel Osborne, M.P., Miss Jefferys, Mrs Somers Cocks, Dowager Lady Somers, Sir Robert Burnet, Bart., Richard Somers Cocks, Esq., R. Lambton, Esq., Miles Peter Andrews, Esq., M.P.' John Parker, Esq., O. Price, Esq., Mrs Pilkington, Mrs Thompson, Miss Shannon, Hon. Miss Irby, Miss Hallam, Lady Heathcote, Countess of Clonmel, Lady Jane Scott, Lady Jane Houstone, Mrs Crosbie and family.

The departures comprise the following :—

Marchioness Dowager of Donegal and family, Earl of Lucan, Countess De Vaudreuil, Lord G. Seymour, G. Johnson, Esq., M.P., D. Vander-heyden, Esq., M.P., Mrs Locke, Lady Anne Bingham, Countess Spencer, Thos. Smith, Esq., John Currie, Esq., John Ayles, Esq., Mrs Tryherne, James Rock, Esq., Countess Dowager of Jersey, Lady E. Villiers, Charles Moore, Esq., M.P.

On Wednesday evening a grand ball in celebration of the birthday of the Hon. Miss Seymour was given to a number of the young nobility and gentry, at the Pavilion. The Prince honoured the ball room with his presence for a considerable time, and participated in all the pleasures of the juvenile party, with that amiable condescension for which His Royal Highness is so eminently conspicuous.

The friends of Mrs Fitzherbert's domestics were, on the same occasion, entertained with a ball at that lady's house on the Steyne.

His Royal Highness the Prince of Wales and suite left the Pavilion at a quarter before two yesterday after-noon, in two travelling carriages, for London, thence to proceed (for a residence of some time) to his newly-fitted up apartments at Windsor.

The unusual assemblage of nobility and other persons of distinction at this place, we understand, will occasion the balls at the Castle Tavern to be kept open till Christmas.

BRIGHTON, DEC. 26, 1808.

The fashionable visitors to Brighton are as follows :—

His Grace the Duke of Leinster, Lord Viscount Boyne, Hon. Miss Hamilton, Lord R. E. H. So.nerset, Viscountess Boyne, George Henskell, Esq., Josh. Hunter, Esq., and Richard Launder, Esq.

The departures include the following :—

The Hon. Mrs W. W. Pole and family, Hon. Mrs Bouverie, Hon. Mrs W. Villiers, Lady Ann Wyndham, Lord Viscount Petersham, W. Ellice. Esq., Col. Ruller and family, Hon. John Byng and family, Thomas Crookenden, Esq., Miss Lambton, and Charles Scott Murray, Esq.

The Prince, contrary to what was lately understood, does not spend his holidays at the Pavilion. His Royal Highness is, however, expected here shortly after the ceremony of his laying the first stone of the New Theatre, at Covent Garden, for which the present weather is rather unpropitious.

On Saturday morning, at eight a.m., a large dismasted vessel was observed in the offing, towed by a man of war brig to the westward. A boat was immediately put off to observe the motions of the brig and her apparent prize, and to see whether she was a friend or an enemy. On the boat approaching, she found the brig to be an English vessel, and that the ship in tow was a transport, No. 177 (the Nelson, of London), which had been picked up at sea, without a soul on board, about 12 leagues south of Fairlight. It is supposed she had been captured by a French privateer, who, after plundering her, and taking out her crew, &c., had turned her adrift.

On Wednesday, as a fisherman was standing on the East Cliff, he observed a cock pheasant flying along the shore, to which he and several others immediately gave chase, and soon secured. A lady who happened to be a spectator of the chase, and admiring the extreme beauty of the feathered captive, purchased him of his pursuers, and sent him to her residence to be taken care of.

On the 6th instant a gang, consisting of about twelve persons, armed with guns and bludgeons, assembled and shot through the woods and plantations of Mr Poyntz, of Cowdray, and barbarously beat one of the keepers.

BRIGHTON, APRIL 18, 1809.

The Prince will not honour this place with his presence during the Easter Holidays, as was expected ; but His Royal Highness, we understand, has signified his intention of residing at his Pavilion at an early period of the summer season.

Lieutenant-General Lord Charles Somerset, accompanied by his brother Lord John, arrived here on Wednesday, but stopped only till Saturday, when they took their departure for London.

The Earl of Egremont, Earl Nelson, Lady Charlotte Nelson, and Sir James Poultney, Secretary of War, also arrived here on Saturday last.

The last week's arrivals were :—

The Marchioness of Downshire, Lord Bruce and family, Lady Charlotte Greville, Lady Ann Wombwell, Sir George Wombwell, Hon. H. Pierrepoint, Hon. C. P. Pierrepoint, Sir W. and Lady James, Colonel Wheatley, Henry Greville, Esq., Charles Greville, Esq., B. Pugh, Esq. and family, Hon. Wm. Broderick, Mr Crosbie and family, Mr Adamson and family, Miss Williamson, Mrs Markett and family, Major Olney and family, Lieut. Stephenson, Mr Arthur, S. T. Russell, Esq., Richard Wellesley, Esq., Miss Williams, Wm. Jones, Esq , Mrs Forbes, Mrs Skinner, — Sandys, Esq., and John Day, Esq.

And our departures :—

General Harcourt and Lady, Capt. Millman, T. H. Sitwell, Esq., Samuel Croft, Esq., Mrs Prideaux and family, Miss Courtenay, and Mr Begbie.

Captain Downman's troop of Royal Horse Artillery, which has occupied our permanent barracks for several years past, have received their route to move from hence to Woolwich, for which place they expect to march in three divisions, in the course of next week. The behaviour of the officers and men belonging to the above excellent corps has been such, during the whole of their stay here, as will render their departure a matter of regret to the inhabitants.

A French cutter privateer appeared off this place on Friday afternoon, dogging two large merchant vessels; but as she soon after altered her course and stood from them, it is supposed she thought them too formidable for her successful attack. The privateer was soon after seen in chase of a small English brig going up channel; but as they both got out of sight about sun-set, we know not how the French succeeded.

Same day, as between 40 and 50 sail of fishing boats, belonging to different sea-port towns in this county, were fishing on what is called the Diamond Ground, they were alarmed by the appearance of two large French lugger privateers, on which they instantly quitted their useful occupation and sailed off in different directions, and we are glad to hear they all effected their escape. Had the Frenchmen concealed themselves till night, they would probably have caught a fine shoal of fishers!

The London coaches have for the last week been greatly loaded on their journey down; and all about us has a lively appearance.

BRIGHTON, AUGUST 5, 1809.

This morning the weather being uncommonly fine, and great expectation being entertained of this day's sport, everything was in motion at an early hour. Donaldson's Library was crowded with sporting gentlemen ; bets were 5 to 4 on Mr Grosvenor's Meteora; and among the most spirited gentlemen the odds were much greater upon this favoured horse, who won the gold cup given by His Royal Highness the Prince of Wales. It was a most interesting race, the horses kept so close together, that a table-cloth might have covered them ; but Meteora, notwithstanding, was never pressed, being evidently able to win at pleasure. The course had a most brilliant appearance. His Royal Highness the Prince of Wales (who was dressed in the Hussar uniform), the Countess Berkeley, the Hon. Miss Seymour and Mrs Fitzherbert, arrived on the ground at a quarter-past one, in the Prince's barouche and six beautiful bays. His Royal Highness then mounted his grey charger. The Duchess of Marlborough also honoured the ground with her presence. Her Grace was accompanied by Lady E. Spencer, and came in an elegant landau-barouche, drawn by six horses, with three out-riders. The servants wore new riding dresses, richly trimmed with silver. As soon as Her Grace arrived on the ground, His Royal Highness went up to the carriage, and conversed with her and Lady E. Spencer. The racing was over by half-past three, when His Royal Highness dismounted and got into his barouche, and returned to the Pavilion. Several were detained on the hill by the attraction of a large fleet of transports which appeared in the offing, steering to westward. They made signal at our port, and were to be seen during the whole of this evening, it being quite calm and clear. We expect that the review, which will take place on the 12th instant, will be one of the grandest ever seen here. It is supposed that the troops will amount to upwards of 12,000, which will consist of the Royal Artillery, 10th Light Dragoons, and Second and Third Dragoon Guards, on the right and left of the line, commanded by Major Hugonin ; the Royal North Gloucester, West Essex, Royal Bucks, Royal Berkshire,

Royal Montgomery, and South Hants will compose part
of the right wing, under the command of General Dyott;
the Royal South Gloucester, Sussex, Nottingham,
Northumberland, and Royal East Middlesex will form to
the left.

The following is a description of the Sham Fight of
the 12th August, 1809, before alluded to :—

On Saturday last, Lord Craven's Brigade, consisting
of the South Gloucester, the West Essex, the Nottingham,
and the Cheshire regiments of Militia, stationed in the
vicinity of Brighton, assembled at Goldstone Bottom, for
the purpose of being reviewed by Lieutenant-General
Lennox, who commands the District. In addition to the
above regiments, there were likewise a detatchment of
Flying artillery, and a squadron of the 1st Dragoon
Guards, making the whole number of troops on the
ground upwards of 4,000. The General and his
attendants appeared about eleven, when the business of
the day immediately commenced, without the ceremonious
compliments usually observed upon such occasions. The
enemy was represented by some small detachments of
Infantry and Cavalry, and was supposed to have taken
possession of a little village, flanked by a corps, at no
considerable distance. To dislodge him from this fastness
was conceived to be the object of the attacking party.
The Grenadier companies, which had been previously
formed into a distinct battalion, proceeded to assail him,
covered by a proportionate number of Dragoons and Light
Infantry, who scoured the thicket. Some skirmishing
now commenced between the advanced posts, and the
Artillery maintained a well-directed fire against the village.
The main army, with their light companies in front, and a
corps of reserve in its rear, was next formed into four
close columns, consisting of the battalion companies of

each regiment. The columns now advanced, and then formed line in a spacious valley, where platoon firing commenced from right to left. The Dragoons and Light Infantry were still skirmishing in front, and keeping up an independent fire at extended distances. A variety of manœuvres were now performed, and several new alignments taken up, by the *echelon* march of companies, as advantageous positions presented themselves. The army still continued, at intervals, to push forward, sometimes in line and sometimes in column, occasionally firing by companies and grand divisions. Having, at length, approached the village invested by the enemy, it again made a stand, and formed in the rear of a quarry, which effectually protected it from a furious charge of heavy Cavalry, who were suddenly obliged to halt on the brink of it, and were exposed to a galling fire from the whole of our line. Some retrograde movements were next deemed expedient, and the line began to retire by alternate battalions, covered in its retreat by our Artillery, Dragoons, and Light Infantry. After numerous other judicious operations, as circumstances occurred, and difficulties rendered necessary, the line formed again, fired a volley, and made a rapid charge under the cover of its own smoke. To attempt anything like a detailed description of the different movements and evolutions which were practised on this occasion would require the talents of an able tactician. With truth, we may say that the General in command appeared to display a profound military judgment, with an accurate knowledge of the country. After the charge of the bayonet, which has, at all times, proved as glorious as successful to the British arms when on actual service, the line wheeled back into open columns of companies, and passed the General in quick time, who was again pleased to dispense with the accustomed formalities of a salute. When over, the different regiments filed off to their respective quarters having acquitted themselves much to their own credit, and highly to the gratification of several hundreds of spectators, all of whom declared that the *tout-ensemble* formed one of the grandest and most interesting spectacles of the kind they had ever beheld.

We are concerned to add that, in the course of the review, one of the dragoons was dismounted, and, we fear, mortally hurt, by the rear ranks riding over him. His skull is said to have been fractured by one of the horses treading upon it. He was conveyed away in a cart, on a litter, and, notwithstanding the best surgical aid was offered to him, is reported to have died of the hurts he received.

———————

At this period Rustic Fetes and Public Breakfasts were much in vogue in fashionable society, and one of the principal places of rendezvous was the Chalybeate and grounds on the Wick Estate,—at that time much resorted to by the affluent to partake of the waters. Many interesting stories are related in connection with the Chalybeate, one in particular, in which royalty figured conspicuously.

Nocturnal outings were also the fashion in early summer, ladies frequently, in their carriages, making midnight journeys to the neighbourhood of Dale Gate or Stanmer Park, for the purpose of listening to the sweet warbling of the nightingale. These journeys were taken to the no small inconvenience of servants in attendance and others employed in the stable yards: in consequence they determined, if possible, to put a stop to these eccentricities, and concerted the following plan:—Two or three of the stable-helpers disguised themselves and secreted in hedges near the spot where carriages and occupants drew up to listen to the 'sweet feathered songsters of the grove," and at a given signal they emerged from their hiding places, discharged blunderbusses, and made an attack upon the carriages, in fact, a mock assault of highwaymen, in turn they were apparently over-powered by the coachmen and footmen in attendance, yet contrived to escape from their clutches. The trick succeeded admirably; the servants were complimented and rewarded for their great courage, the ladies feeling they were under the greatest obligations to those who had preserved their lives and property from these ruthless marauders. We need not add that this adventure was the climax to these midnight wanderings.

To this latter incident in connection with "old Brighton" could be added very many of equal interest, in which the fashionable residents were concerned in these " royal days " of our favourite watering place.

PHŒBE HESSEL.*

This remarkable woman, and one of the most promi-nent of Brighton characters about half a century ago, as the inscription on her tombstone in the Parish Church yard will indicate, was born at Stepney, in the year 1713. She served for many years as a private soldier in the 5th Regiment of Foot, in different parts of Europe, and in the year 1745 fought under the command of the Duke of Cumberland, at the Battle of Fontenoy, where she received a bayonet wound in her arm. Her long life, which commenced in the reign of Queen Anne, extended to that of George the Fourth, by whose munificence she received comfort and support in her latter days. She died at Brighton, where she had long resided, December 12th, 1821, aged 108 years.

---

* Quoted from *Erredye's History of Brighton*, with additions by the Author of this Work.

PHYRN   HUPSEL

She was born ? (page?) ? ?? 1711 and ?? ???? ??
??? ??? 1?1? aged 1?? years

This woman in early life fell in love with a man of the name of Samuel Golding, a private in the regiment called at that time " Kirke's Lambs." She was then only 15 years of age, but being, as she frequently remarked, a fine lass for her years. Her maiden name was Smith. The regiment to which Golding belonged was ordered for foreign service,—the West Indies,—in 1728 ; but such was Phœbe's attachment for him, that donning the garb of a man, she enlisted in the 5th Regiment of Foot, commanded by General Pearce, then under orders for the West Indies likewise (in the hopes of joining her lover). There she served five years without making her sex known to any one, she then returned to England with her regiment, and soon after her return it was ordered to join the forces of the Duke of Cumberland abroad, and fought in the battle before mentioned. Golding's regiment and hers were afterwards at Gibraltar, where he got wounded and was invalided home to Plymouth. She then informed the wife of General Pearce of her sex and story, who obtained her immediate dis-charge, and she was at once sent to England. She then proceeded to the Military Hospital at Plymouth and there nursed Golding, and on his recovery they were married and lived, until his death, happily together for more than 20 years, on his pension from Government.

After being a widow a short time she came to Brighton, and was married to her second husband, William Hessel, and in 1792 they must have been in indigent circumstances, from the fact of its having been recorded in the parish books of the 5th of December of that year, " That, at a Meeting of the Churchwardens and Overseers, it was ordered that Phœbe, wife of William Hessel, be paid three guineas to get their bed and nets, which they had pledged to pay Dr. Henderson for medicine."

Her husband died the year after, and she then, by the assistance of a few of the inhabitants, purchased a donkey, and travelled with fish and other commodities to the villages around Brighton, and it was on one of these journeys westward that she obtained the capture of Rook and Howell, for robbing the mail on the night of the 30th of October, 1792, the extent of the same being half-a-sovereign, transmitted in a letter from a soldier stationed in Steyning barracks to a friend residing in this town.

The spot on which the robbery took place is situated about a mile on the high road to Shoreham, and westward of Goldstone Bottom, already mentioned as the place of the military execution of Cooke and Parish for mutiny.

Their apprehension and capture was through Phœbe calling at the Red Lion public-house at Old Shoreham (kept at that time by a man of the name of Penton), as was her frequent custom, to take refreshment, and soon after Rook came in and ordered some beer. In the course of conversation with the persons present, the subject of the mail robbery came up, and from some observations made by Rook, Phœbe in her own mind, was convinced that he was one of the party in the affair. She, in consequence, went out and gave information of what had transpired to the parish constable, Bartholomew Roberts, who was well acquainted with Rook, then living with his mother in a small cottage close by, on the spot now occupied by Adur Lodge. On being taken into custody, Rook, whose age was about 24, a simple, inoffensive fellow, who had been the dupe of his companion in the crime, admitted the offence, and afforded such intelligence as led to the apprehension of Howell, at Old Shoreham mill, where, at the time, he was reading a pamphlet to the miller. Howell was 40 years old, and by trade a tailor.

Some of the stolen property was found upon them; and their identification by the mail-boy being complete, they were committed from the Fountain Inn for trial at the Spring Assizes, at Horsham, when, being found guilty, they were sentenced to be executed at the spot where the robbery had been effected. They were conveyed to Horsham on horseback, and for their safe custody, not only were they handcuffed and pinioned with strong cords, but each had his legs roped together under the horse's belly, and, besides the constable that accompanied them, there was a military escort of four cavalry.

An immense concourse of spectators witnessed the execution of these unfortunate men, whose bodies, according to the barbarous custom of the times, were afterwards encased in an iron skeleton dress and gibbeted. The disgusting sight of their decaying bodies remained some time a terror to the timid, but a mark of recreation to the reckless and thoughtless, who were accustomed to throw at them and practise many revolting tricks.

When, however, the elements had caused the clothes and the flesh to decay, the aged mother of Rook, night after night, in all weathers,—and the more tempestuous the weather the more frequent the visits,—made a sacred pilgrimage to the lonely spot; and it was noticed that on her return she always brought something away with her in her apron. Upon being watched, it was discovered that the bones of the hanging men were the objects of her search, and as the wind and rain scattered them on the ground she collected the relics, and conveyed them to her home, and when the gibbets were stripped of their horrid burthen, in the dead silence of the night she interred them, deposited in a chest, in the hallowed ground of Old Shoreham Churchyard.

Besides being found guilty of robbing the mail, the Grand Jury, at the same Assizes, returned a "True Bill" against James Rook, for horse stealing; but he was not put upon his trial for that offence, in consequence of being left for death upon the other charge. They were executed on the 26th of April, 1793, and a barn that was some years after erected near the spot by

Messrs. Hardwick, of Hangleton, is called "Gibbet Barn"; the remains of the gibbet, &c., were in existence till 1822, when they were burnt by some gypsies who frequented the neighbourhood.

It was evident that Phœbe could not exist without parish aid, as the following minute from the Vestry book will show:—"1797.—20th May, at a meeting of the Churchwardens and Overseers held at the Hen and Chickens (now the Running Horse, King Street),—Ordered, that Phœbe Hessel's rent be paid from the present time, and that her weekly allowance be discontinued."

In the early part of the present century the infirmities of age began to tell upon her, and, being no longer able to get about the country, she was taken into Brighton Workhouse; from which, however, at her own request, she was discharged in August, 1806, as a minute of the Vestry held on the 14th of that month states:—"That Phœbe Hessel be allowed a pair of stockings and one change on leaving the poor-house."

After this period she obtained a subsistence by selling fruit, bulls-eyes, pin-cushions, &c., at the bottom of the Marine Parade, near Old Steine Street, where, in sunny weather, she used to sit in a chair with her basket of wares beside her, and obtained a good amount of custom. Her costume would, at the present day, form a great attraction. She wore a brown serge dress, a white apron, —always clean,—a black cloth cloak with a hood, surmounted by a red spotted with white handkerchief. Her head-dress was a black antique shaped bonnet over a mob cap. Her shoes were for service and not look, without any regard to "rights and lefts;" and her hands and arms were usually encased in a pair of long woollen mittens. Her walking-stick, was formerly in the possession of Mr Edward Blaker, of Portslade; his father, a resident of Brighton and Churchwarden of the Parish at the time of Phœbe's death, having received the same. During one

of the lectures on "Old Brighton," at the Royal Pavilion
in the present year, by Mr Alderman Henry Martin, he,
on Mr Blaker's behalf, presented the same to the Brighton
Museum.

Hone, in *The Year Book*, date Sept. 22, 1821, says,
"I saw this woman to-day in her bed, to which she is
confined from having lost the use of her limbs. She has
even now, old and withered as she is, a fine character
of countenance, and I should judge, from her present
appearance, must have had a fine though perhaps mascu-
line style of head when young. I have seen many a
woman, at the age of sixty or seventy look older than she
does under the load of 108 years of human life. Her
cheeks are round, and seem firm, though ploughed with
many a small wrinkle. Her eyes, though the sight is
gone, are large and well formed. As soon as it was
announced that somebody had come to see her, she
broke the silence of her solitary thoughts and spoke.
She began in a complaining tone, as if the remains
of a strong and restless spirit were impatient of the
prison of a decaying and weak body. 'Other people
die and I cannot,' she said. Upon exciting the recollection of her former days, her energy seemed roused,
and she spoke with emphasis. Her voice was strong
for an old person, and I could easily believe her when,
upon being asked if her sex was not in danger of
being discovered by her voice, she replied that she
always had a strong and manly voice. She appeared
to take a pride in having kept her secret, declaring
that she told it to no man, woman, or child, during
the time she was in the army; 'for you know, Sir,
a drunken man and a child always tell the truth. But
I told my secret to the ground. I dug a hole that
would hold a gallon, and whispered it there.' While
I was with her the flies annoyed her extremely : she
drove them away with a fan, and said they seemed

to smell her out as one that was going to the grave. She showed me a wound she had received in her elbow by a bayonet. She lamented the error of her former ways, but excused it by saying, 'when you are at Rome, you must do as Rome does.' When she could not distinctly hear what was said, she raised herself in the bed and thrust her head forward with impatient energy. She said, when the King, George IV., —saw her, he called her a 'jolly old fellow.' Though blind, she could discern a glimmering light, and I was told would frequently state the time of day by the effect of light."

Phœbe had nine children, but none of them attained any age except the eldest son, who was a sailor, but she had neither seen nor heard of him for many years prior to her decease.

On the 12th of August, 1814, at the festival which took place at the Royal Cricket Ground, to commemorate the peace on Napoleon Bonaparte retiring to Elba, Phœbe, as the " Oldest Inhabitant," sat on the left of the Vicar, the Rev. Robert James Carr, and was an interesting object, then 100 years of age, and many presents in silver and one pound notes found their way to her from the opulent and enquiring part of the crowd, and she cheerfully joined in the National Anthem.

This incident brought her into great notoriety; and several ladies, being struck with her appearance, and pleased with the respectable character she bore, raised a subscription, each subscriber being presented with Phœbe's likeness, beneath which was inscribed, "An industrious woman living at Brighton, with very slender means of support, which she can only earn by selling the contents of her basket, for whose assistance this etching is sold."

On the celebration of the Coronation of George IV., July 19th, 1821, Phœbe, at the age of 107, and totally blind, took part in the ceremonies, being present on the Level in a carriage with the Vicar.

For some few years previous to her decease, which took place on the 12th of December, 1821, she was allowed half-a-guinea weekly by the King. It is related that His Majesty offered her a guinea per week, but she refused it, saying that half that sum was enough to maintain her.

Phœbe, in support of a good old Sussex custom, regularly, on St. Thomas's Day, December 21st, went out "Goodening," visiting well-to-do parishioners, to gossip upon the past, over hot elderberry wine and plum cake, and to receive doles, either in money or materials, to furnish home comforts for the celebration of the festivities of Christmas.

Mr Hyam Lewis, of Ship Street, silversmith, erected the tomb stone in the Old Churchyard, near the chancel door, where the remains of Phœbe are deposited. At the foot of her grave is interred, likewise, the remains of another character well known in the town prior to his admission to the Workhouse, where he died, and his last wishes were that he might be buried close to her. His name was Corporal Staines, of the Marines, and he served on board the Victory (the flag ship of the immortal Nelson), at the battle of Trafalgar, where that illustrious hero closed his mortal career, and the subject of this anecdote was wounded. He afterwards came to Brighton and fitted up a small hut in a bank about south-west of the commencement of the Upper Lewes Road, close to the angle of a wall, where he made a chalk battery, inter-spersed with gravel paths, with a flag staff in the centre, and had on view a collection of figures, rudely fashioned by himself from chalk, the principal being the hull of the Victory, and upon it the funeral bier of the immortal hero, dressed with sombre drapery, and a small flag bearing the motto, "Britons strike home." It was his

L

custom during the years he resided in his hermitage (for such in reality it appeared) to fire off daily, on the setting of the sun and on occasions of importance, a small cannon and generally to an assemblage of children. This he did with some difficulty, as the Corporal supported himself on crutches. On the Coronation of George IV., July 19th, 1821, festivities took place on the Level and the spot that now forms Park Crescent (which the following year was laid out as Ireland's Tea Gardens), when the Corporal and his colony were jeopardised by a huge bonfire in close proximity to his dwelling. In its centre was a pole, surmounted by a tar tub, but, fortunately, the wind shifted to another quarter, consequently the threatened calamity was averted, and the burning embers of the same fell outside of the fosse of his fortifications.

At a short space from the graves of these two Brighton characters was buried Schmidt, the celebrated trumpeter of the Prince Regent's Band, already alluded to.

GOVERNMENT OF THE TOWN.—ANCIENT AND MODERN.

In the time of King Alfred, England was divided into Shires, the Shires into Hundreds, and the Hundreds into Tithings, tithing men into Head-boroughs—or heads of boroughs—these were the only guardians of the peace and dispensers of justice within their respective districts, the original limits being the residences of ten *creorles* or freemen, with their families and slaves. Under the Saxon constitution Brighthelmstone had two Head-boroughs, a proof that its population even then was far from being inconsiderable. These Head-boroughs sat alternately or together, at the Borough Court, at which the decenners or free or frankpledges (friborgs), who had no causes to be tried there, attended as jurors or sworn assessors to the presiding officer. These free pledges were the origin of " The Society of Twelve " already spoken of in this work, and which continued in this town to the commencement of the present century. By the statute of Winchester, 13th Edward I., the Borough of Brighthelmston had a constable appointed for itself exclusively, an indication of its extent at that period. According to Alfred's division the Hundred to which Brighthelmston belonged contained, besides those of Ovingdean and Rottingdean,— called in *Domesday*, Welsmere, the Boroughs of Preston (Prestetune) and Patcham (Patchame),—which were originally hundreds of themselves, and were, under Edward I., united to the borough of Brighthelmston, and composed a new hundred called Wellsbourne, since corrupted into Whalesbone (as already named, with its origin, in the early part of this book). The boroughs of Ovingdean and Rottingdean were then united to the small hundred of Falmer, under the name of Ewensmere.

The leet or law day, the view of frankpledge for this hundred was held on Easter Tuesday, when the High Constable, Headboroughs and Officers were elected; among the officers were two called respectively the ale-conner, and a searcher or sealer of leather. These offices were of great importance, until they became obsolete; the ale conner's duty was to taste the ales at the respective inns in the town, with a view of preventing adulteration. The searcher and sealer had to examine all hides and skins flayed in the town, and calculate the number of cuts thereon, in order to obtain from the hide or skin owners the penalty of one shilling each recoverable by law,—an Act now repealed.

Since the town became incorporated in 1854, the only appointment of High Constable has been that of Mr James Martin, which took place at the Court Leet of the Earl of Abergavenny, on Easter Tuesday, in the year 1855, and he still holds the office of High Constable of the Hundred of Whalesbone; his duties however are but trifling, merely consisting of taking charge of the Parish Jury List and presenting it to the Clerk of the Peace for the County. He also retains his "staff of office," which he intends presenting to the Town Museum.

The parish books give the names of those who served the above office from Henry Gunn, in 1589, to the last appointment above-mentioned in 1855, a period of nearly 300 years, and the only record to be found relating to any sum being allowed for expenses is the following resolution, passed at a Vestry Meeting, at the Town Hall, April 4th, 1793, when it was ordered "That in future the Constable (High) be allowed twelve guineas, to be paid in full, for all expenses during his office, including four guineas for a dinner."

In 1773 an Act of Parliament was obtained empowering the appointment, in addition to these High Constables and Headboroughs, of 64 persons as Commissioners, who held office during their life-time, and on the decease of a member of the body a meeting of the inhabitants was convened, and his successor appointed thereat by vote. Upon these Commissioners devolved the securing of better government of the town, their power extending to lighting and cleansing the streets, lanes and other places within the parish; also the removal and prevention of nuisances, arranging for the holding and regulation of the Market,* then open daily; the govern-

---

* In the early pages of this work it is mentioned that Brighton possessed a Charter from Edward II. for the holding a weekly market on Thursday. The site of this market place was on the Cliff, commencing at the Town House and fortress (situated about the western corner of the Junction Road, the site of the Queen's Hotel); and on this spot it remained from 1373 until 1703, when the Cliff whereon it stood was sapped by the waves, and the building destroyed and demolished. In the year 1734, the Market was established, as at present, in the Bartholomews,—which at that period, by purchase, became the property of the town.

ment of public groynes, their building and repair,—an important duty at this period,—in order that the coast might be safe and commodious for vessels to approach and unload coals for the consumption of the inhabitants. That the said Commissioners might effect all the above public and desirable ends, they were empowered by the before-mentioned Act to levy a duty of sixpence on every chaldron of coals or culm so landed.

With reference to the cost of the erection of groynes, it is stated that so incapable were the inhabitants,—owing to their poverty,—of the means to make groynes for the preservation of their property, that in 1722, by virtue of letters patent under the Great Seal, there was raised by charitable contributions for the then deplorable sufferers (the inhabitants of the town) money for building groynes, bulwarks and fortifications against the inroads of the sea, in order to preserve such part of the said town then remaining. In 1757 other letters patent,—or a brief,—for alms to be collected from house to house, was obtained for the support of groynes. This brief is still in existence, and after stating that the collection under the former one had been appropriated and applied to the safety and preservation of the place, proceeds thus:—" And the said money being now expended, the groynes and defence that have been made are decayed and worn out, and in all probability, should the next winter prove stormy, great part of the said town will be destroyed if not timely prevented: that the petitioners are not able to support and relieve themselves in this important and weighty affair, being burdened with numerous poor, their rates for the relief of the poor amounting to near *six shillings* in the £ rack or full rent. That the said petitioners, by reason of these calamities, are now become real objects of compassion,—that the money immediately wanted to erect new groynes, supporting such as remain, and the other necessary fortifications, on a moderate calculation will amount to £2,250, which sum the petitioners are unable to raise." It may here be stated that the best house in the town, at this period, was not rated at more than 40s. per annum.

The Act of Parliament of 1773 remained in force between thirty and forty years, and under its operation Brighton experienced most important advantages; but in the year 1810 it was repealed in favour of a new Act, and the management of the place, with very enlarged powers, subsequently invested in twenty-four Commissioners, the necessary qualification for a membership of the body being the occupation of a house of the annual value of £50, and the *bonâ fide* receipt of £50 per annum from landed or household property. The newly-appointed Commissioners held their first and subsequent meetings at the Old Ship Hotel on the 2nd of May, 1810, and they not only possessed the management of the town and its funds, but also had the power of appointing the Directors and Guardians of the Poor, Coal Meters, the Patrole, &c. By the new Act the town duty on coals was increased from sixpence to three shillings per chaldron, and the fund accruing therefrom was at the sole disposal of the Commissioners, and it is evident, from the great power entrusted to them, that the office of the same was considered of no mean importance.

The Act of Parliament of 1810 remained in force until 1825, when it was again deemed requisite to give a fresh impulse to the spirit of improvement that was rapidly, in buildings and otherwise, developing itself in all parts of the town; in consequence, application was made to Parliament for a new Act (which was granted) containing additional powers, without the obnoxious clause of election for life,— existing in the old Act regulating the town, — a new clause therein providing that a portion of the Commissioners should vacate their seats yearly, thereby giving the inhabitants the power of re-electing or otherwise the .

out-going members. The number of Commissioners to bo
appointed under this improved Act was increased to 112.
The power formerly possessed by the Commissioners of
appointing Directors and Guardians of the Poor was, by
the same Act, transferred to the inhabitants, such appointment to take place in Vestry assembled for that purpose
during the Easter-week in every year. This was a salutary
alteration, which has proved of benefit both to ratepayers
and the poor, inasmuch as it brought about the constitution
of another important local body, acting irrespective and
independent of the other, and in possession of better
supervision and surveillance over the poor and their relief.
Brighton's yearly-increasing growth both in size and
importance, brought pauperism with attendant evils in its
wake, and it became the practice of the Board to examine
quarterly, at the Workhouse, on Church Hill, the out-door
poor in receipt of parochial relief, who attended to answer
the interrogations with reference to their means of
subsistence. These Guardians of the Poor commenced
"the relief" at the hour of ten, and with a short
interregnum of one hour for refreshments, comprising
plain joints and vegetables,—partaken of at the House,—the
object of this being the retention of a sufficient
number of the body to recommence business again at the
appointed time, thus avoiding inconvenience to applicants,
which from experience had been found to result from
separation of the Board for their homes, or elsewhere, to
obtain light refreshments. Many of its members lived at
a considerable distance from the Workhouse, and it
frequently happened that on the resumption of business
there was not a quorum present to proceed with the same,
some of the Guardians finding, on arrival at their
respective homes, matters requiring more immediate
personal attention, hence their non-return. These Board
dinners, like other matters, fell into abuse, as the sequel
proved, inasmuch as the plain joints, &c., adopted in 1837,

were discarded for something of a more *recherche* description, and gave rise to the following well-penned satire, which illustrates the revelry in those days of these "substantial and discreet" Guardians:—

THE GOOD OF THE POOR!!!

A DEFENCE OF THE DIRECTORS AND GUARDIANS, BY ONE OF THE BODY.

Dear Brother Electors, when chosen Directors,
    In order your suffrage next year to ensure;
We all began eating and drinking and treating,
    At the parish expense—for the good of the poor!

At first our suggestion was call'd into question,
    And objections were made by the low and obscure,
But we carried our points for fish, fowl, and joints,
    And feasted away—for the good of the poor !

And with salmon and dory wer'nt we in our glory—
    When we'd dined with the zest of a real epicure?
We, like glorious elves, drank our own noble selves,
    With hip, hip, hurrah !—for the good of the poor!

Then we order'd fresh brandy, we found twasn't handy
    To drink common brown like the low or impure,—
'Twas thick and looked dirty, so we got some at thirty-
    Five shillings a gallon—for the good of the poor !

We next gave up port and all wines of that sort
    As only designed the vile paupers to cure ;
And resolved to be merry, got glorious with sherry,
    And staggered to bed—for the good of the poor !

We next built a summer-house, ne'er was a rummer house,—
    'Twas an old boat vamp'd up, 'twasn't meant to endure ;
We determined next quarter to get something smarter—
    A snug smoking box—for the good of the poor.

Meanwhile our retreat for the present look'd neat,
    The site was so pleasant, the air was so pure,
Each served by his lackey ; we puffed off our backey,
    In sight of the paupers—for the good of the poor !

And for fear that our banker should bring us to anchor,
    " Cut off our supplies," and refuse to give more ;
We resolved to raise money like bees making honey,
    And spend it in feasts—for the good of the poor !

So we sent out our letters to poor parish debtors,
  To tell them that, brimful of anger and fur—
Y, we'd sell all their chattels, their goods and their cattles,
  If they didn't pay up—for the good of the poor.

There was first Muster Barnes, he's the gemman wot larns
  How to make Norfolk pies that no stomachs endure ;
But we wash'd out our throttles, with jolly full bottles,
  And swallow'd the pie—for the good of the poor !

And next Muster Griffin sent fish for our tiffin—
  We though 'twas a gift, but 'twas only a lure ;
For when he'd sent dollops of lobsters and scollops,
  Why he sent in his bill—for the good of the poor !

And then Muster Hewitt, O didn't he do it
  Like a gent or a nobleman ?—yes, to be sure !
In nought to be lacking, he bought parish blacking,
  And shone in his shoes—for the good of the poor !

Thus, Electors of Brighton, we beg to enlighten
  Your minds on our merits ; we now say no more ;
But we hope that next Easter, each jolly good feaster
  Will be chosen again—for the good of the poor !

For with feasting and dining and drinking and shining
  We've the Scripture fulfilled, our election made sure,
And, in spite of the papers exposing our capers,
  We shall claim all your votes—for the good of the poor !

As may be supposed, the abuse brought about its own remedy, the outcry against these gourmands was great on all sides, and a new order of things prevailed. It may be here justly remarked of the Board of Guardians : for many years past no body of men has striven more indefatigably in the carrying out of the onerous duties of rendering assistance to and relieving their less fortunate brethren, by the dispensing to them of necessaries and comforts so far as is compatible with the interests of the ratepayers. The present worthy Chairman, Mr James Flowers, has been for many years most assiduous in the discharge of his duties, in which he has been assisted by the very able Clerk to the Board, Mr Alfred Morris, and his officials. The management of the Workhouse also claims our compliment: it has been entrusted to Mr Edward Sattin (the Governor) and his wife (the Matron), who are assisted by a numerous staff of subordinates, and, in order to show the extent of means at the disposal of the Board, the following respectively represent the two poor's rates of last year :— First Poor Rate of 1s 4d in the £, made March, 1870, £28,713 7s 5d ; Second Poor Rate at 1s 6d in the £, made September, 1870, £32,252 14s 4d. A great anomaly exists in the appropriation of money raised for relief of the poor to the payment of salaries and other expenses which justly belong to the Corporation, viz. :—The Recorder, Town Clerk, Stipendiary Magistrate, Accountant, and Crier of the Court; the expenses incurred in the election of members of the Corporation, Coroner's inquests, criminal prosecutions; the maintenance of prisoners in the County Gaol, a proportion of the cost of building the same, also that of the Lunatic Asylum, at Hayward's Heath; the School Board, County liabilities, and a host of others, which amount to and absorb a very considerable sum of money. We trust the time is approaching when the Legislature, in its wisdom, will see the necessity for the passing of an enactment providing that no payments shall be made from the rate for the Poor beyond those strictly within its province, and for which the rate is solely intended. Another reason for the repeal of this defect is the fact that it has a tendency to lower us in the scale of nations, in that it might be inferred therefrom that our poor tax is an immense one, by reference to the great sum collected annually for the use of the poor,—thus representing a large per centage of paupers of the whole population of this kingdom, when it is well known among us that the bulk of the sum ostensibly raised for the poor relief is diverted into other channels.

In 1854 Brighton underwent a very important change, by the introduction of municipal government in the incorporation of the town. Many ineffectual attempts to secure the same had been previously made, as we find it recorded that, in 1806, the desirability of adopting the Act was considered, at a numerously attended public meeting presided over by the Vicar, the Rev. Robert James Carr (afterwards Bishop of Chichester). After a debate of several hours it was resolved that "It is inexpedient to introduce that form of Government." From that period until the year 1852 the subject of incorporation remained in abeyance, but this year many residents, thinking that the amended Incorporation Act of 1835 was well adapted for the requirements of the town, inasmuch as its adoption would place Brighton on a footing with other large cities and towns in the kingdom, with the advantage also that its Chief Magistrate would be at the head of town affairs, again agitated for "the Charter," but met with a refusal from the Privy Council. On a change of ministry the application was renewed and the Charter of Incorporation granted on the 19th of January, 1854, it being received in Brighton on the 3rd of April following. The number to constitute the Council to be 48; the borough was divided into six wards, the number of members elected to the same by the Burgesses at the first election being 36. After this election of the Councillors, the latter proceeded to the election from their body of the Mayor, also two Aldermen to represent each Ward. The Burgesses of each Ward were then called upon for the election of two more representatives to fill the vacancies caused by such elevation; and on the election of twelve other Councillors the municipality was erected.

It will occasion no surprise when it is stated that a contest of this nature, involving a thorough change in the administration of the affairs of the town, created the greatest excitement. Antagonistic Committees were

formed,—Corporationists and Anti-Corporationists,—each
side submitting lists of six candidates for the different
wards,—the required number to be elected,—and no
single competitor entered the lists with the exception of
Mr Henry Martin, who announced himself as a candidate,
and fought successfully the battle, independent of the
party nominees, he being returned for the Pavilion Ward.

The following were the successful candidates at this
memorable election, which took place on the 30th day of
May, 1854 :—

PAVILION WARD.	PARK WARD.
J. Cordy Burrows,	W. Hallett,
I. G. Bass,	Jno. Fawcett,
E. Burn,	T. West,
D. M. Folkard,	E. M. Phillips,
W. Catt,	T. Warner,
Henry Martin.	Geo. Kennedy.

ST. PETER'S WARD.	ST. NICHOLAS' WARD.
H. Schilling,	W. Beedham,
G. Attree,	W. G. Sawyer,
W. Stevens,	T. Cooper,
J. Soper,	W. Bentley,
J. Andrews,	A. Cobbett,
D. Friend.	M. B. Tennant.

PIER WARD.	WEST WARD.
W. Alger,	E. Taylor,
W. D. Savage,	J. Ellis,
R. M. Webb,	W. Silverthorne,
Wm. Hill,	P. Walton,
Charles Stone,	G. Cobb,
E. Sattin.	F. Wright.

The first meeting of the new body took place on the
7th of June following, at which Major John Fawcett was

elected Mayor, and the two Councillors highest on the poll for each Ward were elected Aldermen, viz. :—

PAVILION WARD.—Messrs Burrows and Bass.
PIER WARD.—Messrs Alger and W. D. Savage.
PARK WARD.—Messrs Hallett and Fawcett.
ST. PETER'S WARD.—Messrs Schilling and Attree.
ST. NICHOLAS WARD.—Messrs Beedham and Sawyer.
WEST WARD.—Messrs Taylor and Ellis.

The vacancies occasioned by the election of the above Councillors as Aldermen were filled up as follows :—

PAVILION WARD.—Messrs Cox and Bull.
PIER WARD.—Messrs Brigden and Fiest.
PARK WARD.—Messrs Chamberlain and B. Webb.
ST. PETER'S WARD.—Messrs E. J. Burn and J. Martin.
ST. NICHOLAS WARD.—Messrs J. Patching and S. Saunders.
WEST WARD.—Messrs Harris and H. S. Turrell.

At the same meeting * Charles Sharood, Esq., received the appointment of Town Clerk.

The machinery of the Corporation having been fully set in motion, it soon became evident that the body of Commissioners (which still existed) could not continue to act, as the powers exercised by each would soon come into collision; and, again, it was incompatible with the interests of the town that two bodies antagonistic to each other should exist. Active measures were therefore taken by the inhabitants to secure the election to fill the vacancies yearly occurring in the Commission (one-third of the body retiring) of persons who were favourable to the power of the Commissioners being merged into that of the Corporation, and this desired object was finally brought about on the 9th day of May, 1855, at a Meeting of the

---

* Succeeded on the 6th March, 1863, by David Black, Esq., who was appointed Clerk to the Local Board, April 23, 1863, on the introduction of the Act. He has also held the office of Borough Coroner since the 1st of January, 1855. Mr Francis John Tillstone, Chief Clerk, was appointed to his office on the 2nd May, 1863.

Commissioners,—the following report of the Transfer Committee being presented in confirmation thereof :—

"Your Committee report that the Brighton Commissioners' Transfer Act, 1855, has passed through both Houses of Parliament, and received the Royal Assent on Saturday last, the 5th inst., and that the Act will come into operation and take effect on and from Tuesday, 29th day of May instant," and the following resolutions, consequent thereon, were passed :—

"That the acting Clerk do take the necessary measures, under the direction of the Monthly Finance Committee, for procuring the settlement of all accounts due to the Commissioners, and also for obtaining the bills of all persons having claims against the Commissioners, in order that the same may be examined and discharged as far as may be previously to the 29th inst," and the Meeting be adjourned at its rising to the 28th inst., it being the last of the "Old Commission," and at which the following resolutions were passed unanimously :—

"That the Solicitor and Acting Clerk be directed to hand over to the 'Town Clerk' the deeds, papers and writings set forth in the inventories now presented.

"That the Commissioners have much pleasure in expressing their approval of the obliging and efficient manner in which Mr Lewis Slight, Jun., has discharged the duties of the office of Clerk to this body, and to express a hope that as the said office is about to expire he may succeed in obtaining some other appointment commensurate with his abilities."

With this meeting all the powers and functions that had been exercised under the Act of June 22nd, 1825, by the 112 Commissioners, which comprised the body, ceased and determined, and during the existence of "the Commission" vast improvements had been effected,—but not without bickerings and divisions among its members, an influential portion of whom were called "The Fourteen," the name originating at one of the meetings convened for matters relating to the management of the police, to the following effect :—

TOWN OF BRIGHTON, At a Special Meeting of the Commissioners hold at July 27th, 1827. the Town Hall, on Friday, the 27th day of July, 1827 —For the purpose of taking into consideration the propriety of rescinding a resolution passed on the 15th of August last, relating to discontinuing the payment of salaries to the Police or Headboroughs, and other business connected therewith.

At this Meeting a letter was received from the Vestry Clerk, enclosing a copy of a resolution passed by the Vestry on the 21st instant, requesting the Commissioners to appoint Police Officers at salaries as heretofore, to be paid out of the consolidated rates, and that they direct them to be under the sole controul of the Magistrates.

Resolved.—That William Pilbeam, Charles Penfold, James Thoburn Thomas Harman, Junr., and John Wise, be and are hereby appointed Officers of the Commissioners, to keep the peace of the town.

After the passing of the above resolution, the meeting apparently broke up, — but fourteen of its members remained and passed the following resolution :—

Resolved.—That in the opinion of this Meeting, the Commissioners have no funds out of which they can pay the salaries of a Police, and therefore that no monies be paid for such purpose.

This rendered nugatory the former ; and at a subsequent meeting it was confirmed, the effect of it being that the control of the police remained in the hands of the Commissioners,—hence the cognomen of "The fourteen."

The first Clerk appointed under the Act of Parliament spoken of was Mr Swaysland : he was succeeded by Mr Lewis Slight on the 3rd of November, 1826, and who resigned the appointment on the 25th of January, 1854, a few months prior to the introduction of the Charter of

Incorporation. He died on the 28th day of March, 1869, and the following extract from the *Brighton Examiner* of the period is here inserted as a tribute to his merits and in justice to his memory :—

"It has become our painful duty this week to record the death of Mr Lewis Slight, a gentleman whose name will long be remembered as associated with all the local reforms and improvements of Brighton from about fifty years ago up to the time of the Incorporation of the borough in 1854. Leicestershire was, we believe, his native county, and in taking up his residence in Brighton he opened, in conjunction with Mrs Slight, his first wife, a small and unpretending shop in Poplar Place (Lanes), where for some years they carried on a respectable, although not extensive business. At this time Mr Slight entered with much energy into local matters, and was distinguished as an able and somewhat eloquent, although not showy speaker at public meetings on every question of local economy and reform, and an uncompromising opponent of extravagance and jobbery of every kind. From Poplar Place Mr and Mrs Slight removed to a more eligible situation in North Street, the premises at present occupied by Mr Noakes, chemist; and afterwards to more private premises in Ship Street. In the meantime Mr Slight had received the appointment of Clerk to the Commissioners of Brighton, a post for which he was, by his natural talents and local experience, eminently qualified; and which had hitherto been held by a professional man,—in other words, a lawyer,—an arrangement which had been always opposed by Mr Slight,—and a few more local politicians, —as extravagant and inefficient. It was in the position of Commissioners' Clerk that Mr Slight was enabled, more than any other individual, by his foresight, tact, and business qualifications, to promote the great public local improvements which have from time to time been effected, and

which have mainly assisted in giving to Brighton the
proud title of "Queen of Watering Places." His talent
as a negociator was of eminent service to the town in
obtaining loans on favourable terms, and in nothing
perhaps was this quality more strikingly displayed than
with regard to the purchase of the Royal Pavilion
property from the Commissioners of Woods and Forests,
and which he obtained for the town at a price far below
what would have been gladly given by private speculators.
As an acknowledgment of his services to the town, in
this and other respects, a marble bust of Mr Slight, an
excellent likeness, by Pepper, our talented local artist, the
fund for which was raised by a subscription chiefly among
the members of the Town Council, has been placed in the
entrance hall of the Royal Pavilion, where it holds a
conspicuous position beside those of the Rev. F. W.
Robertson, Sir David Scott, and several other Brighton
worthies and notabilities. Placed in so prominent and
critical a position in the eyes of his fellow-townsmen,
he was on various occasions made the mark of malicious
or ignorant attack, and in these encounters his opponents
always came off second best. When the town was incorporated, an attempt was made to damage him by an
inspection and scrutiny of the public accounts under his
charge; but the scrutiny failed to elicit anything to his
prejudice, the only discovery made being that they were
kept by a system of his own, and not in exact accordance
with methods generally adopted in keeping public accounts.
About a year before the town was incorporated, Mr Slight
resigned the office of Clerk to the Commissioners, and was
succeeded by his son, Mr Lewis Slight, jun., his former
assistant, who held it *pro tem.* until the Incorporation
came into effect, and was then retained in the position of
Borough Accountant until his death in 1862. At a
subsequent period Mr Slight entered into some unsuccessful business speculations, by which his circum-

M

stances were reduced to a very low ebb, the property
of his second wife, who survives him, having been
barely sufficient to maintain them. Subsequently to
this, too, when pecuniary misfortunes were heaped on
him, the estimation in which he was held was evinced
by a private subscription being voluntarily entered
into among his old friends and acquaintances, and
others who had had opportunities of appreciating his
value, by which a considerable and very acceptable sum
was raised for his benefit. To the rest of his misfortunes
was added the death of his younger son, Mr Frederick
Slight, late Secretary to the London, Brighton and South-
Coast Railway Company (his elder son, Samuel, having
died some years previously). His death took place on
Sunday evening, at his residence in Upper Brunswick
Place, aged 77. Few men have had talents and opportunities for achieving what Mr Slight has done in the
course of a long life, and few, perhaps, have received
less in the way of pecuniary reward; and no one
who remembers what Brighton was fifty years ago, as
compared with what it was fifteen years since, and
who recollect the share which was taken by him
in effecting its improvements during that time (the
details of which would exceed the limits of the present
notice), can fail to be grateful to his memory for his
persevering efforts to render this town one of the most
favoured and famous of the places of public resort in the
kingdom."

The first Petty Sessions of Magistrates was held in
September, 1812, at the Old Ship Hotel,—Mr Serjeant
Runnington being the Chairman. They were next
removed in 1822 to the New Inn Tavern, now the
Clarence Hotel; afterwards to the Sea House Hotel;
and subsequently to the new Town Hall, the first stone
of which was laid by Thos. Read Kemp, Esq., in the
year 1830, and the first public ball after its opening was a

Fancy Dress. All Magisterial business prior to the establishment of the Petty Sessions was transacted at Lewes, to the serious inconvenience of those persons who required such aid and assistance. And at a Vestry Meeting, held in 1796, it was resolved that all vagrants and beggars were to be apprehended by the Town Crier, who was to receive 1s. per head for their capture, and whose duty was to carry the same to Lewes for incarceration, and many were the jovial outings in consequence by the "Marmaduke Magog" of the period and his friends (at the parish expense) in carrying out the raid made upon the delinquents who were included in the category of this imperious decree. Mr Serjeant Runnington, before spoken of, acquired some notoriety on the celebration of the 5th of November in 1817, having, in conjunction with the High Constable (Mr Williams, of the Baths), and Mr White, of Castle Square, taken the unwise step of calling out the Military to stay the usual annual demonstration on the Steine. A portion of a Foot Regiment that had arrived in the town from a long march, *en route* from the disturbed manufacturing districts, the same evening,—many of whom had retired to rest, were called out and ordered to charge the mob, after the Riot Act had been read, which they accordingly did, and Thomas Rowles, one of the Headboroughs, was run through by a bayonet and unfortunately killed. An inquest on the deceased commenced, at the King and Queen Inn, on the following day, and was continued for a fortnight, the jury eventually returning a verdict of "Wilful Murder" against the parties implicated, but they were acquitted at the Assizes following. Serjeant Runnington died a few years afterwards and was interred in Preston Churchyard in the presence of a large concourse of persons.

This occurrence was the subject of some cleverly-written verses, by Thomas Herbert, entitled "The Battle of the Tar Tub," lampooning the persons concerned in this sad affair.

It is generally admitted that the introduction of the Charter of Incorporation has proved beneficial to the interests of the town, although taxation will doubtless increase from the great outlay consequent on its requirements being carried out. One of its most extensive works, now in progress, is the great sewer, commencing at Old Hove Street and terminating at its outlet at Portobello, a distance of upwards of seven miles, which will, it is estimated, cost about £80,000, the greater portion of such outlay falling upon this town. This work is being constructed by Mr Matthew J. Jennings, an eminent contractor, who has had great experience in public works,—both at home and abroad. The section drainage of the town, now being completed, will cost £102,500. Street improvements, recently carried out, cost £71,000,—£18,000 of the latter sum being devoted to the improvement of the King's Road and its esplanade. During the past year local taxation has amounted to 5s. 4d. in the £ (the rateable value of the property, according to the present poor-rate assessment, being £410,834 16s.); not an excessive sum when we take into consideration the large sums of money that have been borrowed both by the Town Council and the Guardians. The Corporation debt amounts in the whole to upwards of a quarter of a million pounds, inclusive of the debt of the late Commissioners and the purchase of the Royal Pavilion and grounds. Among many causes that have operated to give this town the pre-eminence over other watering-places, is the salubrity of the air and healthfulness of the place, also its situation contiguous to the sea; and although the inland parts of this kingdom may more nearly resemble the continent, in the degrees and duration of heat and cold,—although it is true the changes are often sudden and unforeseen,

but not excessive, yet we are constantly refreshed in
summer by a temperate breeze, and have in winter a
warm wind from the sea, which speedily puts an end
to frost and snow. We are totally free from the vapours
of running and the impurities of stagnant waters, the
nearest river being six miles distant,—alike beneficial to
the health and comfort of our inhabitants. Another
advantage may likewise be mentioned, the proximity of
Brighton to the emporium of the world, of which it is
within one hour and a quarter's ride. The railway system
is also so admirably conducted, with both safety and
convenience to its passengers,—under the able supervision
of Samuel Laing, Esq. (the Chairman), and its General
Manager, J. P. Knight, Esq. In order to promote the
accommodation of the eastern part of the town, the late
Directorate constructed a branch line to Kemp Town, the
first turf of the same being turned by the Mayor of the
period (Mr Alderman Martin) on the 17th day of
February, 1866, and completed by him on the 6th of
August, 1869. In honor of the occasion he was presented
by the contractors, Messrs. William and John Pickering,
with a massive silver trowel, bearing thereon a suitable
inscription, in commemoration of the event. This branch
line will prove of the greatest utility to the inhabitants
in the neighbourhood of the Cemeteries and Cavalry
Barracks, when a Station is established in their locality.
The opportunities afforded by the London, Brighton,
and South-Coast Railway Company to the public to visit
adjacent towns and villages on its system cannot be too
highly praised.

Attractions are constantly held out for the gratification of our numerous visitors, who, in the zenith of
the season, on reliable authority number 50,000, a convincing proof that Brighton is a most attractive place of
resort. Its capabilities are so extensive that double the
above number might be accommodated, and its Hotels can

vie with any in the kingdom, both for the admirable manner in which they are conducted and the provision made for the comfort of guests. The largest and most extensive of these is The Grand Hotel, a noble building on the western sea frontage,—King's Road. An engraving of this really elegant hotel is here inserted and will illustrate the great extent of its resources.

Brighton was enfranchised under the Reform Act of 1832; the first election of Members to represent the same took place on the 11th and 12th of December of that year; and the Members returned were Isaac Newton Wigney, Esq., and George Faithfull, Esq.; the present Members are James White, Esq., and Henry Fawcett, Esq. The Parliamentary Borough includes Hove, but by the provisions of the recent Reform Act of 1868, the Parish of Preston has been annexed thereunto.

Preston is a pretty suburb of Brighton, pleasantly situated; the high road to London passes through it, and on each side are erected spacious villas, to which attractive grounds are attached. Recently a station has been opened, and it has proved of great convenience to those who reside there. Buildings are being rapidly added, more especially in the district of Prestonville. At Preston Place, lately in the occupation of Wm. Stanford, Esq., Anne of Cleves, the unfortunate consort of Henry VIII., once resided, and here formerly might be seen a large portrait of this unhappy lady. From Preston Place she retired to a Convent at Falmer, where she died. This Convent was converted into the farm-house now adjoining the Church, and is occupied by R. R. Verrall, Esq.

The population of the Parliamentary Borough of Brighton, which now includes the parishes of Hove and Preston, numbers 103,760, (this town comprising 90,013 of the number,) and the register of voters for the same amounts to 9,626. Of these 8,700 have qualified for Brighton, 683 for Hove, and 243 for Preston, and we

THE GRAND HOTEL KINGS ROAD BRIGHTON

think the time will arrive when these parishes must
be united to the Municipal Borough, as it is obvious
that by such annexation advantages would accrue which
cannot be obtained under differently-constituted authorities.
One disadvantage especially connected with the administration of justice calls for immediate remedy, viz.: the
cases that arise in Hove, if a committal takes place
from the Hove Bench of Magistrates, are sent to Lewes,
there to await trial at the Quarter Sessions for the
Eastern Division of the County, thereby incurring a large
outlay of time and money, by reason of the distance
being greater; whereas, if Hove was incorporated with
this Borough, prisoners might be tried at its Quarter
Sessions in Brighton, thus obviating the inconvenience
and extra expense consequent upon witnesses' attendance
at Lewes. The ill-effects of a divided jurisdiction
are also very glaring with respect to hackney carriages, the drivers of such not being amenable for over-
charging when hired from the stand to go out of the
parishes for which they are licensed, either Bench of Magistrates not being able to adjudicate in such cases. Other
benefits might be pointed out, but we feel that our neighbours in Hove will, on the score of taxation, object to
this step being taken, though perhaps, in the course of
time, matters in this respect will be assimilated; but, if
otherwise, the benefit of the common weal should pre-
ponderate over all other considerations, as, without doubt,
Hove is an integral part of this town, enjoying a common
benefit therewith.

The Mayor and Corporation, in furthering all
improvements, assist materially the development and
advancement of the town, thus making it in reality the
"Queen of watering places" and London super-mare.
The Corporate body have recently resolved to pay £7,000
towards the Aquarium now in progress, which when
completed, coupled with the new road southward of the

same, will still further improve our sea-frontage. It is also in contemplation to extend the road to Kemp Town, which will resemble somewhat the Rotton Row of the metropolis and also form an agreeable resort for invalids, &c., especially during the winter months, when, from its salubrious position, it may be likened to the Undercliff of the Isle of Wight. On completion this work will prove a most advantageous and attractive one for the town generally, the eastern portion of it in particular.

The following gentlemen have filled the important office of Chief Magistrate, viz. :—

1854—Lieut.-Col. Fawcett.	1862—Richard Wilson, Esq.
1855—William Hallett, Esq.	1863—Jno. L. Brigden, Esq.
1856—Isaac Gray Bass, Esq.	1864—Jno. L. Brigden, Esq.
1857—Jno. Cordy Burrows, Esq.	1865—Henry Martin, Esq.
1858—Jno. Cordy Burrows, Esq.	1866—William Hallett, Esq.
1859—William Alger, Esq.	1867—William Hallett, Esq.
1860—William Alger, Esq.	1868—Thomas Lester, Esq.
1861—Henry Smithers, Esq.	1869—Arthur H. Cox, Esq.

1870—Richard Mallam Webb, Esq

On the incorporation of this town, the following gentlemen were selected by the Town Council to be submitted to the Lord Chancellor for approval by him as Magistrates for the Borough, and eight of them were appointed by that functionary :—

I. G. Bass, Esq.,	D. M. Folkard, Esq.,
J. Cordy Burrows, Esq ,	W. Furner, Esq.,
W. Catt, Esq.,	E. M. Philipps, Esq.,
W. Coningham, Esq.,	M. D. Scott, Esq.,
Jno. Fawcett, Esq.,	T. Warner, Esq.

These were afterwards supplemented by F. A. Argles, Esq., and W. F. Smithe, Esq., thus forming the first Bench of Magistrates for the Borough under its Incorporation.

The rapid increase of population and extent of Brighton can compare with any town of modern growth, in proof of this we may state that on the first census taken in 1801 the population numbered but 7,514, whilst the census of the present year shows an increase over this number of 82,499, making the total, as before stated, 90,013.

TOWNS AND VILLAGES OF INTEREST IN THE NEIGHBOURHOOD OF BRIGHTON.

(CLOSING CHAPTER.)

In concluding this work we have thought it not out of place to devote a chapter to towns and villages within twelve miles of Brighton, and we trust our brief historical account of them will interest our readers,—the first claiming our notice is the ancient town of

LEWES.

Large, populous, of great antiquity, situated about fifty miles from the metropolis, and eight from Brighton. Here is its etymology:—"Lewes has been thought to come from the French *Les eaux*, the waters; and the latest invention of a meaning for it is Ljod hus — pronounced lodge hus—a landing place: and it is argued therefrom that Lewes was once a seaport, and was settled by Norsemen, as it is a Norse name. Lewes is, however, nothing whatsoever of the kind; it is a pure Celtic name, still pronounced exactly right, and as it must have been two thousand years ago. It is Lle wysg: the river place, or place on the wysg, or uisge, — that is, the Ouse, as the river is still called. There is the fellow-name to Lewes in Wales. A little distance above Hay, in Radnorshire, is Lowes, on the River Wye; Wye is short for Wysg. Uisge, or Wysg, forms part of many of the names of places on the Ouse: Ashcombe is the combe of the stream, or uisge; Isfield, is Uisge, and the Anglo-Saxon field, or Celtic faes, meaning the same thing. Uckfield is the same. Buxted is Ben ux, or uisge: the place on the river; stead is the Anglo-Saxon for a place.

Hastingford is Uisge or Is; tynn, valley; fford, a way or passage: the river valley crossing. Swanboro is from Uisge and Afon, both meaning a river or stream, and byrrhos, a low meadow, or the Anglo-Saxon burgh. Iford and Itford are both the river crossing. Upper Rise is from Yr uisge, the river: Northease is North uisge; and Southease South uisge; Asham is uisge and the Anglo-Saxon ham, a town. Piddinghoe is Pen dwyn—the bank place—and the Anglo-Saxon or Danish hooc, a little rise." *

We find it recorded that in Lewes Athelstan established two Mint-houses, also that it was the chief town and mart in this shire, and is mentioned in the King's ordinance for prohibiting the coinage of money except in towns of especial note.

Here is an interesting relic of the past in relation to the Mint and other matters,—"During the Reign of the Saxons, King Athelstan, after he had repair'd divers Monasteries, and endow'd them with divers Privileges, Lands and Reliques, betook himself to such Methods by which he might also beautify and advantage the Cities and Towns of his Kingdom; and to that End made a Law, that no Money should be coin'd but in Cities and Towns only, and among others appointed two Mint-houses to be set up here. When in the reign of William the Norman, Domesday-Book was compos'd, it is there observ'd, that this Town, in the Reign of King Edward the Confessor, paid 6l. 4s. for Tax and Toll, and that the King had here 127 burgesses. It was also their Custom, that if the King had a Mind to send his Soldiers to Sea without them, of all of them, whosoever the Lands were, there should be collected 20s. to be given to those that served the Ships. That whoever sold an Horse in the Borough should give the Provost one Penny, and the

---

* For this quotation we are indebted to an able article in the *Brighton Herald* of some time since.

Buyer another ; for an Ox or Cow an Half-penny, and for
a Man four Pence, wheresoever in the Rape he buys ; that
he that sheds Blood should pay 7s. and he that commits
Adultery or a Rape 8s. 4d. and the Woman as much, and
the King should have the Adulterer, and the Archbishop
the Woman ; that when Money was new-made, every
Mint-master should pay 20s. Of all these payments, two
Parts went to the King, and a third to the Earl."

Lewes is situated on the banks of the Ouse, within six
or seven miles of the sea. It is included in the Hundred of
Swanborough and Rape of Lewes, and possesses a Castle,
which was formerly the residence of the Lords of Lewes, and
at one time the citadel of the town, until the failure of the
male line of the De Warrennes, in 1347, when it became
the property of the Earl of Arundel, and was allowed to
decay. Originally an oblong fortification guarded by
two keeps or fortresses,—these on artificial mounts. Of
the eastern keep scarcely a vestige remains, and other
portions of this once famous building are fast succumbing
to the ravages of time. The Castle in the days of ancient
warfare might have been considered almost impregnable,
but the war engines now in use would speedily raze it to
the ground, an opinion ratified by that illustrious warrior
and great military authority, Sir Hope Grant, whilst in
company with the author of this work, upon the Castle's
summit, — the early part of the present year, — both
spectators of the picturesque scenery surrounding.

Under the Saxons, Lewes Castle flourished, and gave
the title of Earl to its possessor, and the only case
analogous hereunto, we believe, is that of Arundel Castle,
which gives the same privilege to its owner,—this latter
feudal right being still in existence. The double gateway
leading into the Castle is of mixed architecture, and the
inner arch has every appearance of Saxon origin, whilst
the outer is, probably, of the more modern style,
somewhat resembling that of Henry III.

Lewes is a borough by prescription, and has, since the 23rd of Edward I., sent two members to Parliament; but by the operation of the Reform Act of 1868 was deprived of a seat. The last representatives were the Hon. Henry Brand and Lord Pelham: the former resigned his pretensions in favour of His Lordship, who now remains the sitting member. There are two Constables for the Borough; these are chosen at the annual Court Leet, and act as Returning Officers. Lewes has, at present, seven parish churches—formerly it had twelve,—including those attached to the suburbs of Southover and the Cliff, although the number has been reduced to the following, viz. :- -St. Michaels', St. John's-sub-Castro, St. John's (Southover), South Malling, St. Mary's, Westover (commonly called St. Ann's), St. Thomas-in-the-Cliffe, and All Saints.

Upon what is called Spittal Hill, about a mile west of the town, Lewes has a capital Race Course. A commodious Stand was built by subscription in 1772,—and recently another, upon a more extensive scale, has been erected. Races take place here on the two days following those of Brighton,—under the able superintendence of J. F. Verrall, Esq., the much esteemed Clerk of the Course and Manager,—and excellent sport is afforded.

This Spittal Hill was the scene of the memorable battle of Lewes, fought on the 12th of May, 1264, between the forces of Henry III. and the army of the Barons, the latter headed by Simon de Montfort (Earl of Leicester). Henry was worsted in the fight, and, together with the King of the Romans,—who fought on his side, —and several nobles, taken captive, and incarcerated in the Priory. The royal army, on the morning of the battle, was divided into three bodies,—that on the right under the command of Prince Edward; the King of the Romans commanded the left wing; and Henry in person the main body. The Baron's army was divided into four bodies ;—the first led by Henry de Montfort (the Earl of Leicester's son) ; the Earl of Gloucester commanded the second ; the Earl of Leicester the third ; and the fourth army, which consisted of Londoners, was commanded by Nicholas Segrave.

Prince Edward began the fight,—attacking the Londoners, who, being unable to withstand his vigorous onslaught, immediately fled. A London mob had some time previously insulted the Queen, his mother, an affront which the Prince resolved on avenging, and the moment being opportune, he, flushed with his success, pursued the London troops for four miles, and gave them no quarter. On his return in triumph, to his amazement he found the Royal army dispersed, and discovered that Henry and the Roman King were prisoners. He resolved on the attempt to liberate them,—but his exhausted troops would not second his ardour, and he was compelled to accept mortifying terms from the conquerors, viz., that himself and Henry his cousin should remain as hostages in custody of the Barons until all their differences were settled by authority of Parliament.

Of the fight at Lewes,—during Edward's pursuit of the Londoners, it is related that the Earls of Leicester and Gloucester gained advantage over Henry III. and the Roman King, and put to flight their troops. Henry surrendered to the Earl of Leicester ; Richard to the Earl of Gloucester, and both were conducted to the Priory in Lewes, situated at the foot of the Castle, and there imprisoned.

An eminence near the Race Course,—formerly used as a beacon,—has from the above memorable battle retained the name of " Mount Harry,"—and most of the slain were interred in large pits or burgs near the spot, evidence thereof being still traceable. About eighty years ago, as workmen were making the turnpike road from Lewes to

Brighton, they dug into one of these pits, and exhumed a great quantity of human bones.

In the year 1805, whilst preparing the foundation for a new Church, at Lewes, it became necessary to disturb a leaden coffin containing the remains of one long since committed to earth: after the disinterment, the coffin was opened, and therein lay a perfect skeleton, the leg and thigh bones being covered with myriads of flies, of a species perhaps totally unknown to the naturalist. The spectators of this extraordinary sight were astounded, still more so at the wonderful activity of these singular insects,—in being as strong on the wing as gnats on a summer evening. The wings of this nondescript were white, and, for the sake of distinction, the spectators christened it "the coffin fly." A fleshy moisture still clung to the bones of the occupant of the coffin, and his fallen beard lay on the under jaw. The lead of the coffin had kept perfectly sound, presenting not the least chink or crevice for the admission of air, and this circumstance increased the wonder of all at the presence in the coffin of such strange companions of the dead.

At Malling, near Lewes, there was at one time a collegiate Church said to be as old as Cadwaller, King of the West Saxons, whose death took place in the year 688. Its patrons were the successive Archbishops of Canterbury, and in 1805, whilst some labourers were levelling a piece of ground near Malling Church, some human skeletons were discovered,—amongst them one much larger than the rest. Curiosity in the workmen led them to ascertain its length, and it proved, by accurate measurement, to be exactly 8ft.

In the early pages of this work allusion is made to the extensive and magnificent Priory erected in Southover by Gundrada and Earl de Warrenne,—but it will be of interest to our readers if we here give an outline of this spacious monastery at its dissolution, after an existence of over 500 years. The last Prior was Robert Crowham, and he, on the 16th November, 1537, surrendered the Priory unto Henry VIII. In the King's book it was valued at £1091 1s. 6d.,—a sum far below its real revenues. The community possessed £2000 per year, an income equal to £13,000 per annum of the present value of money. The destruction of this edifice was entrusted to Thos. Cromwell, who deputed John Portmarus to carry out the same, and he proved a very active agent in the demolition of this Gothic edifice. The following letters will afford some idea of the extent of the buildings, and the savage industry with which they were demolished :—

"March 24th, 1538.
"My Lord,—I humbly commend myself to your Lordship. The last I wrote to your Lordship was the 20th instant, March, by the hands of Mr. Williamson, by which I advertized your Lordship of the length and greatness of this Church and the sale ; how we had begun to pull down the whole to the ground, and what manner of fashion they had used in pulling down. I told your Lordship of a vault on the right hand of the high altar that was borne with four pillars, having about five chapels, which were compassed with the vaults, 70 steps in length, that is 210 feet. All this is down Thursday and Friday last. Now we are pulling down a higher vault, borne up by four thick and lofty pillars, 14 feet from side to side, in circumference 45 feet. This shall be done for our second week. As it goes forward I shall advertize your Lordship from time to time. And that your Lordship may know with how many men we have done this, we brought from London 17 men, three carpenters, two smiths, two plumbers, and one that keeps the furnace. Every one of these keeps to his own office. Ten of them hew the walls, among which are three carpenters, these make props to underset when the

others cut away. The others cut the walls. These are men exercised much better than the men we find here in the country, wherefore we must have men, and other things also that we need of, the which I shall, in a few days, shew your Lordship by month. They began to cast the lead, and it shall be done with as much diligence and saving as it may be. So as our trust is, that your Lordship will be much satisfied with what we do, when I most heartily commend myself, much desiring God to maintain your health and your heart's ease.

" Your Lordship's Servant,

" JOHN PORTMARUS."

" Underneath your Lordship shall see a just measure of the wide Abbey ;—

" Length of the Church 150 feet; height 68 ; the circumference 1558 feet ; the wall of the front ten feet; thickness of the steeple wall ten feet ; thickness of the walls in torno four feet.

" There be in the church 32 pillors standing equally from the walls ; a high roof made for the bells; eight pillors' very high, 13 feet thick ; and 45 feet about. The height of the greatest sort is 42 feet, other 28 feet.

" The height of the roof before the great altar is 93 feet ; in the middle of the church where the bells did hang, 105 feet ; the height of the steeple in front is 90 feet."

Thus, after this structure had stood 460 years, its sacred walls now echoed to the strokes of the hammer, instead of the chanting of hymns ; and a few crumbling ruins are all that the curious traveller can now discover of that once celebrated scene of monkish splendour and piety. The ashes of its noble founders and benefactors were insulted and scattered : its fairest monuments wantonly destroyed ;

and the stable or cottage rudely ornamented with the fragments of its grandeur.

After the completion of this work of destruction, Cromwell was created Earl of Essex, and received a grant of the manor of Southover. This nobleman was formerly a blacksmith's son, and was born at Putney.

The site of the Priory is now called the Lord's Place, and formerly the Earl of Dorset had a mansion here, which was burnt down 130 years ago. The building adjoined the church yard, near to which stood the great church of St. Pancras, and the other buildings of the Priory. Here also were the remains of a large elliptical oven, 17 feet wide at the mouth, and vestiges of two subterraneous passages, now choked up with filth, which are supposed to have been applied to the use of aqueducts or sewers.

Of the Priory gate there is still enough to give an idea of the grand and expensive style of architecture which this wealthy community affected in all their buildings. It consisted of Caen stone and Sussex marble, adorned with nail-headed quarterfoils, and other ornaments, in the best style of the 15th century.

In the Chapter-house were monuments of the founder, his wife and son, bearing date 1085; of William, Earl of Moreton and Surrey, 1240; of his great nephew, 1379, and doubtless others of the family. As already mentioned the remains of Gundrada and her husband, Earl de Warrenne, were exhumed on excavating for the railway, and these remains were re-interred in Southover Church. A journey to these interesting ruins of a former magnificent structure would amply reward both antiquarian and visitor.

This Priory formerly covered a space of 40 acres, and was inclosed with a stone wall of considerable height. Within this inclosure, or rather fortification, stood these extensive buildings, among which was a water-mill, that was supplied with water from the Cockshut Stream, also

N

from another spring, a subterraneous water course, which may still be traced to the head of the pool, and was formerly the reservoir of the mill on the north side of Pigeon-house Croft.

The Pigeon-house, though clearly another monument of monkish wealth and luxury, was probably one of the last of their labours, and had not been erected many years before the dissolution of the Priory. It was built in the form of a cross, and still discovers much ingenuity and labour in the construction of the pigeon-holes, which are all of hewn chalk stone. These holes were numbered considerably above 8000. The flight of pigeons which such a dove-house must have contained impoverished the land. To the husbandman they were as sacred as the divinity they typify : conscious of security, they anticipated the sickle from field to field.

These dove-cotes were formerly more numerous, and of much greater extent than at the present time, inasmuch as they were the means of affording fresh food to the owners and occupiers of the land at a period when the gun and chase were the only means of providing it, irrespective of this source, for use in the winter months, as it was the custom to slaughter animals intended for winter consumption in October ; and on the occasion of farms being let, to stipulate conditions as to the number of birds to be sent to the owners from the respective dove-cotes on them. This no doubt was a heavy tax in those days to the tillers of the soil. Dove-cotes were frequently placed in the vicinity of each other,—an instance in this neighbourhood may be adduced : on a farm occupied by Messrs John and Richard Brown, adjacent to Patcham Church (Lord Abergavenny being the owner), may be seen one of these dove-cotes, which has existed for centuries, the holes of which are of hewn chalk stone ; and another similar in character formerly existed not far from this, and near the site on which is erected the new Vicarage, occupied by the Rev. John Allen, the Vicar. There are instances on record of its being formerly part of the agreement, on the letting of farms situated near the sea, for tenants to send to their respective owners, during the season, a crock or two of potted wheat-ears,—called by many the English ortolan. These birds annually visit our shores in Sussex; they were formerly much more numerous than at the present time, and may be seen on the hills near Brighton *en route* to Lewes *via* Newmarket Hill,—a most beautiful and diversified prospect. The season for them is the autumn, and in the old coaching times the heat of the weather would scarcely allow this delicate creature to be carried fresh to London, unless taken alive. They are about the size of larks, but lighter brown, and have more white in their feathers; the rump and the lower part of the tail are white, the upper half black, the under side of the body white, tinged with yellow, the neck inclining to red, the quill feathers black edged with brown. They arrive in England about the middle of July (the females a fortnight before the male), grow fat in August, and disappear in September. They frequent the Downs for a certain fly which breeds among the wild thyme and other herbs thereon. Being very timid birds the motion of a cloud will drive them for shelter into holes in the ground.

The manner in which these birds are deprived of liberty and life is simply thus :—The shepherds, while they attend their flocks on the hills, cut sods of earth; each trench is as long as a middle-sized man's leg, and as wide at the top as the smaller part thereof, inclining towards the bottom nearly to an angle. These sods they lay carefully on the turf side across, and not far from the left corner of the lower part of the trench. Open to the top of the trench, and crossways, another turf not so long but wider, is cut out in like manner, and laid with the bottom upwards, across and over the near part of the trench (that is close up with the communication part), and underneath the latter turf, upon a small flat stick that lies

across, hang two horse-hair nooses ; the victims, timid by
nature to the last degree, and with the view of shunning
even the shadows of passing clouds upon the grass, hop
along the angular cut at the bottom of the trench, which
is several inches deep, and are snared in passing under
the fatal covering. These traps, ranged in great numbers,
—at equal distances, though several yards asunder,—along
the ridges of the Downs, look not much unlike small
artillery; and their form, being in the rude shape of a cross,
might, in ancient times, have been adopted by direction of the Romish priests, to supply the shepherds and
way-faring travellers with frequent objects of devotion.
At stated times in the day, the snarers go round and
collect their captives. When the season is over they put
their sods in their former places ; and time, that grand
restorer as well as destroyer, cures all.

The old County Gaol is situated in the centre of the
town of Lewes, but has for many years ceased to be the
prison-house of criminals. During the Crimean war it
was occupied by Russian prisoners, who were visited by
hundreds of persons, many of whom became purchasers
from them of their skilfully-made boxes, puzzles,
&c., fashioned from wood during their bondage. The
Gaol is now used as a Naval Prison.

The New Gaol, erected a few years since, is of an
extensive character. It is situated at the western entrance
of Lewes, on the turnpike road from Brighton. Towards
its erection Brighton contributed a large quota, a short
time since entering into an agreement with the authorities
to maintain its prisoners for a number of years, whether
under committal or otherwise. The Assizes are held at
the County Hall—a conspicuous structure in the heart of
the town.

It will not be out of place here to mention that
Lewes is the centre of a good hunting district and within
three miles of the kennels of the South Down Foxhounds,

at Ringmer ; respecting the establishment of these hounds
we publish a copy of the original document in relation
thereto, which we have obtained since the chapter on
racing and hunting was written. For this we are indebted
to the kindness of W. C. Tamplin, Esq., the respected
Treasurer to the Brighton Hunt, and hereto append the
same :—

(CIRCULAR.)

" It being proposed to establish a Pack of
Fox Hounds by Subscription in the Eastern part of
Sussex (extending from the Shoreham River to the
neighbourhood of Eastbourne, Hailsham, and Hellingly)
of which Major Cator has undertaken the management,
the following Gentlemen have formed themselves into a
Committee, to carry the above intention into effect."

> Viscount Gage.
> W. Campion, Esq. (of Danny.)
> C. C. Cavendish, Esq.
> Capt. Shiffner.
> H. Campion, Esq.

——o——

My Dear Sir,—I send you the proceedings of the temporary
Committee. I meant to have asked you to be one of them, but
I always forgot to do so when I saw you, and we had delayed
so long in sending anything round to the country that it was
thought better to form the present one, and hereafter it may be
thought advisable to call a meeting of the subscribers and let them
appoint a permanent one.

I shall be obliged to you if you will make out a List of Names
in your neighbourhood to whom it would be proper to send the
Circular.

You will perceive I have put you down as a 25 guinea subscriber.
I do not know if I have done justice to you in it, but I consider what
you do equal to that.

I wish to get the Hounds in next week. I should be obliged to you if you would collect those in your neighbourhood, and if you let me know where to send for them or come for them I will do so.

I think we shall have a pretty good lot of Foxes.

> Believe me,
> My dear Sir,
> Yours very faithfully,

Ringmer, 14th August, 1821.   WILLIAM CATOR.

———

Lewes, 1821.

I am directed by the Committee to forward to you a list of Subscribers, and to request the favour of you, to grant permission for the Hounds to hunt your country; and further to acquaint me if it is your pleasure to become a subscriber, in support of the Establishment.

* I am directed also to inform you, that this application for your country is with the concurrence of Col. Wyndham.

> I have the honour to be,
> Your most obedient, humble Servant,

WILLIAM NEWMAN, Secretary.

———0———

PRESENT SUBSCRIBERS.

	Guineas.		Guineas.
Lord Gage	100	Troop of Artillery	25
C. C. Cavendish, Esq.	50	H. Campion, Esq.	10
Captain Shiffner, R.N	25	Reverend P. Crofts	10
W. Campion, Esq., of Danny..	25	Charles Craven, Esq.	10
Reverend W. Courthope	25	J. M. Goble, Esq.	10
Robert Todd, Esq.	25	—— Russell, Esq.	10
King Sampson, Esq.	25	James Eyre, Esq.	10
Henry Doughty, Esq.	25	T. Hobson, Esq.	10

SUBSCRIPTIONS to be paid into the hands of Messrs HURLY and Co., Lewes Bank; or Sir JAMES ESDAIL and Co., London; half immediately (being due on the 25th of March) the other half to be paid on the 29th of September.

---

* This paragraph is only sent to the neighbourhood of the Shoreham River.

WORTHING AND NEIGHBOURHOOD.

We now give a brief description of Worthing,—called in Domesday Book " Wordinges." It is a very pleasant town and watering-place, about eleven miles distance to the west of Brighton. In the reign of Edward III. this place must have been of some importance, it being on record that at that time Sir Thomas Hoo, Knight,—whose seat was at Hoo, in Bedfordshire,—was Lord of the Manor, and obtained a grant for a market to be held every Tuesday, and an annual fair to be held on the 20th, 21st, and 22nd July, the latter the eve, day, and morrow of St. Magdalene. From these circumstances we presume Worthing to have been, in the past, an important town,— otherwise a market and an annual fair of three days would not have been deemed necessary. We cannot discover when these Institutions were abolished,—but it must have been many years since.

Sir William Hoo,—a descendant of the before-named Knight, deserved so well of King Henry VI.,—by his suppression of a rebellion in Normandy and for his services in the wars with France, that that King, in reward, advanced him to the dignity of a Baron of this realm, by the title of Lord Hoo and Hastings in this county, the title to descend to heirs male of his body lawfully begotten. The year following his succession to the title he was summoned to Parliament to take his seat among the Barons, and continued in the enjoyment of his honors and title until the 31st of Henry VI., when his death is supposed to have taken place. On his decease he left to the Abbot and Convent of Battle, in this county, 80 marks per annum, a proviso in the gift being that two monks should, at the altar of St. Benigni, perpetually sing for the saving of his soul and those of his ancestors.

In all probability the encroachments of the sea in the past very materially contributed to the reduction of Worthing and the number of its inhabitants, as it is stated that within the last century houses stood whereon what is now known as low water mark, and which are supposed to have been washed away by the inroads of the sea.

The Government of the town is under the jurisdiction of a High Constable and officers, appointed at an annual Court Leet holden for that purpose, and the town affairs are well regulated, offering every inducement to its numerous visitors. The country in its neighbourhood is varied and very attractive, and the drives are unsurpassed by any in the kingdom. Within a short distance of the town is High Down Hill, and from here there is a delightful prospect of land and sea: the hill can be plainly seen from Brighton, and serves as a landmark to navigators.

On the hillside is what is known as "The Miller's Tomb,"—it is surrounded by a railing; at each corner a yew tree is planted. There is an inscription upon the tomb which certifies that it was erected in the year 1766 by John Olliver, miller,—for the reception of his body after death. On the slab of the tomb appears these quotations from Scripture :—

For as in Adam all die, even so in CHRIST shall all be made alive,— 2 *Cor.* xv. 22.

For the law was given by Moses, but grace and truth came by JESUS CHRIST.—*St. John* i. 17.

That whosoever believeth in Him should not perish, but have eternal life.—*St. John* iii. 15.

Wherefore I perceive that there is nothing better than that a man should rejoice in his own works; for that is his portion; for who shall bring him to see what shall be after him.—*Eccles.* iii. 22.

Knowing that shortly I must put off this tabernacle, even as our LORD JESUS CHRIST hath shewed me.—2 *Pet.* i. 24.

On the eastern end of the tomb is engraven the following, almost obliterated by the hand of time :—

Why should my fancy any one offend,
Whose good or ill on it does not depend ;
'Tis at my own expense except the land
(A gen'rous grant) on which my tomb doth stand ;
This is the only spot that I have chose,
Wherein to take my lasting—long repose,
Here, in the dust, my body lieth down :
You'll say it is not consecrated ground :
I grant the same; but where shall we e'er find
The spot that e'er can purify the mind ;
Nor to the body any lustre give ;
This more depends on what a'life we live.
When the trumpet shall begin to sound,
'Twill not avail thee where the body's found.

A MORAL.

Blessed are they, and only they,
  Who in the Lord their Saviour die ;
Their bodies wait *redemption's* day,
  And sleep in peace where'er they lie.

The western end bears the following :—

Death! why so fast? pray stop your hand,
And let my glass run out its sand :
As neither Death nor Time will stay,
Let us improve the present day.

Why start you at that skeleton ?
'Tis your own picture which you shun :
Alive it did resemble thee ;
And thou, when dead, like that shall be.

But though Death must have his will,
  Yet old Time prolongs the date,
Till the measure we shall fill,
  That's allotted us by fate.
When that's done, then Time and Death
Both agree to take our breath.

The Scripture sentences were selected by Mr Olliver, and the verses are the production of his muse. About ten yards from the tomb a variety of flowering shrubs were planted, and an alcove existed, whereon Death's heads were painted. In this retreat the miller, during his life, spent most of his leisure hours. We here mention another circumstance expressive of the whimsical disposition of this extraordinary character : he had, some years previous to his death, prepared a coffin, on which were inscribed the words,, *memento mori;* it run upon castors, and was every night wheeled under the bed of its intended possessor. Mr Olliver's residence was about a quarter of a mile from the tomb, on the declivity of the hill. Near the miller's house, in a tree, was fixed a curious piece of machinery (the production of his own hands) representing an old woman and her dog endeavouring to rescue a smuggler from a custom-house officer. The figures were formerly put in action by four sweeps, like those of a mill, and turned by the wind; but eventually they became so much out of repair, that only one had any motion.

Mr. Oliver's remains were committed to this tomb May 1, 1793, in the presence of above 3000 spectators. The body was borne from his house to the place of interment by eight men dressed in white ; and the funeral service, according to the rites of the Church of England, and also a sermon, adapted to the occasion, were read by a girl of twelve years of age. Mr. Oliver died in his 84th year.

Here let us remark that this novel mode of interment, unconnected with any religious establishment, was not without an imitation, inasmuch as there lies buried in a small piece of ground belonging to the mill, on the west side of and near to the station at Worthing, the bodies of Thomas Moore, his wife and two daughters ; the grave is enclosed with iron railings, it is situated within a few feet of the down line to Portsmouth, and passengers by train may see the tombstones erected to the memory of Moore and his family.

In the chancel of Broadwater Church there is a tablet to the memory of Thomas Lord De la Warr, who was of great eminence and employments in the reigns of King Henry VII. and King Henry VIII. By his last will and testament this nobleman bequeathed his body to be buried in a tomb of freestone, appointing also that his executors should bury him according to his honor, ordaining that every poor man and poor woman who attended his corpse to Church should receive twopence, and that his burial expenses should be defrayed by the sale of his collar and chain of gold. To the Church he left his mantle of blue velvet and gown of crimson velvet, the same to be made into altar cloths. Eleanor, his wife, survived him about ten years, and by her will appointed that her body should be buried in the same tomb with that of her husband,—in the chancel of Broadwater Church,—also that a priest should for one year after her decease sing mass for her soul, and receive ten marks from her executors as salary.

BRAMBER.

At Bramber there are the remains of an old castle from which the Rape takes its title. It was built by De Braose, in the reign of William the Conqueror, and history records that an arm of the sea formerly flowed past its walls and onwards as far as Knepp Castle, the seat of Sir Percy Burrell, whose father, the late Sir Charles Merrik Burrell, represented the Rape for many years, attained a very advanced age, and was known as "the father of the House of Commons." At the foot of the Castle nestles the village of Bramber, which returned its representatives to Parliament as early as the reign of Edward I., but was disfranchised under the provisions of the Reform Act of 1832.

The Castle at one period was an immense structure, and in feudal times a powerful barrier. The remnant of this relic of bygone grandeur stands upon a circular elevation, and its former strength and importance may even now be justly estimated by an inspection of the noble ruins. To those fond of exploring the works of former ages, an hour here may be agreeably devoted. It is remarkable that, in Domesday book, (which was begun in 1086, by order of William the Conqueror), the Castle retains its ancient name, for it is there written *Brember Castle.* The rape of Bramber at the conquest was given to William de Braose. The descent of the Castle continued in that family, through successive generations, until October 19, 1672, the 24th of Charles II, when it was restored to Henry Howard, Earl of Norfolk, hereditary Earl Marshal, — this nobleman succeeding his brother as Duke of Norfolk, which title had been dormant for 107 years, owing to the attainder of Thomas Howard, Duke of Norfolk, who was executed on Tower Hill, June 2, 1573, 15th Elizabeth. The Castle and rape of Bramber descended with that of Arundel, in 1819, to Edward Bernard Howard, Duke of Norfolk. It is scarcely to be believed that, so late as the Protectorate of Cromwell, this Castle contained a numerous garrison of the Parliamentary forces.

The rape of Bramber contains thirty-two parishes, extending from Worthing to Shire Mark Mill (which forms the boundaries of Surrey and Sussex, beyond Horsham), north to south, 32 miles. From Edburton to Upper Burpham Farm, east to west, eleven miles. The principal places in this Rape are Old and New Shoreham, Worthing, Horsham, Steyning, &c.

During the summer months, gypsy-parties, picnics, and the like, are common at Bramber Castle, and it is a favourite, much-patronised resort. With scholastic establishments it is a frequent retreat,—the study of books deserted for a peep into the past afforded by this remnant of antiquity. A few years since, it was honoured with a visit from the Sussex Archæological Society, and a paper on "its history" was read on the occasion by Durrant Cooper, Esq. It is certainly one of the prettiest and most sought pleasure retreats in Sussex, and is surrounded with lovely scenery.

There is a Station of the South-Coast Railway at Bramber, about half-a-mile from the town of Steyning, and within a short distance of Shoreham.

LANCING.

Ten miles from Brighton and within two of Worthing, is situated the village of Lancing, which skirts the sea. It contains several lodging houses, also an old-established and excellent scholastic establishment for young gentlemen, conducted by W. W. Pyne, Esq.

This village won the admiration of the late Princess of Wales, — consort of George IV., and here she occasionally resided, and from this place, on the 12th of August, 1814, after a brief sojourn, took her departure for the continent, The Jason frigate, commanded by Capt. King, lay off the town in waiting for the embarkation of Her Royal Highness,—here is a description relating to the latter event and the Princess while at Lancing, :—

On August 2, 1814, the Princess of Wales arrived at Worthing, previous to her departure for the continent. The Jason frigate, commanded by the Hon. Captain King, lay off that town, in waiting for the embarkation of Her Royal Highness. Between that day and the 9th, the Princess came to this village, and walked to the beach, opposite the Horse Shoes Inn, where she would sit for some time on a capstan, which the landlord of the house used to point out with feelings of affectionate veneration. Sometimes her Royal Highness appeared so lost in contemplation, that she required the frequent admonitions of her attendants, warning her to retire on account of her health.

On the 9th of August, a great concourse of people assembled on the Steyne, at Worthing, to witness the departure of the Princess of Wales. Her Royal Highness arrived at the Steyne Hotel, about quarter-past four o'clock on that day, when, the Hon. Captain King not being ready to receive her, she drove off with Lady Charlotte Lindsay, accompanied by another lady, and Austin (her *protége* boy) to this village, apparently wishing to avoid the people who were waiting to see her embark, but all the carriages, horsemen, and numerous pedestrians followed Her Royal Highness to Lancing. The barge of the Jason frigate proceeded thither, but the attendants and domestics of the Princess were taken on board at Worthing.

On the arrival of the Princess of Wales, she waited with some impatience for the barge, which was to bear her to the frigate destined to convey her from Albion's shores. Her Royal Highness was dressed in a dark cloth pelisse, with large gold clasps, and a cap of velvet and green satin, with a green feather,—the Prussian hussar costume. When on board the barge, the Princess kissed her hand to the immense assemblage of ladies, who in return waved their handkerchiefs. The farewell of this illustrious personage was a silent parting, seemingly, as if the spectators intuitively feared that their shouts of affectionate regard might be misconstrued. On quitting the English shores, Her Royal Highness was so much affected that she fainted away and fell in the arms of one of her attendants. This was truly a scene at once solemn and sublime, and the spectators were much concerned thereat.

In the upper portion of this parish there is a College, dedicated to S. Nicholas, established some years since by the Rev. N. Woodard, D.C.L., for the purpose of educating, on moderate terms, boys of the middle class. It is conducted by the Rev. R. E. Sanderson, M.A., who is assisted by other clergymen. Institutions in close relation hereunto have been established at Shoreham, Hurst, and Ardingly in this county.

Lancing is considered by many, from the mildness of its air, to be the " Montpelier" of England. Figs grow in great abundance in this and the adjacent parishes of Sompting and Tarring, and ripen in the open air, such not being always the case in other parts; some years the growth of them is so abundant that the choicest are sold in Brighton at sixpence per dozen, and quantities are forwarded to different parts of the kingdom. This fruit was first introduced into England by St. Thomas à Becket, who resided at Tarring, at what is now called the Rectory House, built upon the site of the Archbishop's Palace. At the present time there is a large fig orchard contiguous to it, consisting of a hundred trees or more, and it has been known to produce in one season upwards of 2,000 dozens of the fruit, and is visited by the beccafico of Italy, a fig-eating bird.

SHOREHAM.

Is about six miles west of Brighton, and is the smallest village in the rape of Bramber, being only 170 acres in extent. It commands the entrance to the river Adur, and is designated " New " to distinguish it from Old Shoreham, a sister village in its vicinity now much decayed. Shoreham possesses a place in history's pages, it being one of the most ancient towns in England. For many centuries it enjoyed great commercial and political importance, and in 452 was the second landing-place of Ella, who defeated the Britons near this spot, and afterwards founded the kingdom of the South Saxons. In the time of Edward I., the town must have been considerable, for in 1298, it sent members to Parliament.

Camden, speaking of this town, says, "Upon the shore is a place, anciently called Score-ham, which, by a little and a little has dwindled into a poor village, now called Old Shoreham, having given rise to another town of the same name, the greater part whereof is ruined and under water, and the commodiousness of its port, by reason of the bank of sand cast up at the mouth of the river, wholly taken away; whereas in former ages, it was wont to carry ships under sail as high as Bramber, a pretty distance from the sea."

A writer of considerable celebrity, in 1762, speaking of Shoreham, says, "It is a town chiefly inhabited by ship chandlers, carpenters, and all the several trades depending upon the building and fitting-up of ships, which is their chief business. Vessels of a large size, some for the use of the navy, but most for the merchant service, are here constructed. The demands of late for these are so great, and the people so industrious, that it is asserted there is sometimes not so much as a single person who receives alms, a circumstance worthy not only of praise, but of imitation. Shoreham is justly noted for seamen, but mostly for neat and stout sea boats. The builders of ships seem to have settled here, chiefly because the quantity and cheapness of timber in the country behind them is favourable to naval architecture. Vessels of 700 tons burthen have been launched from the ship yard of this town; and although the trade of ship-building declined for several years, owing to the badness of its harbour, there is every prospect of its obtaining a return of prosperity upon the completion of the present improvements."

Shoreham Harbour, for magnitude and capacity, stood in high estimation in 1316, the year in which Edward defeated the French at the memorable battle of Cressy. In that expedition, Shoreham sent to sea 26 ships of war, equipped with 82 men each, at the expense of the inhabitants; and which was a greater proportion of vessels than even London and more than any other port in the kingdom,—except Fowey, in Cornwall; Yarmouth, in Norfolk; and Dartmouth, in Devonshire,—at that time was required to furnish.

The Harbour limits include a large portion of the line of bay which extends westward towards Worthing, and to the east as far as Rottingdean,—including Brighton, and nature seems to have fashioned this spot for its present use, its many prominent features and inland curve well adapting it for the great and valuable purpose of protection to our shipping. At spring tides the water rises to the height of 20ft. up the estuary of the river, a depth sufficient for the formation of one of the first depôts in the world for merchant ships or sloops of war. Docks could be constructed on either side of the river,—and the old bridge made subservient to shipping necessities. The Harbour and neighbourhood possess advantages which would prove in every way equal to the requirements of a large proportion of the shipping trade of our country.

In 1760 an Act was obtained for the formation of a new entrance to the Harbour, and the erection of piers and auxiliaries at a spot near Fishersgate. This project was carried into effect, but the works were so badly constructed, and in such an imperfect manner,—

" Somebody blundered,"

that in less than two years the piers became undermined and were washed away. This disaster, it is believed, was due to the shortening, by the pile drivers, of the timbers, which, on examination, were from six to ten feet short of the foundation, hence the tide soon sapped beneath them. Notwithstanding the defective execution of these works, at spring tides there was a depth of 24ft. of water, and at half-

o

flood sufficient for vessels of 200 tons to pass up: whereas, at the present time, vessels of the same burthen can only enter at spring tides.

Owing to the evils above mentioned, the Harbour was almost ruined, so much so that in the year 1816 the proprietors were determined upon its improvement, and, if possible, to make it a mart for commerce, —the adaptability for which we have above shadowed forth. Energetic steps were at once taken for its improvement, and the proprietors, conjointly with the inhabitants of Shoreham, called in the assistance of Mr W. Clegram, who made a survey of the Harbour, and concerted measures for its improvement; thereupon a committee of subscribers was appointed to consider the same, and what steps were necessary for carrying them into execution. W. Chapman, Esq., C.E., on the recommendation of the Honorable Board of Trinity, of Trinity House, also reported on the Harbour, and very forcibly demonstrated the advantages that would result from the projected improvement. The Commissioners under the old Act of Parliament and the Committee of Subscribers thereupon appointed Mr Chapman as Chief Engineer in connection with the new undertaking, and on the passing of the Act of Parliament, in 1817, Mr Clegram was appointed Resident Engineer, and for his eminent services he was afterwards selected to fill the responsible post of Harbour Master. William Wigney, Esq., brewer, of Brighton (father of Mr Isaac Newton Wigney, who was returned as one of the first Members for Brighton, under its enfranchisement by the provisions of the Reform Act of 1832), was one of its principal promoters, and materially assisted the progress of the Bill, exerting himself to the utmost to facilitate the project.

The work was undertaken by contract, and on the 22nd of April, 1817, amidst a great concourse of spectators, the highly-interesting ceremony of driving the first pile took place,—the spectacle enhanced by a full Masonic procession; but the contractors, from want of capital or other causes, delayed progress of the works until the December following, and then abandoned them. Mr Mackintosh, of Bloomsbury Square, London, next entered into arrangements for the completion of the Harbour, successfully carried out the same, and on the 26th of January, 1818, the ceremony of opening took place.

Our readers, from the foregoing statement, will be fully able to appreciate how easily a great national Harbour might here be made, and the incalculable importance such a safe haven would be, at all times, to commerce. When it is considered how frequently, and oft with fatal results, our coasts are visited by storms and gales, more especially between Portsmouth and the Downs or Ramsgate Harbour, also that excepting the Port of Newhaven no place of shelter offers itself to the distressed mariner when weathering a desolating tempest,—it must be seen how much it is an object of national importance that more places of refuge should be created, as there cannot be one harbour too many for the rescue of our sailors from the fury of the waves.

Shoreham is most advantageously situated, in the centre of a bay formed by two headlands, viz., Beachy Head on the east and Selsey to the westward. It possesses every desirable advantage for a safe and commodious haven, the anchorage in the bay is excellent, there are five or ten fathoms of water, and the sea bottom is chiefly of stiff blue clay. The tide at this spot is soon down, nor does it rise very high. The Harbour entrance is about a mile and a quarter to the west of the old one already spoken of as at Fishersgate, and is rendered permanent by the erection of two substantial piers, 60 yards distant from each other. It opens into two spacious arms, one to the eastward towards Brighton, the other

towards Shoreham. These arms, or reaches were
sufficiently capacious (with proper moorings laid down)
to contain a number of vessels of as large as 400 tons
burthen. In order to prevent the formation of a bar at
the entrance to the Harbour, piers were placed at right
angles with the shore, both of equal length, and extending
to near low water mark at spring tides. This extension
of uniform length confines the ebb tide into a narrow
compass until it passes the Pier heads; and there being
but a weak ebb and flow in the bay, the tide will continue
rapidly eastward. The mouth of the Harbour is formed
by two curves, eastward and westward, on which are placed
six dolphins (three on each side); rows of piles are driven
and wattled at the bottom of the slope, and finished
with a facing of chalk: these curves were a wise
invention of the Engineer, as they give the current of the
tide a true and direct course between the two piers, which,
jointly, are not unlike a trumpet-mouth, and thus a
quantity of water is collected and forces itself out
with great rapidity. According to the report of
Mr Chapman, the improvements before enumerated
amounted to £36,432. In this state matters relative
to the Harbour remained till the year 1851, when it
was thought expedient to make considerable alterations, with a view to extend the eastern reach
or arm to the "Wish," near Hove, for the purpose of
bringing it as near Brighton as possible (which
was rapidly extending itself westward), for the convenience of landing coals, &c., and with the desire to
compete with the Railway Company, who had erected a
wharf at Kingston for the same purpose, and were bringing
large quantities of coals into Brighton by railway
transit from thence; also from their wharf at Deptford,
—coals being brought from the north to the Thames by
powerful screw steamers, which thus reduced considerably
the price of that article of daily need. Inland coals

brought direct from the pit's mouth, by railroad, also contributed materially to the latter result.

The river Adur, to which Shoreham Harbour owes its origin, rises at Nuthurst near Horsham, and derives its name from Aweddwr, the running of flowing water. It passes close to the Church of the latter town, and in its course receives a tributary stream from Cowfold and Shipley; it afterwards flows between Beeding and Bramber and onwards by Old Shoreham Church into the port of Shoreham.

In 1781, a wooden bridge was erected over the estuary at this spot at a cost of £5,000, the money raised by a tontine. The river could be forded at low water, and at high tide a ferry-boat was resorted to. Previous to the erection of this bridge, communication between the eastern and western sides of the county was extremely difficult, inconvenient, and frequently dangerous, and the uncertainty of a passage either way induced the greater number of passengers to the western parts of the county to select the circuitous route by the Upper Shoreham Road, via "Bramber Gorge," over Bramber Bridge, onward to Steyning, thence up the Bosthill, and back to Sompting Church (which is within three miles of this bridge, and on a level road). This occasioned a great loss of time, and entailed extra labour for travellers, also other disadvantages, inasmuch as, at this latter point, had the bridge been in existence, more than half the distance could have been saved by passing over it, instead of resorting to the hilly road before mentioned. The tolls payable at the bridge were considerable, and on the expiration of the tontine the bridge reverted to the Duke of Norfolk.

The great inconvenience experienced from the uncertainty of crossing the river during a contested county election which took place at Chichester, about 1774, was the immediate cause of the erection of this bridge,—freeholders from the extreme eastern parts of the county having to travel to the western to record their votes, an enormous expense to the respective candidates, which loudly called for remedy. The ferry tolls were heavy, and the property of the Priory of Hardham.

In 1832, a suspension bridge of truly handsome design, and known as " Norfolk Bridge," was built by Bernard Edward, Duke of Norfolk,—the purpose of its erection being the shortening of the distance to Worthing by the South Lancing route : but in consequence of the incursions of the sea, it has for years failed to realise the object of its founder. Between this bridge and the old tontine bridge before alluded to, the London, Brighton, and South-Coast Railway have constructed one expressly for the passage of their Portsmouth traffic,—this step necessitating the purchase from the Duke of Norfolk of its aged contemporary above.

Shoreham Church is an edifice remarkable for its richness, elegance, and diversity, and may justly be said to present an excellent school for the study of our ancient architecture. This grand and venerable building stands near the entrance of the road from Brighton, and is the remnant of a truly sublime structure; but it has lost a magnificent portion in the nave, only a small part of it remaining, which has been walled up in such a manner, as not only to preserve fragments of what is destroyed, but to save the appearance of an ancient end,—an instance not very common. The present west entrance, — probably the original, is a pointed arch, decorated in every respect with Saxon ornaments, and supported by Saxon capitals. The design is curious, but much mutilated. Over this is a small pointed window, of four or five divisions, not of very early date. The walls of the edifice are Saxon, and the windows, buttresses, &c., of this work remain unusually entire.

The tower, at the intersection of the great cross aisles, is in two stories, and not lofty, the first having two Saxon windows on each side; the second two pointed of the same mouldings, probably built at the same time, surmounted by a block cornice and parapet. On the north and south sides are two handsome flying buttresses, terminated by pinnacles. A great portion of the Saxon work remains; but the north side appears to be less altered. The eastern end is particularly elegant, having three beautifully pointed windows, supported by handsome clustered columns, over three recessed Saxon arches. Under the pediment is a circular window, now blocked up. A small fragment of the western extremity of the nave, surrounded by shrubs, still remains, also the foundations of the intervening walls.

The Choir is a noble specimen of the mixed style of building that prevailed before the dissolution of the Saxon and the introduction of the pointed arch. The capitals which support the arches are various and very artistic. The font is on the north side, near the entrance, of a square form, supported by a stout centre column and four smaller ones at the angles. The upper half of the south transept is separated from the lower, and forms a commodious school-room. The whole edifice is extremely beautiful, but the ornaments not destroyed by white-wash are filled with dirt.

On the south and north sides of this Church are private doors, of a very diminutive size, which communicate with the pulpit and the reading-desk.

This edifice was formerly Collegiate, but is now a vicarage, in the patronage of Magdalene College, Cambridge. Recently an attempt was made to raise funds in support of the restoration of this splendid old Church, and many, both wealthy and others, came forward to help the praiseworthy motive: but we regret to write that, from the indifference and parsimony of some residents who possess the power to assist and should have been foremost in the good work, this effort to restore God's House became fruitless. We know that the hope of its restoration is still cherished by the inhabitants, and trust that so necessary an act in remembrance of the piety and devotion of our ancestors will not long remain in abeyance, and that this fine specimen of early English architecture, which has been in existence for many centuries, will be restored to its former grandeur.

Edward II. founded a Carmelite or White Friars' House opposite the east end of the Church, and some years since the whole edifice and land adjoining were sold to George Irving, Esq., M.P., a London merchant, for £600. He thoroughly renovated and improved the property, gave a noble appearance to the mansion, and named it " Cupola House."

Before concluding this brief history of Shoreham, it will not be amiss to speak of its political character. Like other boroughs, it has not been free from the grossest bribery that could possibly be committed ; and, being a place of some importance, its representation was eagerly sought for by contending parties, more especially as a return might be expected for the outlay they incurred consequent on contested elections, in the shape of a . degree of patronage that exists in seaport towns, viz. :— obtaining from the Government of the day the appointments connected with the Customs, Tide-waiters, &c.,— vacancies supposed to be in the gift of Members representing these boroughs. In Shoreham this kind of patronage was made use of to the greatest extent possible,—we will, therefore, now proceed to speak of this Borough from the earliest period ; not that we consider it in this respect worse than its more fortunate neighbours, but they had the misfortune to have their delinquencies discovered. In this respect the custom of England coincides with the Spartan law: the crime consists not in the committal of the offensive act, but in the awkwardness of keeping it secret,—not in the act itself, but in the discovery of it; and as in Sparta so in

England, the most condign punishment assuredly follows the disclosure.

The right of voting for this Borough was first granetd in the 23rd Edward I. to the inhabitant householders paying scot and lot, whose number, however, was very small, and who appear very early to have addicted themselves to the commission of the crimes for which they afterwards suffered; for we find that on the 26th of February, 1700, certain of the inhabitants petitioned the House and complained that their free right of Election had been invaded. On the 25th of November, in the same year, the inhabitants petitioned against the sitting Member who had treated; and on the 16th of November, 1709, a similar petition was presented from the same persons; but it was not till the year 1771 that the whole of the infamous system pursued in this place was brought to light.

In the latter year, however, the Returning Officer returned a candidate with only 87 votes, instead of another for whom 87 had been tendered, but of which number the Returning Officer had queried 76, and made his return without examining the validity of the votes he had so questioned. Against this return a petition was presented, and the Returning Officer was called to the Bar to answer for his conduct. "It appeared," says Oldfield, "from the defence made by him, that a majority of the freemen of that Borough had formed themselves into a society, under the name of the Christian Club, the apparent ends of which institution were to promote acts of charity and benevolence and to answer such other purposes as were suitable to the import of its name. Under this sanction of piety and religion and the cover of occasional acts of charity, they profaned that sacred name by making it an excuse for carrying on the worst purposes; making a traffic of their oaths and consciences, and setting their Borough to sale to the highest bidder;

while the rest of the Freemen were deprived of every legal benefit from their votes."

The Members of this Society were bound to secrecy and to each other by oaths, by writings, by bonds with large penalties, and by all the ties which could strengthen their compact ; and they carried on this traffic by means of a Select Committee, who, under the pretence of scruples of conscience, never appeared or voted at any election themselves ; but having notwithstanding sold the Borough and received the stipulated price, they gave directions to the rest how to vote, and by this complicated evasion the employers and their agents having fully satisfied their conscience, shared the money without any scruple as soon as the election was over.

The Returning Officer had belonged to this Society, and having taken some disgust to his associates, quitted the party. The majority of legal votes which he objected to, was, he said, in part owing to his experimental knowledge of their corruption, and partly founded upon some improper acts which had come within his knowledge as a Magistrate upon the late Election ; particularly an affidavit of a very considerable sum of money, which had been distributed among them. Upon these grounds, though they had the hardiness to take the oath against bribery and corruption, he looked upon them as disqualified ; and having besides taken the opinion of Counsel, which it seems coincided with his own, he returned the Candidate who had the smaller number of votes, as they were free from these objections.

Upon these principles he rested his plea for the justification of the illegality of his conduct ; but the House thinking that by tolerating such an act of power they would be setting a very bad precedent, the Returning Officer was placed on his knees and reprimanded at the Bar of the House. A further inquiry was afterwards made into the case, the allegations of the Returning Officer were fully proved, and at length a Bill was passed for the correction of the abuses.

This Act, the famous 2nd Geo. III. cap. 55, after reciting that a wicked and corrupt Society, calling itself "The Christian Club," had for several years subsisted in the Borough, and consisted of a great majority of persons having the right to vote ; and that the chief end of that Society appeared to be for the purpose of selling from time to time the seat or seats for that Borough, and that John Burnett and 80 others were members of such Society, it was enacted that the said 81 voters were thenceforth disqualified from ever giving a vote at any Election for Members to serve in Parliament; that the right of voting should thenceforth be exercised by every 40s. Freeholder within the Rape of Bramber, as well as by the Burgesses of New Shoreham.

The right of Election was thereby extended to a body of 1300 Freeholders ; and although a complete check was placed upon the bribery, yet the nomination of the Members became immediately vested in the Duke of Norfolk and the Earl of Egremont, whose large landed possessions in the Rape gave them immense influence. And this was the sort of Reform then held out to the people of England as the only safe, proper and practical species ! ! The substitution of nomination for corruption was the only good which it effected in any of the places where it was tried; and yet this was all the Reform which Englishmen at that period were led to wish for or expect ! ! !

The Norfolk and Egremont interests continued quietly to return the Members till 1808, when they were opposed without success in the son of Sir Cecil Bishop, afterwards Lord De La Zouch. From this time till 1820 these same interests rested secure ; but in the latter year Henry Webster, Esq., endeavoured to open the representation, and determined to stand a contest. Mr John Smith, a Brighton celebrity, supposed that he should be able to make a stand in conjunction with Mr Webster; but on the day of Election he found himself quite unsupported. He could not even obtain a person to put him in nomination; and finally, having nominated himself, no person tendered a vote for him. J. Marten Lloyd, Esq., stood on the Duke of Norfolk's interest; and Sir Charles Merrik Burrell, Bart, was supported by Lord Egremont; and against them was Mr Webster's attack directed. He was however defeated, the numbers at the close of the poll being,—for J. M. Lloyd, Esq., 383; Sir C. M. Burrell, 251; Henry Webster, Esq., 167.

Within the compass of six miles from Shoreham, there were formerly two other borough towns,—viz., Bramber and Steyning, — both disfranchised by the Reform Act of 1832. It is on record that so mercenary were the proceedings connected with the elections for the three boroughs, that more money was expended on them during the reign of George III. than all the land in the parishes was worth at 20 years' purchase. On one of these occasions, the landlord of the Star, at Shoreham, long since deceased (although a " Deadman" when living) boasted that at an election at that time he had made £300 of a pipe of wine. In 1826,—prior to the Reform Bill coming into operation, there was a sharp contest for the Rape of Bramber between Sir C. M. Burrell, Bart., Henry Howard, Esq., and E. B. Sugden, Esq. (afterwards Lord St. Leonards, and High Chancellor of England). The latter gentleman sought the seat vacated by the retirement of Sir J. M. Loyd; but was unsuccessful, — the numbers at the close of the poll being: for Sir C. M. Burrell, 865; Henry Howard, Esq., 545; E. B. Sugden, Esq., 483. Since that period, with but one exception, that of 1857, there has not been a contest worth recording, and on this occasion

Mr Pemberton came forward in the independent interest. At the close of the poll, William Greaves, Esq., High Constable of Shoreham, and the Returning Officer, declared the numbers to be: for Sir Charles Burrell, 994 ; Lord Alexander Lennox, 805 ; and Mr Pemberton, 489.

The Protestant Grammar School of W. H. Harper, Esq., also deserves allusion to,—it has a good reputation, and is one of the best educational establishments in Sussex.

In concluding our chapter on Shoreham, that delightful pleasure seat, the Swiss Gardens, claims our tribute. It is conducted in the most praiseworthy manner by Messrs. Goodchild and Son ; presents as great a variety of amusements as can be met with in any other place of its kind in England ; is patronized by thousands during the summer season; and in the winter is largely attended by ladies and gentlemen for its skating, the frozen lakes being admirably adapted for this healthful and agreeable exercise.

THE DEVIL'S DYKE.

In a north-westerly direction from Brighton, and at about five and a half miles' distance is the well-known Devil's Dyke, a very extensive oval entrenchment, about one mile in circumference, accessible by an inlet to the south. It is fortified by a narrow ditch, the earth thrown inwards, and forming a very high rampart, which is known as "The Poor Man's Wall."

Dr. Tabor, in speaking of this strange birth of nature, said he could not learn whether it had ever had any other name, also that its present one derived its origin from the " wall " having been a security to the distressed Britons : it is even now a valued shelter to shepherds. We find it written that " The Devil's Dyke " is a corruption of *Diphwys dynchel*, *i.e.*, the high and stately precipice.

From the Devil's Dyke the whole Weald of Sussex, adjoining parts of Hampshire, Surrey, and Kent, may be viewed, and the prospects are picturesque and beautiful. On a clear day the scene is truly romantic at this most salubrious spot. Thousands court the Dyke for its scenery, and it is known far and wide as one of the sights of Sussex. The old Dyke House, of which Mr Thacker has been "mine host" for so many years, has recently been re-built, and under his admirable supervision the creature comforts for which it is famed are dispensed with all their known good qualities. In the hunting season the Dyke is a favourite meet of the Brighton Harriers, at which there is a large muster of lovers of the chase, and Host Thacker drives a busy trade.

It is supposed that the Dyke, in early ages, was the scene of a Roman encampment; and it is conjectured that it belonged to the last of the Roman Emperors, from the discovery in the neighbourhood of an urn filled with coins which were current at the period.

The lands in the neighbourhood belong to the Crown. It may not be out of place to mention that the revenue arising from Crown Lands in England is now nearly all subject to Parliament, which provides for the support of the Sovereign and Government. The annual income from these Lands is about £284,500. The revenues from the Duchies of Cornwall and Lancaster belong to the Prince of Wales, and accumulate during his minority. Henry VII. resumed those which had been given to their followers by the Sovereigns of the House of York. The hereditary estates of the Crown were largely bestowed on their courtiers by Sovereigns, especially by the Stuarts.

In the bottom, almost immediately beneath the hill, is the pleasant village of Poynings,—and horsemen frequently select it in their journey homeward, it being situate on a high road leading to Brighton. Poynings, and its neighbour Fulking, are favourite resorts for the inhabitants of this town. Fulking Fair, which takes place annually on Whitsun Tuesday,—its head-quarters being a roadside public house in that village, situated immediately under the hill, and called "The Shepherd and his Dog,"—prior to the opening of the Swiss Gardens, was the resort of a great many Brightonians, who made the Dyke House, *en route*, their rendezvous.

The Dyke, although nothing more than a precipitous valley, formed by the hand of nature, is ascribed to the Prince of Darkness, in whose honour it has been so-called, and here is the old Sussex legend :—

THE DEVIL'S DYKE.

Five hundred years ago or more,
Or if you please, in days of yore ;
That wicked wight y'clept *Old Nick* ;
Renowned for many a wanton trick,
With envy, from the downs, beheld
The studded Churches of the Weald ;
(Here Poynings' Cruciform, and there
Hurst, Albourne, Bolney, Newtimber,
Cuckfield, and more, with towering crest,
Quae nunc praescribere longum est ;
Oft heard the undulating chime
Proclaim around 'twas service time,
"Can I, with common patience, see
These Churches, and not one for me ;
Shall I be cheated of my due
By such a sanctimonious crew?"
He mutter'd twenty things beside ;
And sure *that* night the foaming tide,
Led through a vast and wondrous trench
Should give these pious souls a drench !
Adown the West the Steeds of Day
Hasted merrily away,
And night in solemn pomp came on,
Her lamp her star—a cloud her throne
The lightsome Moon she was not there,
But deck't the other hemisphere.
    Now with a fit capacious spade,
So large, it was on purpose made ;
Old Nick began, with much ado,
To cut the lofty downs in two :

At every lift his spade threw out
A thousand waggon load, no doubt
O! had he labour'd till to-morrow,
His envious work had wrought much sorrow;
The Weald, with verdant beauty grac'd,
O'erwhelmed—a sad and watery waste!
   But so it chanced, a good old dame,
Whose deed has long outliv'd her name,
Wak'd by the cramp, at midnight hour,
Or just escaped the night mare's power,
Rose from her humble bed, when lo!
She heard Nick's *terrible ado*!
And by the star-light, faintly spied
This wicked wight, and dike so wide?
She knew him by his mighty size,
His tail, his horns, his saucer eyes;
And while, with wonderment amaz'd,
At workman and at work she gaz'd,
Swift cross her mind a thought then flew,
That she, by strategem, might do
A deed, which luckily should save
Her country from a watery grave;
By his own weapons fairly beating
The father of all lies and cheating!
   Forth from her casement in a minute,
A sieve, with flaming candle in it,
She held to view:—and simple Nick,
Who ne'er suspecting such a trick,
(All rogues are fools) when first his sight
A full orb'd luminary bright
Beheld—he fled—his work undone—
Scar'd at the sight of a *new Sun;*
And smuttering curses that the day
Should drive him from his work away!
   Night after night, this knowing dame
Watch'd—but again Nick never came!
Who now dare call the action evil
To hold a Candle to the Devil?

"The Brighton fisherman at the Dyke," is a somewhat amusing anecdote. It is told that a fisherman
accompanied a bird-catching party, and, during the time
they were engaged in their pursuits, strolled from
them, lost his way, and eventually found himself at this

romantic spot. Here he was so astonished at the inland
view presented of the weald and adjacent counties that
the scene bewildered him, and he had to solicit the
guidance of a shepherd into the road for Brighton. Both
kindred and neighbours wondered at his non-return with
his companions, and were anxious as to his whereabouts,
he having been absent *many hours*. On the return of the
"lost man" there was much rejoicing, and all assembled
around to hear him relate his adventures,—the more
anxiously from the fact of his exclaiming that "He had
been to the Devil's Dyke." After allaying their amazement
and interrogations as to what sort of place it was,—none of
his listeners having ventured so far,—he concluded with
the somewhat quaint rejoinder, "That he ne'er beleft the
world was half so big afore." The fishermen of bygone
times were remarkable for their love of home, but when
not engaged in fishing they occasionally accompanied bird-
catchers to the hills around old Brighton,—bird catching
being a favorite pursuit of the aborigines,—though it was
a very rare occurrence for them to venture far beyond their
habitations into the country district,—the farthest distance
being the Preston, Hove, and Southwick Fairs, which
were annual events. Even to this day many of their
descendants can be found who have not ventured ten
miles inland.

ALDRINGTON.

Adjacent to Portslade is the so-called parish of
Aldrington, which is within a mile of Hove, and
without an inhabitant. It possesses the ruins of a Church,
—nought but tottering walls,—which stand in the centre
of a meadow field. One small window of early date is
the only noteworthy feature in the remains of this edifice,
the remainder comprising but crumbling walls and a

P

narrow fragment of the Church tower. The living is in the gift of Magdalene College, Cambridge : it is a Rectory, and a sinecure. Mr Dodd was appointed thereto in 1812, and held it until his decease : on his preferment the following comments appeared :—

"On reference to the 'blue book,' containing the 'Report of the Commissioners appointed by Her Majesty to inquire into the Ecclesiastical Revenue of England and Wales, 1835,'—(page 266) we find the Rev. P. S. Dodd reported as being appointed the Rector of this place in 1812. The patron of the parish is Magdalene College, Cambridge. There is 'no dwelling-house.' The Church is 'in ruins.' The annual gross average income is £300, out of which payments were made of £6 a year, leaving Mr Dodd in possession of a net income of £294. Mr Dodd was also Rector of Penshurst in Kent, the patron of which is Sir I. S. Sidney. The population of Penshurst is 1499. It has one Church, which holds 450 persons. This living is a Rectory, to which Mr Dodd was appointed in 1819, and the gross income of it is £820 a year ; yearly payments deducted, £54, and £100 a year for a curate, leaving a net income of £666 to Mr Dodd, which added to the £294 a year from Aldrington, gave him a clear income of £960 a year. Mr Dodd is just deceased, and the living of Aldrington, therefore, is vacant. Now, without an inhabitant, without a Church, without a clergyman, clerk, or congregation, what is to be done with the £300 a year ? What will its patron, Magdalene College, Cambridge, do with it ? Is another clergyman to be appointed to receive the £300 a year ? without duties to perform ! a pastor without a cure of souls ! a shepherd without a flock ! How far do the powers of the Ecclesiastical Commissioners extend ? Can they interfere in a matter of this kind, now that the parish is without an incumbent ? The £300 a year is, we suppose, derived from the tithes, which the landlord, be he who he may, has no right to put into his own pocket: and as there is here a considerable ecclesiastical revenue and a complete sinecure if any one be re-appointed to it, it is to be hoped that power exists somewhere to make a proper disposal of the revenue in some way. Has the Bishop of the Diocese any power to interfere? we imagine not. But certainly Magdalene College ought not to confer a revenue on any man who can give, in an uninhabited parish, nothing in return."

A few years since a mariner was drowned in the new basin,—which is near to the Church,—and his remains were interred within its precincts.

Aldrington was the "Portus Adurni of the Romans," and with reference to Portslade, the adjoining village, its derivation is from slade or way to the port,—as before stated.

NEWHAVEN

Is a small town, formerly inhabited chiefly by maritime people. Its Harbour is situate at the mouth of the river Ouse, having a quay on the east side of it, where ships may ride secure in foul weather; here are sometimes a good many vessels which bring coals, deals, and other merchandize for Lewes and neighbourhood, which lies about seven or eight miles up the river, and load from here with corn, timber, &c.

This town, formerly called Meeching, is an important place on our sea-coast, and nine miles to the east of Brighton,—the route thither being through the village of Rottingdean, which is about midway. It is built on the banks of the Ouse, and is close to the sea. Formerly ships of great burthen could harbour here, but owing to neglect of necessary repairs, the piles became rotten and decayed, and in consequence sand and beach encroached upon the harbour domain.

The entrance was formed in the 16th century, prior thereto the river flowed eastward for near three miles towards Seaford, thus forming the Harbour,—and there is little doubt but that its present entrance is the same as when occupied by the Romans, from the fact that whilst excavations were in progress recently near the mouth of the Harbour, for the purposes of a new fort on the west hill of the same, the remains of a Roman encampment were discovered. This encampment, it is supposed, protected the town from invasion.

In the year 1718, an Act of Parliament was obtained empowering the authorities to repair the piers and keep the Harbour in good and safe condition, and the effect of carrying out the object has been a rapid increase in trade. A new quay has been erected on the east side of the Harbour; and a few years since Government built a fort of great magnitude, its cost being upwards of £150,000.

The Parish Church stands on a hill to the west of the town, and is a rectory, formerly in the patronage of the Queen. Its construction varies from accustomed Church architecture, the tower being placed at the eastern end of the edifice, a very rare occurrence; and it has circular-headed windows, which denote its antiquity.

In the Churchyard there is a very neat obelisk, commemorative of the fate of His Majesty's ship "Brazen." It is surmounted by an iron railing, and is an attractive object. There are tablets on the monument which tell its history, and here are copies of the inscriptions :—

" Sacred to the memory of Captain James Hanson, the Officers and company of his Majesty's ship "Brazen," who were wrecked in a violent storm under the cliff, bearing from this place S.W. at five o'clock a.m., Jan. 26, A.D., 1800; one of the crew only surviving to tell the melan-choly tale. By this fatal event, the country, alas! was deprived of 105 brave defenders, at a time it most required their assistance. The remains of many of them were interred near this spot by the directions of the Lord's Commissioners of the Admiralty.

"The waters saw Thee, O God!"

On the west tablet the names of the officers lost, namely, James Hanson, Esq., commander, and ten others, are inscribed.

On the south tablet :—

"The friends of Captain Hanson caused this monument to be erected as a mark of their esteem for a deserving officer and a valued friend ; it was the will of heaven to preserve him during four years' voyage of danger and difficulty round the world, on discoveries with Captain Vancouver, in the year 1791, 1792, 1793, and 1794, but to take him from us when most he thought himself secure,—

"The voice of the Lord is upon the face of the waters."

On the east tablet :—

"The "Brazen" had been ordered to protect this part of the coast from the insolent attacks of the enemy ; and in the evening preceding the sad catastrophe had detained a foreign vessel, which was put under the care of the master's mate, a midshipman, eight seamen, and two marines, who were hereby saved from the fate of their companions."

At one period it stood on the *outside* of the Church-yard, but the requirements of the parish for sepulture necessitating an extension of burial ground, the land around it was enclosed and consecrated.

The town, at one period, was celebrated for its ale brewing, and its "Newhaven Tipper" became a very popular beverage. It was introduced to the public by a brewer named Thomas Tipper. His remains lie buried in the Churchyard, and here are the lines *in memoriam* of this famous brewer :—

TO THE MEMORY OF

THOMAS TIPPER,

Who departed this Life, May yᵉ 14th, 1785,

AGED 54 YEARS.

> Reader with kind regard this grave survey,
> Nor heedless pass where Tipper's ashes lay ;
> Honest he was, ingenious, blunt, and kind,
> And dared do what few dare to :—speak his mind.
> Philosophy and History well he knew,
> Was versed in Physic and Surgery too.
> The best old Stingo he both brewed and sold ;
> Nor did one knavish act to get his gold.
> He played through life a varied comic part,
> And knew immortal Hudibras by heart.
> Reader, in real truth, such was the man ;
> Be better, wiser, laugh more, if you can.

In the royal days of Brighton,—during the times of George IV. and William IV.,—there was a great consumption of this popular " Tipper." It was even partaken of by Royalty, and its sale extended unto the metropolis, but of late years has much declined : it is still brewed on its original premises.

In the neighbouring barracks of East Blatchington the Oxford Militia were quartered at the time of their mutiny and breaking into the tide-mill at Bishopstone (now in the occupation of Messrs. Catt and Stonham), which they plundered, and afterwards wantonly emptied into the river a cargo of corn. Two of the ringleaders,—Cooke and Parish,—were tried for their share in the crime, and condemned to be shot. This sentence was carried into execution at Goldstone Bottom, on the 13th of June, 1795,—and is treated of in "Brighton Camps," a foregoing chapter in this work.

For many years the "Hyperion" frigate, under the command of Captain Mingaye, was stationed here, in the employment of the Coast-Guard service.

The prosperity of the Port has also been fostered by the London, Brighton, and South-Coast Railway Company, and the Ouse Navigation Commissioners, and very important improvements have been effected by them. The *route* from England to France, *via* Newhaven, is the shortest between the two countries and much patronised,—and for the accommodation and comfort of voyagers a large Hotel, &c., has been erected by the Railway Company, at a cost of £10,000.

Since the association of the South-Coast Railway Company with Newhaven, the town has risen considerably in importance. A new and commodious bridge has been constructed at a very large outlay, and the traffic to and from the Continent has developed immensely during late years, the resources of the port and neighbourhood having been much taxed to keep pace therewith.

The Commissioners appointed to enquire into and report on the eligibility of positions for harbours of refuge on the South-coast selected Newhaven as one of the situations best adapted for the purpose; and in the event of the carrying of the same into effect it will conduce still more to the advancement of this thriving town. Observers of its present success, and those familiar with the growth of trade here of late, may fairly prophesy that Newhaven will eventually become one of the principal sea ports of the kingdom.

SEAFORD.

Seaford, or Sefford, the lordship of John Earl de Warrenne and Surrey, who, having no issue by his wife, made over, by special grant, all his inheritance to King Edward II., and among his great estates in this and other counties the Manor of Seaford was included, and in recompence for which settlement the King assigned him the Castles of Coningsburgh and Ferndale, and Manors of Wakefield, Halifax, &c., in Yorkshire. He enjoyed the whole for his life, and at his death, which happened in 21 of Edward III., all reverted to the Crown, with the exception of some few which, by the consent of King Edward, had been re-granted to him, with remainder to his natural son by Maud de Nereford, John de Warrenne, and his heirs male, &c. We find that this Manor continued for a time in possession of the Crown; but in 42 of Edward III. it is recorded that Michael Lord Poynings died possessed of it; it then returned to the Crown, and was given to Richard Fitzalan, Earl of Arundel, who forfeited it for being guilty of treason. Richard II., on account of great services by Thomas de Mowbray, Earl of Nottingham, bestowed it upon him, likewise other large estates, and soon after created him Duke of Norfolk. During the period that the Manor was possessed by the Poynings family, an effort was made by them to build a new town at the eastern portion of the parish of Seaford, the said town to extend over several acres, and although traces of buildings are to be found, no authentic record is in existence of the same, but in the neighbourhood it is still called Poynings Town. The town not only suffered from the French in former times, but was visited by the great plague in 1348, called by many "the black death," which considerably decimated the number of its inhabitants. King John with his suite slept in this place on the 23rd of May, 1216, and afterwards at Lewes.

Seaford is the last of the Cinque Ports of Sussex, eighth on the rolls of the ancient guild or fraternity, although not coming within that designation, being merely a member of Hastings, yet possesses all the privileges and immunities enjoyed by Rye, Winchelsea, and others in the county, but is subject to certain conditions,—it appearing, from records in the Exchequer, that Hastings with its members,

on receipt of forty days' notice, should supply twenty-one
ships for the King's service, each manned by twenty-one
able, fitly-qualified, and well-armed men. On the arrival
of the ships at their destination, they had to remain there
fifteen days at their own cost; but if the King had
further need for them, they were provided for at the
following rate : the Master of each ship, 6d per day; the
Constable, 6d per day; and the men 3d per day.

It will not be unacceptable to readers here to quote
an old record of the origin of the Cinque Ports :—

" The proximity of the Southern coasts of England
to that of France caused our Sovereigns in early ages
to consider the havens along this line of coast of very
superior importance ; and by way of eminence they styled
them ' Quinque Portuus,' since changed into their
present designation ' Cinque Ports ; ' and William the
Conqueror placed them under the command of an officer
called the Warden of the Cinque Ports, who also acted as
Admiral among them. Although this officer was formerly
of much use to the nation, and had full employment, yet
for many years the office has become a complete sinecure.
The late Duke of Wellington held the office, for which he
received £4,000 per annum.

" The inhabitants of these ports were endowed
with many privileges ; the most important of which
comprised the following :—A power to oblige all who
live in their jurisdiction to plead to their Courts, and
to punish offenders in their own bounds; as also mur-
derers and fugitives from justice ;—To be a guild or
fraternity, and to be allowed the franchises of Court Leet
and Court Baron ;—A power to assemble and keep a
portmote or Parliament for the Cinque Ports ; to punish all
infringers of their privileges ; make bye-laws, and hear
all appeals from the inferior Courts ; — their Barons
to have the privilege of supporting the canopy over the
King's head at the Coronation. In return for these

privileges, they were compelled to supply the King with
57 ships, each provided with 21 men and a boy, to attend
the King's service for 15 days at their own expence ; but
if any further service was required, then they were to be
paid by the Crown."

None of these duties, however, have been exacted
for centuries ; but we believe the inhabitants are still
liable, and as every inhabitant who contributes to
the expense of the town, that is, every householder,
would, in case it was required, be obliged to contribute
towards the formation of this force, so ought they,
reasoning by analogy, to be admitted to a share of the
privileges ; and it is extremely probable that formerly
these rights, designated their freedom, were enjoyed by
all those inhabitants who were assessed to the exigencies
of the public.   It is uncertain when these privileges were
first granted ; but it is known that they were confirmed
by Magna Charta, and again by a General Charter of
Edward I., which received confirmation from most of the
Kings and Queens down to the time of Charles II.

The privileged Ports were at first only three, viz.,
Dover, Sandwich, and Romney.   To these Hastings and
Hythe were added by the Conqueror, and these completed the number to five, which were ever after called the
Cinque Ports.   The ancient towns of Winchelsea and
Rye were added before the time of John, and were called
" *Nobiliora membra Quinque Portuum* ; " and from the time
of their addition, they were treated and considered as
original Ports.   Each of these Cinque Ports had some
adjacent places belonging to and incorporated with them ;
and thus Seaford became a member of Hastings, but
returning its Members to Parliament separately.   The
local government of these several places is vested in a
Mayor and Jurats, of whom there ought to be twelve
besides the Mayor ; although of late years it has not been
the custom in any of the Ports, except Hastings, to have

more than five or six. At Seaford, instead of a Mayor, the chief officer is designated bailiff: the chief of the municipality and two Jurats compose a quorum. Before the passing of the 9th Anne, chap. 20, which prevents Returning Officers holding their office for more than one year at a time, the Mayors of the Cinque Ports were seldom, if ever, changed.

Formerly this town had five Churches and a Chapel, four of the Churches were destroyed by the French, in the course of their attack of 1377;—the remaining one, dedicated to St. Leonard, is of great antiquity, and in 1778, on digging up a portion of its foundation, three stone coffins were discovered,— two had handsome crosses on them and the remaining one enclosed sixteen skulls. No aperture was perceivable in these primitive coffins, and they were fixed in the northern wall of the Church. This edifice was restored in 1862, and contains many objects of interest, but none deserving of special mention.

The Chapel before alluded to belonged to Chyngton, and derived its sustenance from Michelham Priory, near Hailsham. This latter place is now occupied as a farm house, and still exhibits remains of its ecclesiastical origin : at one time there was a drawbridge at its entrance. This religious house gave the name to one of the Manors of Brighton, called "Brighton-Michelham," and it is believed derived a substantial benefit therefrom.

Sutton and Chyngton are both within the liberties of Seaford, and James S. Turner, Esq., occupier of the latter, a much-respected gentleman and eminent agriculturist, has on several occasions been placed at the head of the municipality,—which also possesses a Town Hall, lock-up, &c., and holds Petty and Quarter Sessions. The higher class of offences are tried at the County Assizes, at Lewes.

Seaford is situated in a bay formed by the Newhaven Cliffs on the westward, and its own on the east. Some years since the late William Catt, Esq., proprietor of the extensive tide-mills in the adjoining parish of Bishopstone, —an energetic enterprising gentleman, who was the architect of his own fortune, and whose sons, emulating his worthy example, occupy prominent positions in Brighton and other parts of the county,—sought to stay the inroads of the sea by the blasting of a portion of the cliff, and the Government instructed military engineers to assist him in carrying out the project. The blasting was successful, but the object, that of raising a barrier against the sea, was defeated, the tides speedily sweeping away the *débris*. The chasm in the cliff, left by the explosion, is still visible. From this spot may be obtained a beautiful view of the bay and neighbourhood surrounding.

Wrecks were formerly very numerous on this coast, and in the early part of the present century several merchant vessels, under convoy of the "Harlequin," a sloop of war, were wrecked here. The inhabitants of this part of Sussex and other places along the coast formerly bore an unenviable notoriety, owing to their rapacity whenever vessels were wrecked or stranded in the locality, all classes of the people being tainted with a propensity to commit depredations upon persons and cargoes cast upon their shores. In corroboration of the assertion, it is told that on a Sunday morning during the hours of Divine service in a neighbouring Parish Church, the preacher noticed, whilst delivering his sermon, an unusual stir among his congregation, and being familiar with the habits of those whom he was addressing, imagined the reason of the same, also espied a new arrival in the act of whispering to one of the Churchwardens the news that "there was a wreck on shore," information which was speedily conveyed to others present. With electrical rapidity the whole congregation were made acquainted with the same, and forthwith prepared to desert their devotions for the beach. The clergyman immediately shouted out at the top of his voice,

"Hold! four words before *you* go,

"LET'S ALL START FAIR!"

By this time he had divested himself of his gown and left with the rest for the *scene of operations* on the beach.

Many evidences of Roman occupation of the neighbourhood are still traceable. About a mile to the east of the town, and near the cliffs, there is an earthwork which plainly indicates that, in early ages, it was a Roman encampment. Coins and urns have been found belonging to the Roman era, also bones, and other vestiges of mortality.

The author of this work recommends visitors to Brighton, who covet a pleasant ramble, to take a ride to Seaford, by the South-Coast Railway, and then to commence their peregrinations,—following the " Chalk line " to Eastbourne, which will amply repay for the fatigue from mounting " the Charles's"—cliffs so-called,—that will be met with on the way, the journey being so diversified,—hill, dale, and objects of the greatest interest being frequently met with. In the autumn of 1869, the writer, accompanied by an esteemed friend, G. H. Evershed, Esq. (formerly an inhabitant of Seaford), traversed this route, and to him he is indebted for much information in connection therewith.

After passing Puck Church Parlor we arrive at Cuckmere Haven, which derives its name from a small river that flows into the sea from a level at that spot. It rises in the parishes of Heathfield and Waldron, and during the winter months this level assumes the appearance of a " mere " or lake. It was thought, some years since, by the Dutch Government, admirably suited for the purposes of a Harbour on this dangerous coast; and as at that time they were more engaged in maritime commerce than our own nation,—having a number of vessels employed in the Batavia and East India trade, &c.,

they offered a large sum of money for the same, which offer was very naturally and prudently refused.

Proceeding onwards, crossing the Harbour by the shingle, in preference to Exceat Bridge, which is situated to the north, we arrive at the landing place of Crowlink, and shortly reach Birling Gap, — an opening in the Cliff taking its name from the village. An ancient gateway or stronghold formerly stood here, which was used in the wars, and as an entrance into the country,—and at this spot is the junction for the sub-marine telegraph between the capitals of England and France.

This Gap and its neighbourhood in years past was likewise the scene of many fearful shipwrecks ;—one in particular, that of the "Nympha," a Spanish prize, in the year 1747. This vessel was built entirely of cedar, and some of its timber used for the building of barns, &c., in the locality. Articles of furniture made of wood from the same wreck are still to be found in several houses at Seaford, Eastdean, &c., although, from the lapse of time, they are quite black in appearance. The following is copied from a rare print of the wreck in the author's possession :—

" 'The Nympha Americana' was taken by Commodore George Walker, Commander of the 'Royal Family Privateer,' near Cadiz, and carried first to Lisbon, thence to Portsmouth, and after, in her passage to London, she was unfortunately wreck'd near Beachy Head, on the coast of Sussex, November yº 29th, 1747, at eleven o'clock at night. She was built chiefly of cedar, about 800 tons burthen, had ports for 60 guns ; her lading consisted of superfine velvets, cloths, gold and silver laces, and almost every other kind of merchandize. She struck upon yᵉ rocks, and left her bottom some distance from yᵉ shore, which had parted at the rungs ; afterwards broke asunder in yº midships. The fore part overturn'd, by which accident 30 of the 130 men that were on board were drown'd. Her bottom could not be found till December the 24th, from which was taken up, by persons imploy'd with their boats, near 30,000 pounds' sterling value of quicksilver ; great quantities of her cargo were carried off by people from different parts, 60 of whom perish'd on the Beach, Downs, and other places ; one was shot, and one broke his thigh ; but, notwithstanding those accidents, great numbers still continued to search, and often found some of her cargo, so that this may justly be recorded ye most extraordinary wreck that ever happen'd on any part of ye coasts of this Kingdom."

It was the sad loss of life occasioned by these catastrophes that induced the Incumbent of Eastdean and two neighbouring parishes,—the Rev. Jonathan Darby, a man of benevolent and philanthropic ideas, — to avert them if possible. He accordingly caused a cavern of considerable dimensions (consisting of a staircase opening from the beach, a dining room, and inner chamber), to be excavated in the cliff, above the flow of the tide, where unfortunate sailors might escape from the waters on their being cast ashore ; and on many a stormy night did he wend his way to the cave and exhibit a light, to caution mariners on their too near approach. It is asserted that in consequence of his taking these precautionary measures he, on one occasion, saved the lives of 12 seamen from a Dutch vessel. At last he fell a victim to his praiseworthy efforts; in the year 1726 he contracted a cold and died. The cavern is situated about a mile eastward of Birling Gap,—and to this day is called " Parson Darby's Hole."

" The Charles's " before alluded to, are among the highest cliffs on the Sussex coast, being upwards of 500ft. Here great numbers of birds, including the raven, congregate and breed, but many of them at the latter part of the season migrate to warmer climates. The eggs of these birds are considered a great luxury, and in the procuring of them persons run the hazard of losing their lives. The following is the mode in which eggs are collected :

A crow-bar is driven into the earth on the summit of the
cliff, and hereto a rope is securely attached; the egg-taker
then fastens the other end tightly and securely around
his waist, affixes a basket to his person, and descends
down the face of the cliff,—an assistant regulating the
lengthening or shortening of the rope. Having reached
the nests, which are built in the fissures of the cliff, the
adventurer takes possession of all eggs within his reach,
and is then drawn upwards by his mate. Many a poor
fellow has forfeited his life for his temerity in the pursuit
of this daring occupation. It is recorded that about the
end of the fourth century a hermit lived in a cell made in
the cliff. Near the beach in the interstices of the cliff the
samphire grows, the gathering of which is attended by
commensurate reward.

Pursuing our journey we soon arrive at a place called
Belletout, formerly an ancient entrenchment, whereon is
erected Beachy Head Lighthouse (constructed by the late
Mr Fabian, builder, of Brighton). This lighthouse has
proved to be of infinite service to those navigating the
Channel,—which is narrow at this point,—and has been the
means of preserving a number of lives. A man constantly
resides here, who will give every information required by
visitors. It is frequently resorted to by parties from the
fashionable and modern town of Eastbourne, which is
situated about three miles to the eastward. The Cliffs at this
spot are nearly 600ft. high, and the view is most extensive
and charming. A Coast Guard Station is in close proximity.

Charles I. in 1640,—the sixteenth year of his reign,
—restored unto Seaford its former privilege of sending
Members to Parliament,—a power of which it had been
deprived from the first year of Edward IV., anterior to
which it had been a borough of the realm, returning its first
members the 26th of Edward I.

In bringing this sketch of Seaford to a close, it will
interest our readers if we give a brief outline of the election

doings of this immaculate Borough prior to 1832, when it was disfranchised by the Reform Act of that year, by being placed in Schedule A, and sharing the fate of many other rotten boroughs.

Many eminent statesmen have represented this historical borough in Parliament, among them the Earl of Chatham, Lord Brougham, Sir John Leach, the Right Hon. George Canning, &c. From the foregoing list of names it is clear there must have been some attractions attached to the representation of this ancient borough. We find that at a majority of the elections there was a contest for the honor of sitting in St. Stephen's; also, that very frequently successful candidates were petitioned against. In 1670, when a petition was presented, the House of Commons decided that the right of the electors was in the "Populacy," i.e., "Inhabitants paying scot and lot," and none others were allowed to be placed on the rates until the year 1786, when Mr Flood succeeded in compelling the authorities to rate every inhabitant-householder, which provision remained in existence for many years after.

In this Borough "the Treasury" exerted every influence to secure the return of representatives pledged to support its interests, and others locally connected strove their utmost for the same object. The Duke of Newcastle was one of these, and at that time (1747), residing in the neighbouring village of Bishopstone and possessing great influence in the return of representatives for the County, also the elections of Lewes and Winchelsea. His Grace was the instigation of the nomination for Seaford of William Pitt (afterwards Earl of Chatham) and William Hay, Esq.; these candidates were opposed by the Earl of Middlesex and the Hon. W. H. Gage (afterwards Viscount Gage). After the poll, the Bailiff (Mr Chambers), declared the Duke's nominees duly elected. The opposition candidates petitioned against

Q

their return, on the ground of interference of the Duke, and his actual presence at the poll, and a motion was moved in Parliament "that the matter contained in such petition should be heard at the bar of the House," but this motion was negatived by a large majority.

At the election of 1761, the Duke of Newcastle again returned his nominees, and again they were petitioned against, but the House confirmed the return, and thereby the patronage was absolutely vested in the Duke. At two other election contests,—1774 and 1780,—efforts were made to wrest this power from him, but they were unsuccessful. It appears that after the Duke's death, the Pelham interest, which had been allowed to fall into neglect, was revived by the Hon. Thomas Pelham, and the Hon. L. Watson became a candidate under his patronage. Mr Alves, an independent candidate, started in opposition to him, but circumstances transpired which rendered a coalition between the Pelham interest and Mr Alves' party extremely desirable,—and such was accordingly effected.

Mr Alderman Curtis was at this time one of the candidates of the Treasury, but subsequently its support was withdrawn from him and preferred to Lord Neville and Sir Peter Parker. On the day of election the numbers at the close of the poll were as follows :— Lord Neville, 12 ; Sir Peter Parker, 12 ; Hon. L. T. Watson, 11; Thomas Alves, Esq., 11. It appears the bailiff had, pursuant to the statute, omitted to give four clear days' notice of the election, consequently a petition was presented against the return, and the election declared void. This decision being anticipated in the interval after the election just mentioned, and the decision in March, 1785, at the election which followed, the large number of twenty-six candidates offered themselves to the free and independent electors, who only numbered *twenty-four*. A rich harvest was anticipated from so many candidates, and as the proceedings were of such an interesting character, we give them in detail :—

" One candidate in the Ministerial interest, Lord Mount-morris, was removed after the same method as Mr. Curtis had been at the previous election, and Sir John Henderson substituted in his stead. On the day of election, however, there were only six candidates. The Right Hon. Henry Flood and Sir Lawrence Parsons, supported on the interest of the non-rated inhabitants; Sir Godfrey Webster, the father of the Battle Abbey Baronet, on the Pelham interest, united with Mr Alves; and Sir Peter Parker and Sir John Henderson under the Treasury influence. The numbers tendered were, for the Right Hon. Henry Flood, 28, Sir Lawrence Parsons, 24, Sir G. Webster, 19, Thomas Alves, 18, Sir P. Parker, 16, Sir J. Henderson, 14. But the Bailiff again refused the votes of all the non-rated inhabitants, and returned the Treasury Candidates. Four petitions were presented against this return, on the hearing of which it appeared that the correct numbers of Sir G. Webster, Mr. Alves, Sir P. Parker, and Sir J. Henderson were exactly equal, and this second election was therefore declared void.

" Mr. Alves, by this time, had seen quite enough of the immaculate borough of Seaford, and not being willing to incur any further expense, he retired. Mr. Flood's party had an opportunity of again appealing against the poor-rate, and were thus put in a situation to prove their rateability before a Committee of the House ; and on a junction between the Pelham and the Flood interests being effected, on the day of election the numbers appeared to be—for the Right Hon. H. Flood, 32, Sir G. Webster, Bart., 32, Sir P. Parker, Bart, 16, Sir J. Henderson, Bart., 16 ; but notwithstanding this majority, the Bailiff again rejected every person whose name did not appear on the rate manufactured by his own party, and returned the government Candidates. The case, however, was too flagrant to meet the eyes of a Committee, and a petition being presented against the return, the sitting Members declared that it was not their intention to justify their election, and their political opponents were therefore triumphant; the Committee on the 13th March, 1786, reporting —'That the Right Hon. H. Flood and Sir G. Webster, Bart., were duly elected and ought to have been returned.

"The Treasury interest being thus defeated, a great coolness arose between the Government and Mr. Harrison. The Treasury afterwards transferred its confidence from him to Mr. Harben, who, on pretence of being Mr. Harrison's friend, obtained from him the purchase of some acres of his estate within the borough at a very cheap rate, and having built a house, he gradually unfolded as deep a piece of treachery as was ever shown. He procured creatures of his own to be elected Bailiff and Freemen, and then procured the dismissal of Mr Harrison from his appointments, which he divided among his own associates, not at all neglecting his own interest, obtaining the appointment of Receiver General of the Stamp Duties for Sussex, worth £600 per annum, for his son, and other advantages; and immediately afterwards a system of the greatest profligacy was commenced, although strenuously opposed by the independent Mr. James Hurdis, who long lived in the grateful recollection of many of the old inhabitants of Seaford. Still Mr. Harben had not a majority of votes; and in order to obtain that preponderance, he created 19 non-resident Freemen. This did not however ensure his success, and accordingly, on the eve of Christmas-day, 1789, he brought into the town 26 chalk diggers, most of whom were in his own employ, and rated them for the houses of widows and revenue officers, not having votes. The dissolution however took place 17 days before the expiration of the six months' rating; but

by management the poll was kept open until these had
expired and the chalk-diggers were allowed to vote. By
this device the numbers were—for the Ministerial candidates—John Sargent, Esq., 92, R. P. Poddrell, 91, and
for the Pelham and Flood candidates, Sir G. Webster and
John Tarleton, Esq., 48 each. A petition was presented
against this return; and on examination of the votes, it
appeared that there was a majority of one for Mr. Sargent
and Mr. Tarleton, occasioned by the cross polling of some
of the voters, and the Committee, on the 13th March,
1792, reported that they were duly elected, and 'that the
right of election for the port and borough of Seaford, in
the county of Sussex, is in the Inhabitant Housekeepers of
the said Port, paying scot and lot, and in them only.' This
decision rendered completely useless the old corporation,
consisting of the Bailiff, Jurats, and Freemen, which
Mr. Harben had been taking so much trouble to complete.
Mr. Harben did not however approve of this decision, and
accordingly appealed against it. But the Committee
reported to the House on the 19th February, 1795, in
confirmation of the former decision, and Mr. Harben was
defeated.

   " Not long after this decision, Mr Harben made considerable purchases in the town, and thus added to his
interests, which he increased sufficiently to succeed in
sometimes returning one Member. A few years afterwards
Mr Pelham sold his interest to Mr Leach, the Master
of the Rolls, who regularly returned himself and some friend,
till at length, getting tired of it, he sold out to Mr Ellis,
now Lord Seaford, for a sum of £20,000, if we are to believe
report. On Mr Harben's bankruptcy, his estates were all sold,
and the Seaford houses became the property of Mr Pindar,
on whose interest the Hon. Thomas Bowes contested
the borough in 1812, but was defeated; the numbers
being—for John Leach, Esq., 77; — Ellis, Esq., 75;
— Bowes, Esq., 40. From Mr Pindar the interest

was transferred to Mr Fitzgerald, who continued to
divide with Lord Seaford the nomination till 1826,
when they were opposed by Sir Jacob Astley, Bart.,
and William Earl Lytton Bulwer, Esq., who, however,
were unable to defeat the combined local interest, the
numbers being—for J. Fitzgerald, Esq., 55 ; Augustus J.
Ellis, Esq., 54; Sir Jacob Astley, 26 ; W. E. Bulwer,
Esq., 23. At the next election, however, in 1830, two
gentlemen, Captain William Lyon and William Williams,
Esq., determined on rescuing the borough from this nomination, and they accordingly canvassed the electors. Having
obtained many promises of support, they resolved to stand
the poll, which was accordingly entered upon on the
30th July, 1830, when the number of votes decided by the
Bailiff to be good were—for John Fitzgerald, Esq., 44; the
Hon. Augustus Frederick Ellis, 38 ; William Lyon, Esq.,
34; William Williams, Esq., 24; leaving five voters
unpolled. Against this return Messrs. Lyon and Williams
petitioned, and Captain Lyons succeeded in getting five
votes, which had been rejected by the Bailiff, put upon the
poll, but Mr Williams only succeeded in establishing two.
The numbers, therefore, after the decision of the Committee,
were—for John Fitzgerald, Esq., 40; William Lyons,
Esq., 39 ; Hon. A. F. Ellis, 38 ; William Williams, Esq., 26 ;
and the Committee reported that Messrs. Fitzgerald and
Lyon were duly elected and ought to have been returned.
This decision took the nomination out of the hands of
Lord Seaford, who at the last election did not oppose the
return of Captain Lyon.

"The voters in this place were formerly as corrupt as
any place could possibly be. We have heard that at the
election in 1792, a club was formed in the Pelham interest,
similar in many respects to the Christian Club, at
Shoreham, already mentioned in the chapter on Shoreham,
the members of which received £100 each for their *services*:
and for years afterwards the regular price of a single vote

was £50 and for a double one £25 from each candidate. In addition to which the widow of a deceased voter usually received the same sums immediately after her husband's death. The voters themselves paid little or no rent for their houses; their doctor's bills were paid by the candidates' agents; and at Christmas, a regular distribution of coals, bread, and beef took place. The voters of the period declared in their petition presented to the House that they were perfectly free from the sins of their predecessors, and we trust this is the case. We can scarcely however reconcile it with the facts, that it cost Captain Lyon nearly £4000 to poll the 39 voters in 1830 ; that no less than 36 dozens of wine were drunk at one Inn during the contest; and that at Christmas a distribution of meat and coals took place."

Within the last few years Seaford has exhibited considerable vitality, partly owing to the patronage it receives from visitors in the summer and autumn seasons, —for whose accommodation a number of houses have been erected; but mainly due to a branch line that has been constructed thereto (having a station at Bishopstone). This branch is a continuation of the line from London to Newhaven and Quay, the purposes of the latter being the convenience of the large numbers of passengers embarking and disembarking, both by day and by night, at all seasons of the year, to and from the Continent.

T H E   E N D.

W. CURTIS, PRINTER, GAZETTE OFFICE, NORTH STREET, BRIGHTON.

www.ingramcontent.com/pod-product-compliance
Lightning Source LLC
Chambersburg PA
CBHW060610030726
47498CB00005B/1624